VOL. 37
VIZ Media Edition

Story and Art by
RUMIKO TAKAHASHI

English Adaptation by Gerard Jones

Translation/Mari Morimoto
Touch-up Art & Lettering/Bill Schuch
Cover and Interior Graphic Design/Yuki Ameda
Editor/Ian Robertson

Editor in Chief, Books/Alvin Lu
Editor in Chief, Magazines/Marc Weidenbaum
VP, Publishing Licensing/Rika Inouye
VP, Sales & Product Marketing/Gonzalo Ferreyra
VP, Creative/Linda Espinosa
Publisher/Hyoe Narita

Printed in the U.S.A.

Published by VIZ Media, LLC
P.O. Box 77010
San Francisco, CA 94107

VIZ Media Edition
10 9 8 7 6 5 4 3 2 1
First printing, April 2009

www.viz.com

store.viz.com

INUYASHA

VOL. 37 VIZ Media Edition

STORY AND ART BY
RUMIKO TAKAHASHI

CONTENTS

THE STORY THUS FAR

Long ago, in the "Warring States" era of Japan's Muromachi period (Sengoku-jidai, approximately 1467-1568 CE), a legendary dog-like half-demon called "Inuyasha" attempted to steal the Shikon Jewel—or "Jewel of Four Souls"—from a village, but was stopped by the enchanted arrow of the village priestess, Kikyo. Inuyasha fell into a deep sleep, pinned to a tree by Kikyo's arrow, while the mortally wounded Kikyo took the Shikon Jewel with her into the fires of her funeral pyre. Years passed.

Fast-forward to the present day. Kagome, a Japanese high school girl, is pulled into a well one day by a mysterious centipede monster and finds herself transported into the past—only to come face to face with the trapped Inuyasha. She frees him, and Inuyasha easily defeats the centipede monster.

The residents of the village, now 50 years older, readily accept Kagome as the reincarnation of their deceased priestess Kikyo, a claim supported by the fact that the Shikon Jewel emerges from a cut on Kagome's body. Unfortunately, the jewel's rediscovery means that the village is soon under attack by a variety of demons in search of this treasure. Then, the jewel is accidentally shattered into many shards, each of which may have the fearsome power of the entire jewel.

Although Inuyasha says he hates Kagome because of her resemblance to Kikyo, the woman who "killed" him, he is forced to team up with her when Kaede, the village leader, binds him to Kagome with a powerful spell. Now the two grudging companions must fight to reclaim and reassemble the shattered shards of the Shikon Jewel before they fall into the wrong hands...

THIS VOLUME Inuyasha and the crew pass through a town that has been attacked by some kind of dog. When the group stays to help the village, they run into Kohaku, who is hunting this dog. Kohaku conceals the fact that he has regained his memory in order to get a better chance at revenge on Naraku. Meanwhile the intrigue between Kagura and Goryomaru deepens.

CHARACTERS

INUYASHA
Half-demon hybrid, son of a human mother and demon father. His necklace is enchanted, allowing Kagome to control him with a word.

KAGOME
Modern-day Japanese schoolgirl who can travel back and forth between the past and present through an enchanted well.

NARAKU
Enigmatic demon-mastermind behind the miseries of nearly everyone in the story.

MIROKU
Lecherous Buddhist priest cursed with a mystical "hellhole" in his hand that's slowly killing him.

KOGA
Leader of the Wolf Clan, Koga is himself a Wolf Demon and, because of several Shikon shards in his legs, possesses super speed. Enamored of Kagome, he quarrels with Inuyasha frequently.

SANGO
"Demon Exterminator" or slayer from the village where the Shikon Jewel was first born.

SCROLL 1

ROOTS

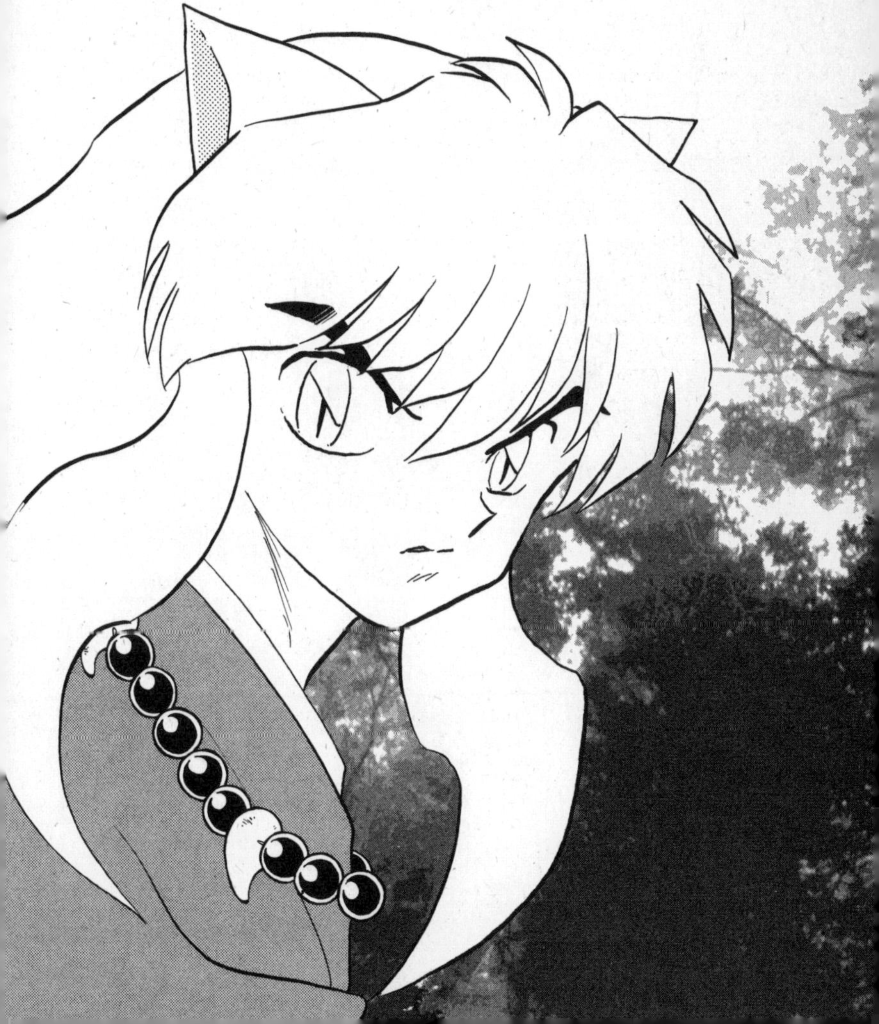

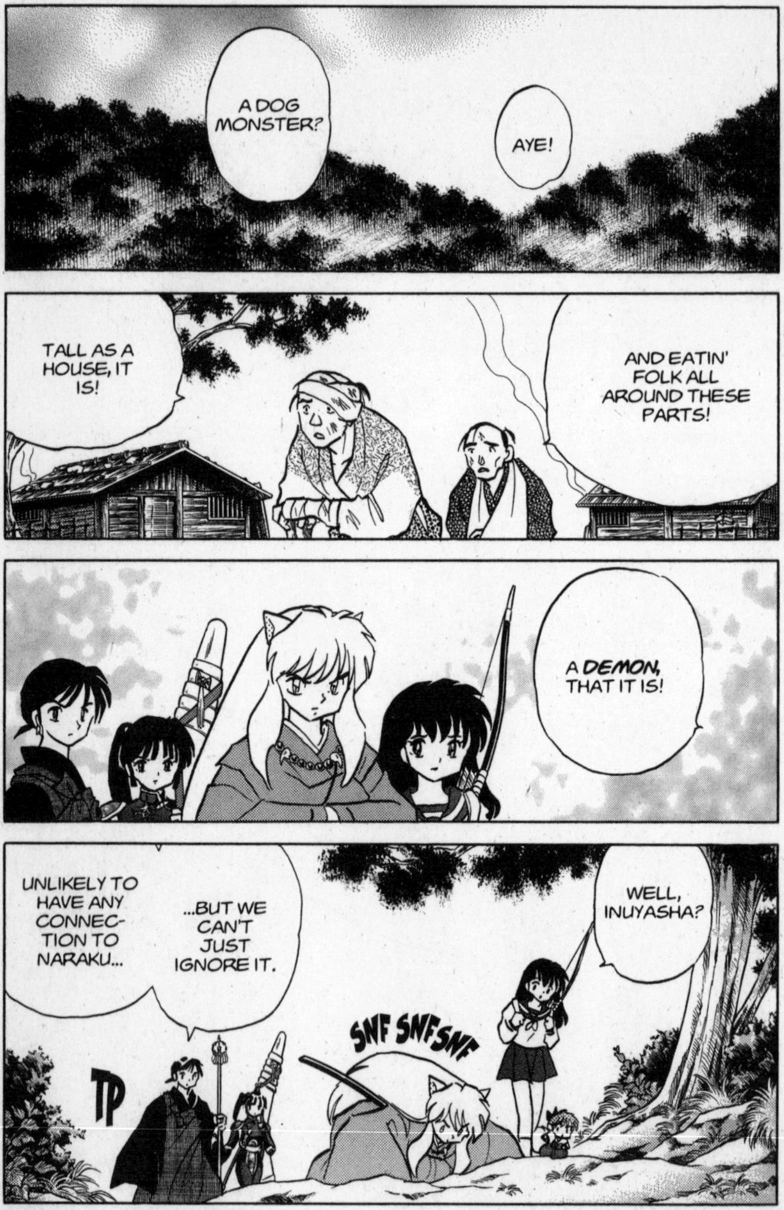
A DOG MONSTER?
AYE!
TALL AS A HOUSE, IT IS!
AND EATIN' FOLK ALL AROUND THESE PARTS!
A *DEMON*, THAT IT IS!
UNLIKELY TO HAVE ANY CONNEC-TION TO NARAKU...
...BUT WE CAN'T JUST IGNORE IT.
WELL, INUYASHA?
SNF SNF SNF
TP

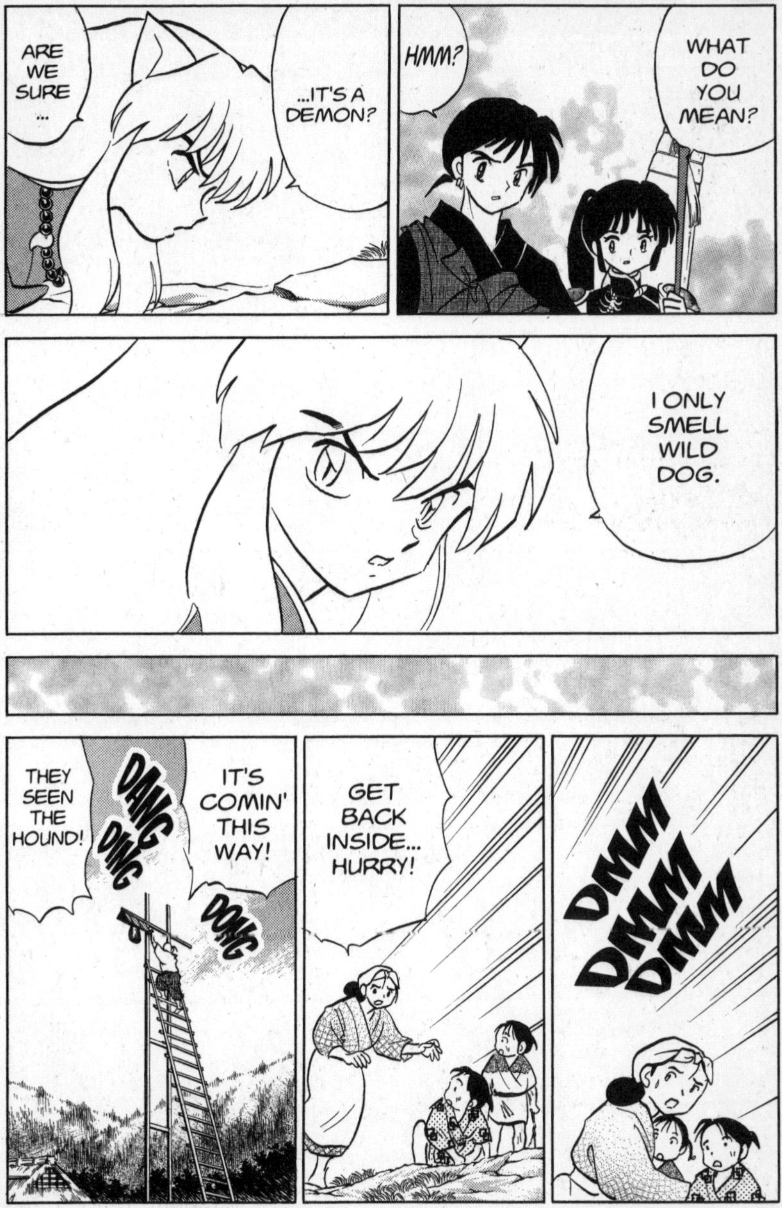
ARE WE SURE ...
...IT'S A DEMON?
HMM?
WHAT DO YOU MEAN?
I ONLY SMELL WILD DOG.
THEY SEEN THE HOUND!
DANG
DING
IT'S COMIN' THIS WAY!
DONG
GET BACK INSIDE... HURRY!
DMM
DMM
DMM

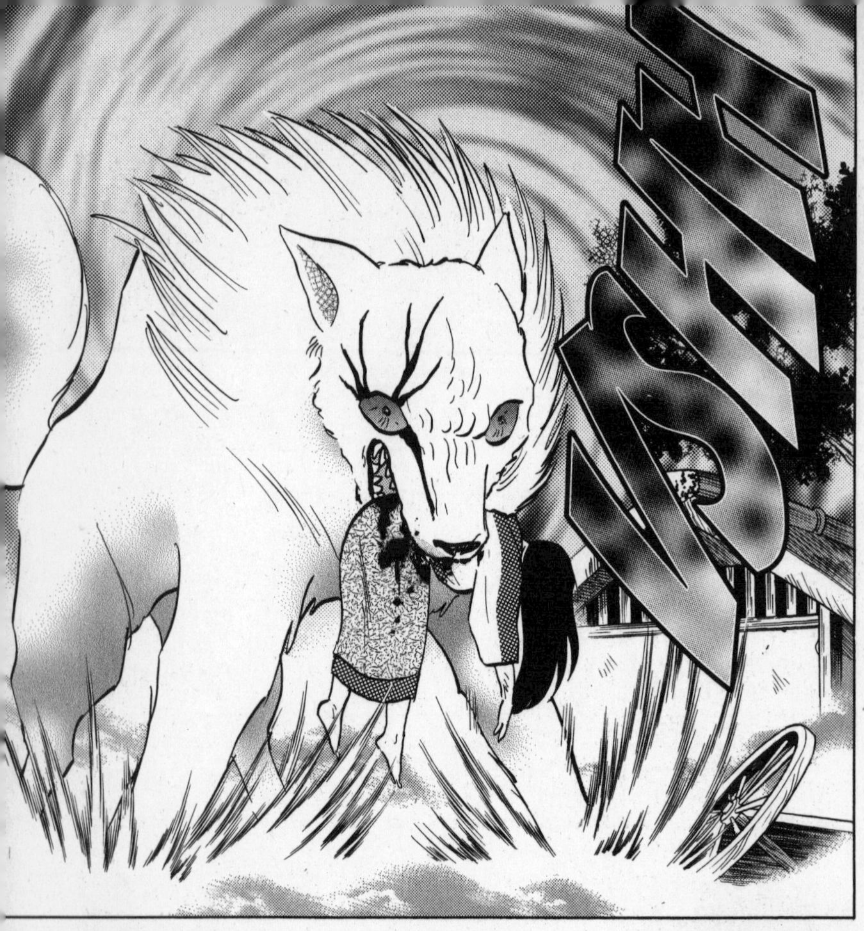
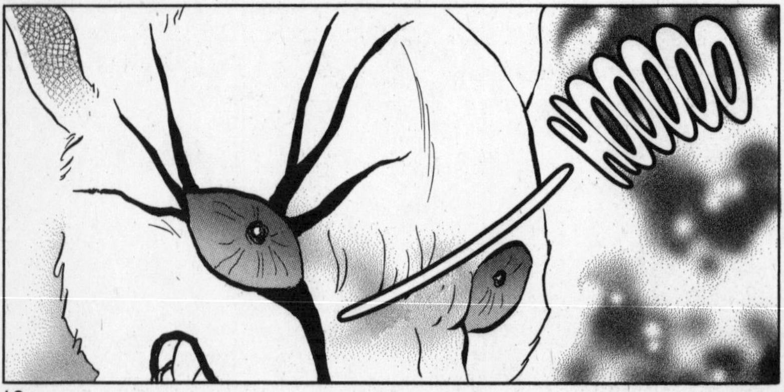

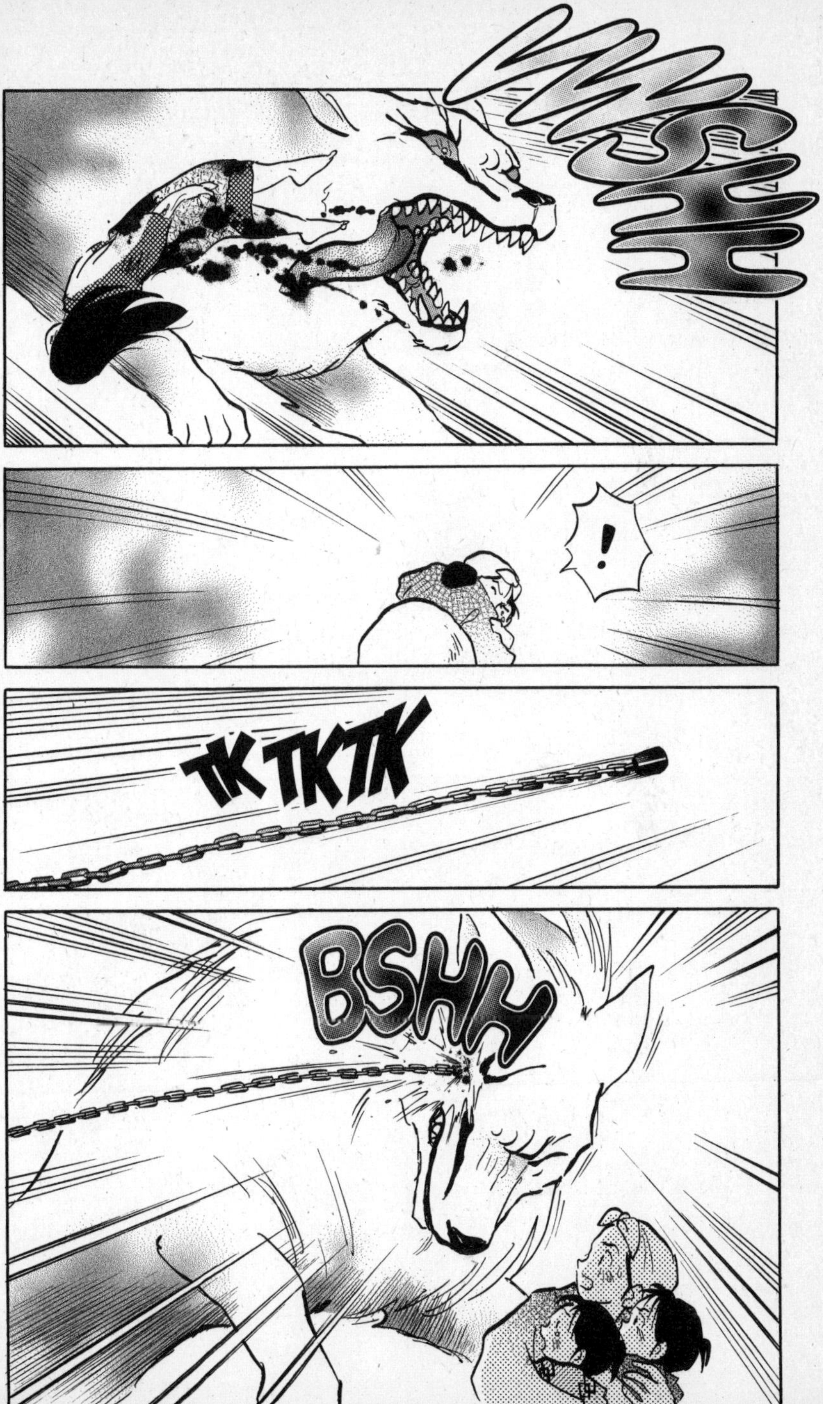
WHSHH
!
TK TK TK
BSHH

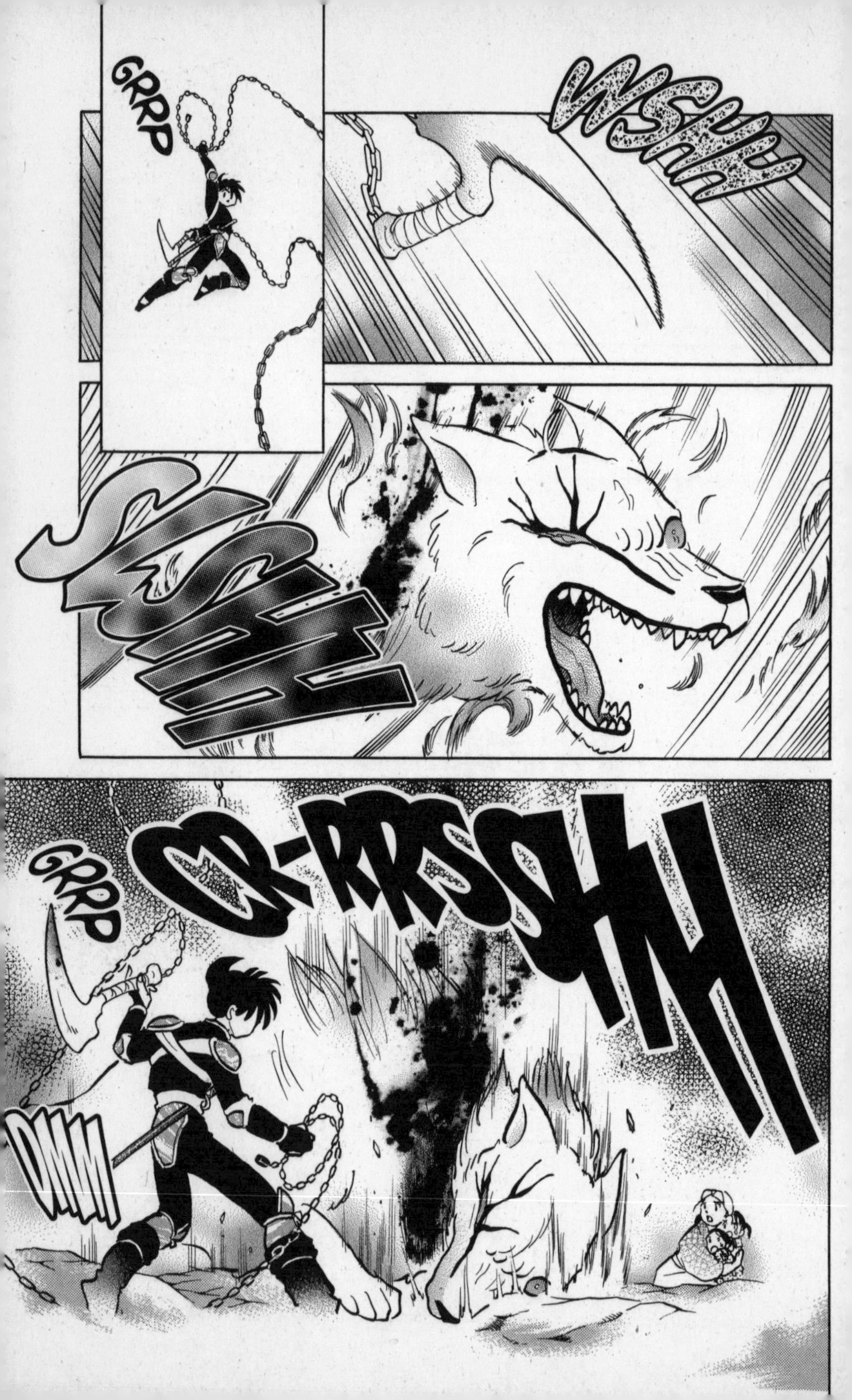
GRRP
WSHUH
GRRP
GR-RRSCHH

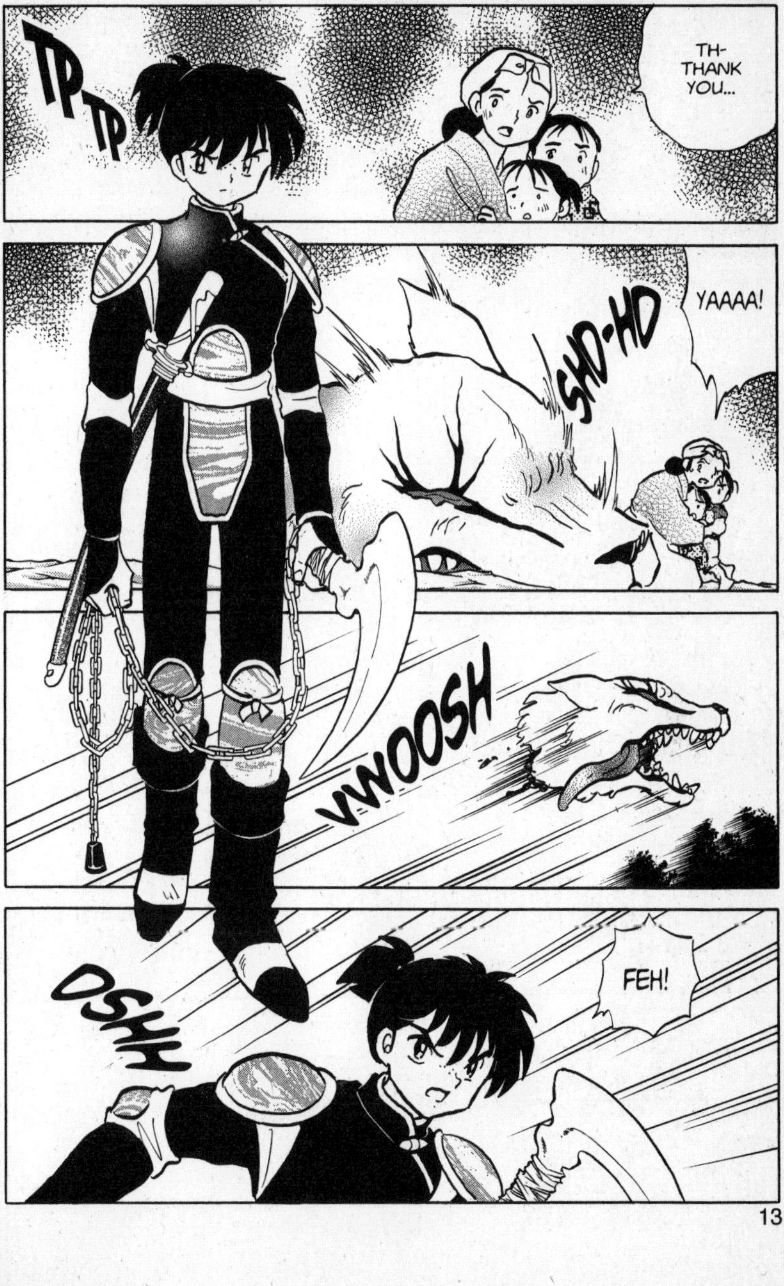
TP TP
TH-THANK YOU...
SHD-HD
YAAAA!
VWOOSH
DSHH
FEH!

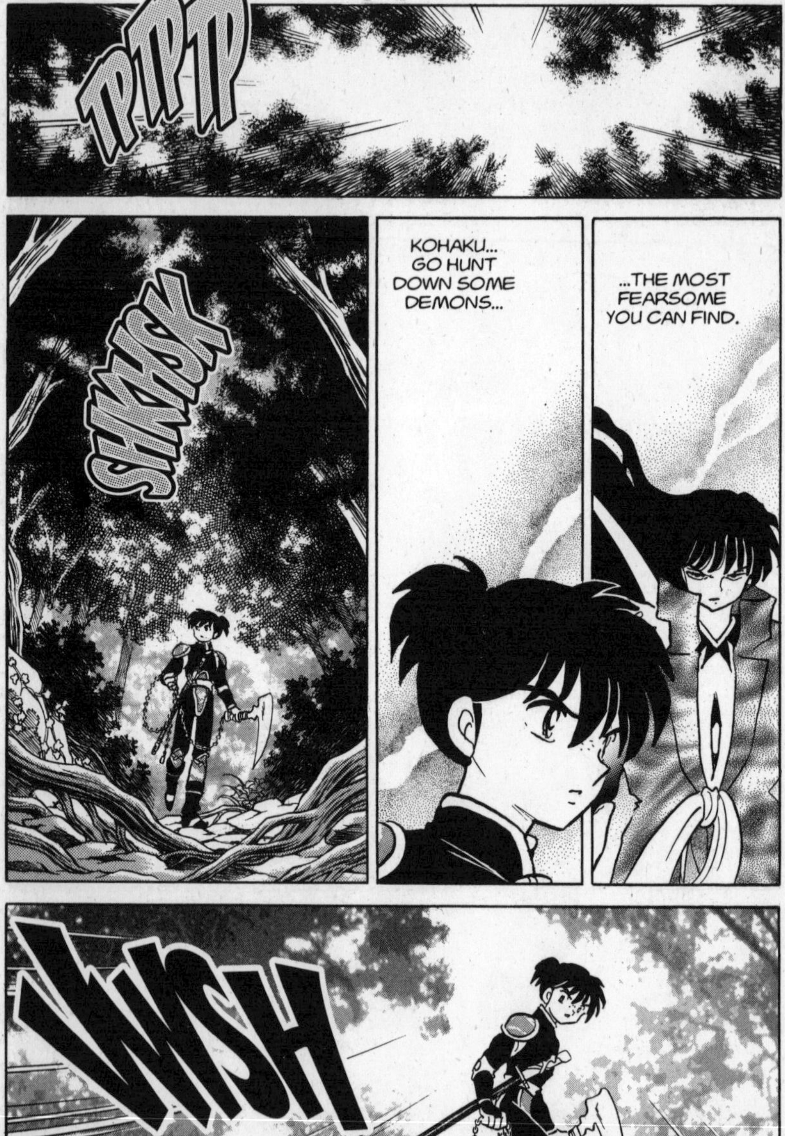
TPTPTP
SHKHSK
KOHAKU... GO HUNT DOWN SOME DEMONS...
...THE MOST FEARSOME YOU CAN FIND.
WHSH

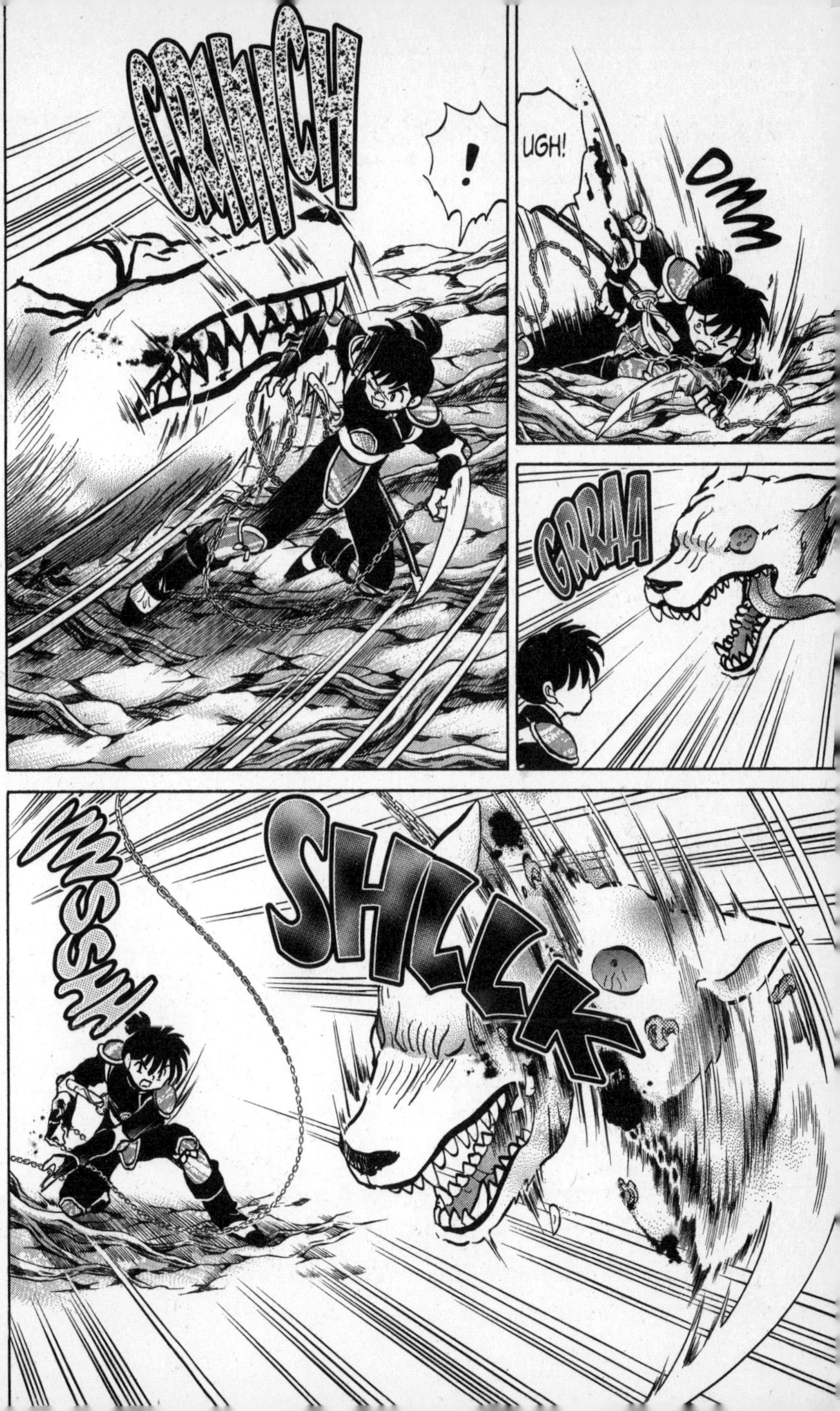

CRUNCH
!
UGH!
DMM
GRRAA
WSSSH
SHLLK

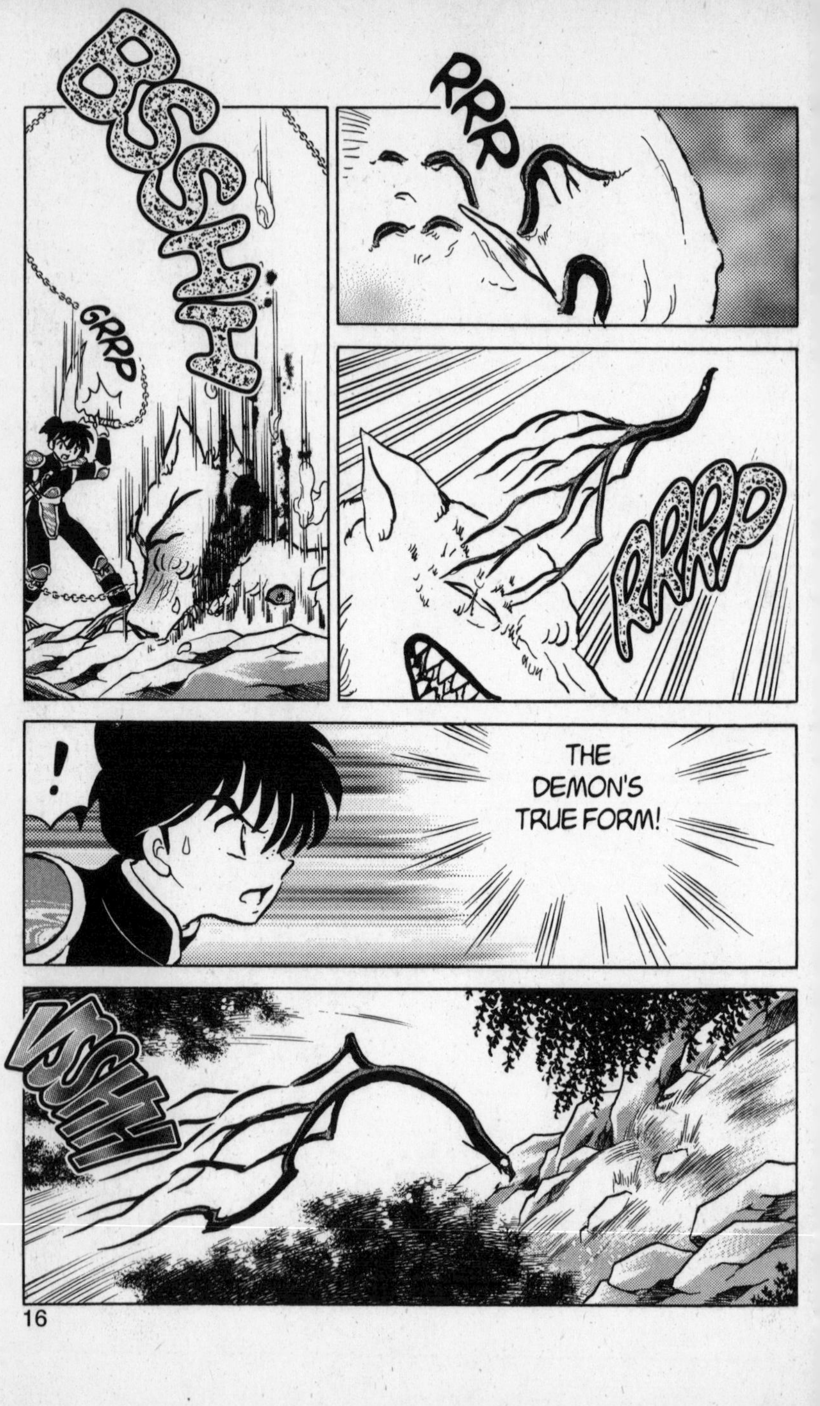
BSSHH
GRRP
RRR
RRRP
!
THE DEMON'S TRUE FORM!
VSSHH!

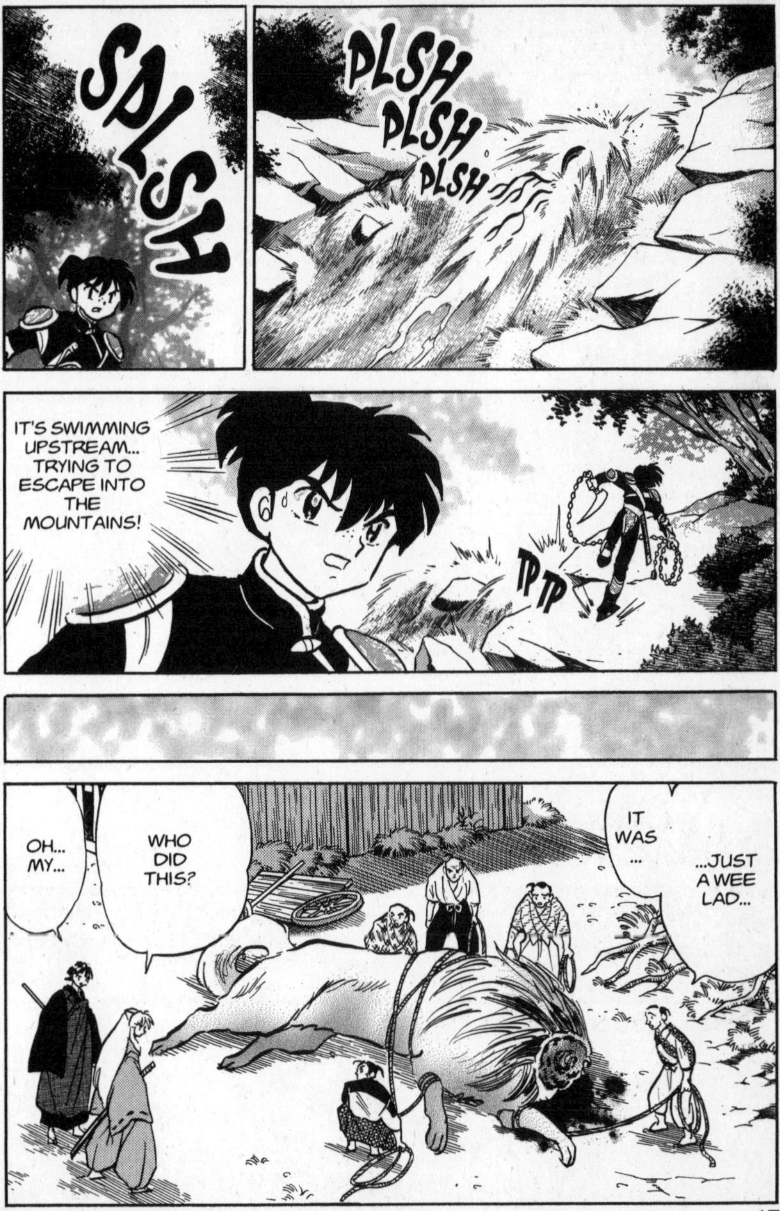
SPLSH
PLSH PLSH PLSH
IT'S SWIMMING UPSTREAM... TRYING TO ESCAPE INTO THE MOUNTAINS!
TP TP
OH... MY...
WHO DID THIS?
IT WAS...
...JUST A WEE LAD...

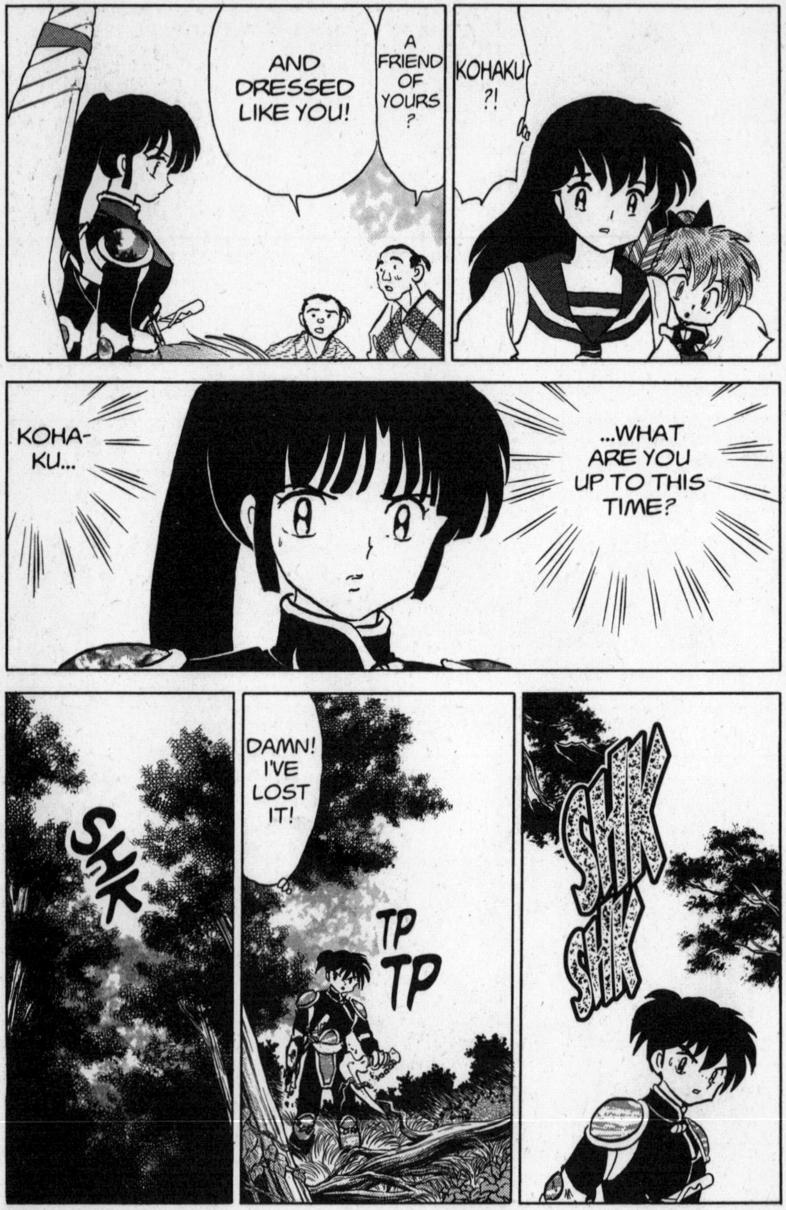
AND DRESSED LIKE YOU!
A FRIEND OF YOURS?
KOHAKU ?!
KOHA-KU...
...WHAT ARE YOU UP TO THIS TIME?
SHK
DAMN! I'VE LOST IT!
TP TP
SHK SHK

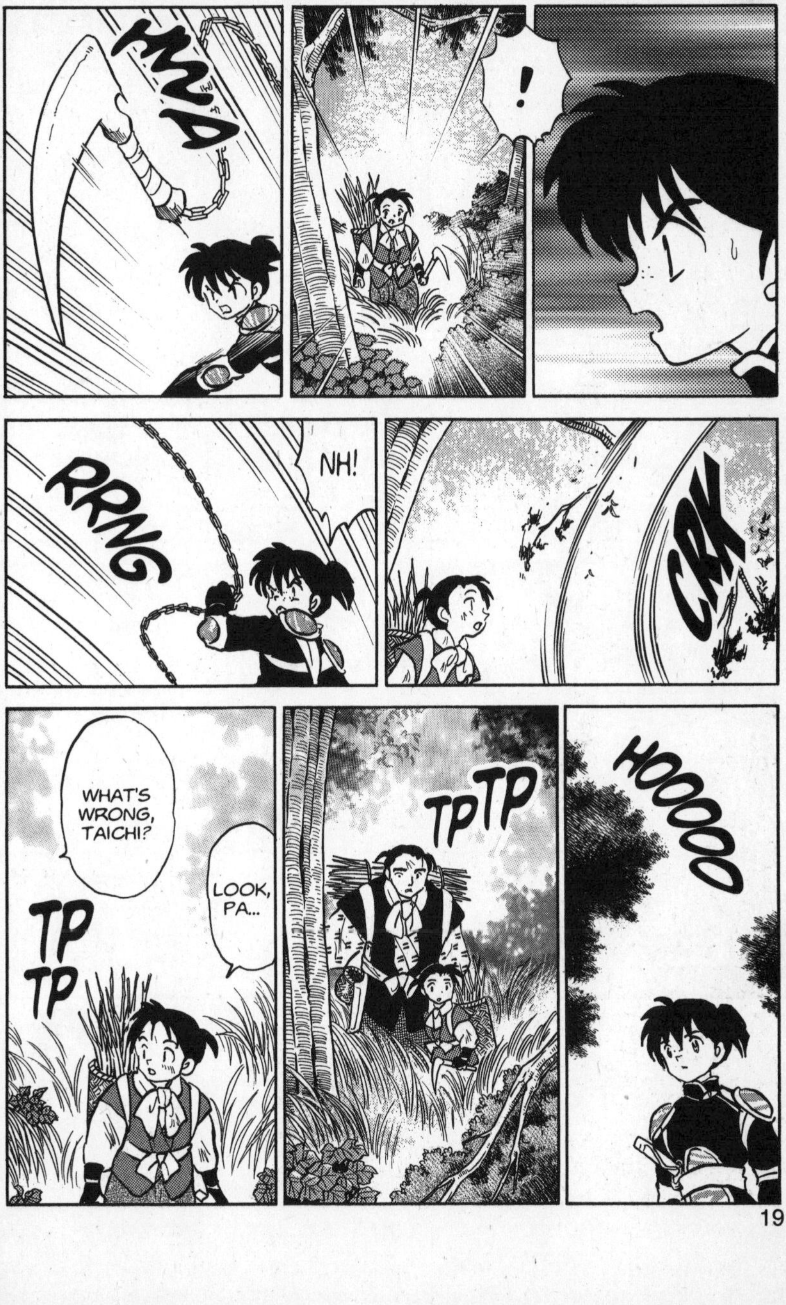
WHA
!
RRNG
NH!
CRK
WHAT'S WRONG, TAICHI?
LOOK, PA...
TP TP
TP TP
HOOOOO

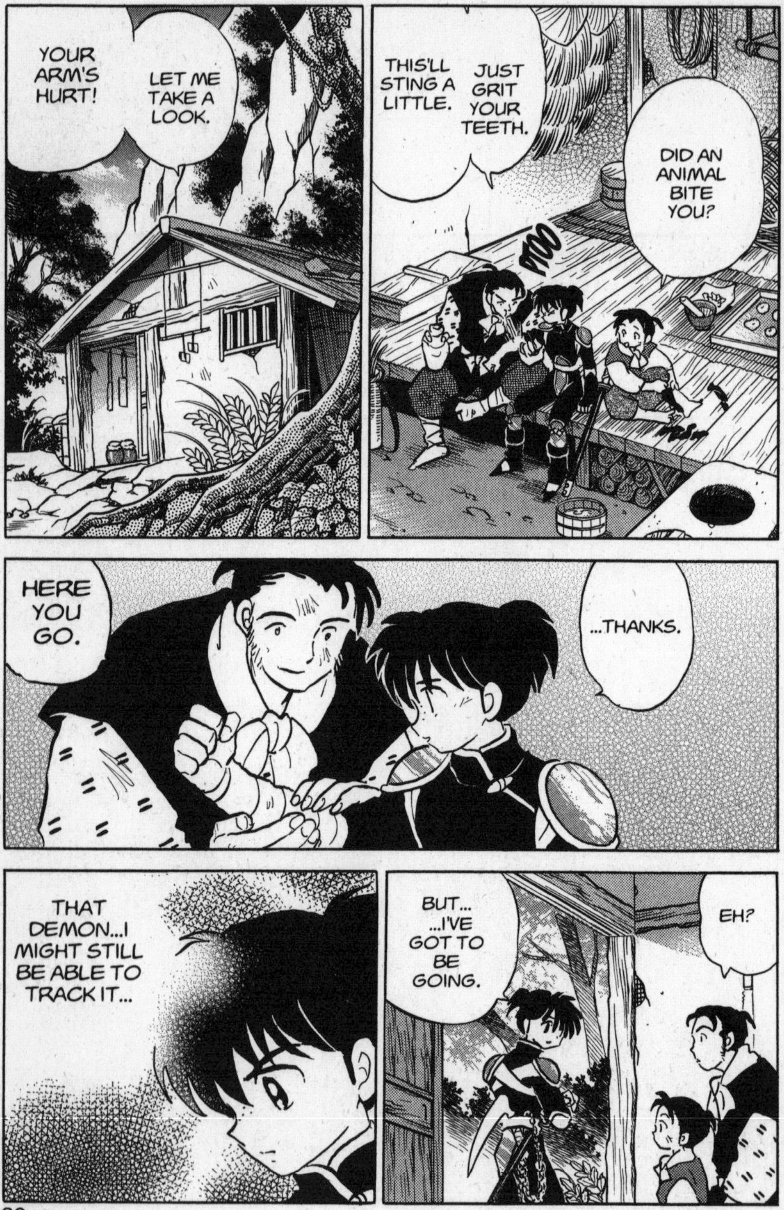
YOUR ARM'S HURT!
LET ME TAKE A LOOK.
THIS'LL STING A LITTLE.
JUST GRIT YOUR TEETH.
PTOO
DID AN ANIMAL BITE YOU?
HERE YOU GO.
...THANKS.
THAT DEMON...I MIGHT STILL BE ABLE TO TRACK IT...
BUT... ...I'VE GOT TO BE GOING.
EH?

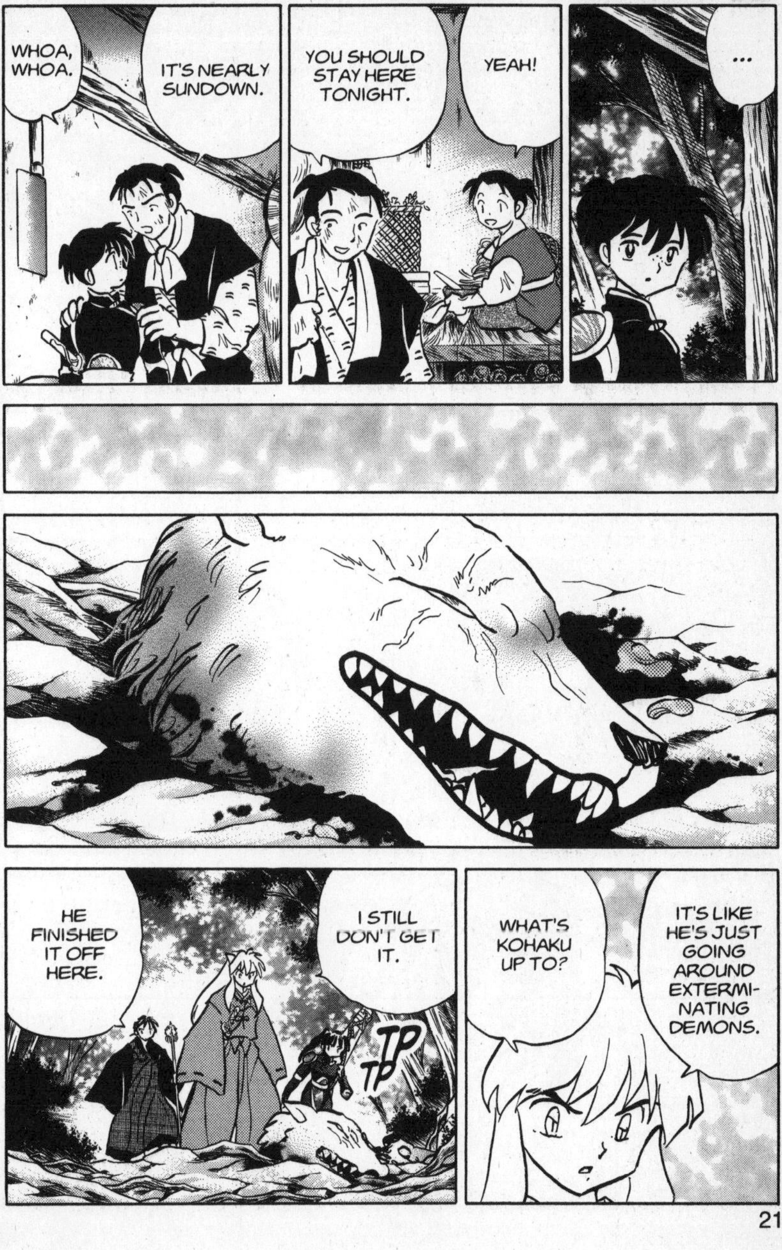
WHOA, WHOA.
IT'S NEARLY SUNDOWN.
YOU SHOULD STAY HERE TONIGHT.
YEAH!
...
HE FINISHED IT OFF HERE.
I STILL DON'T GET IT.
TP TP
WHAT'S KOHAKU UP TO?
IT'S LIKE HE'S JUST GOING AROUND EXTERMINATING DEMONS.

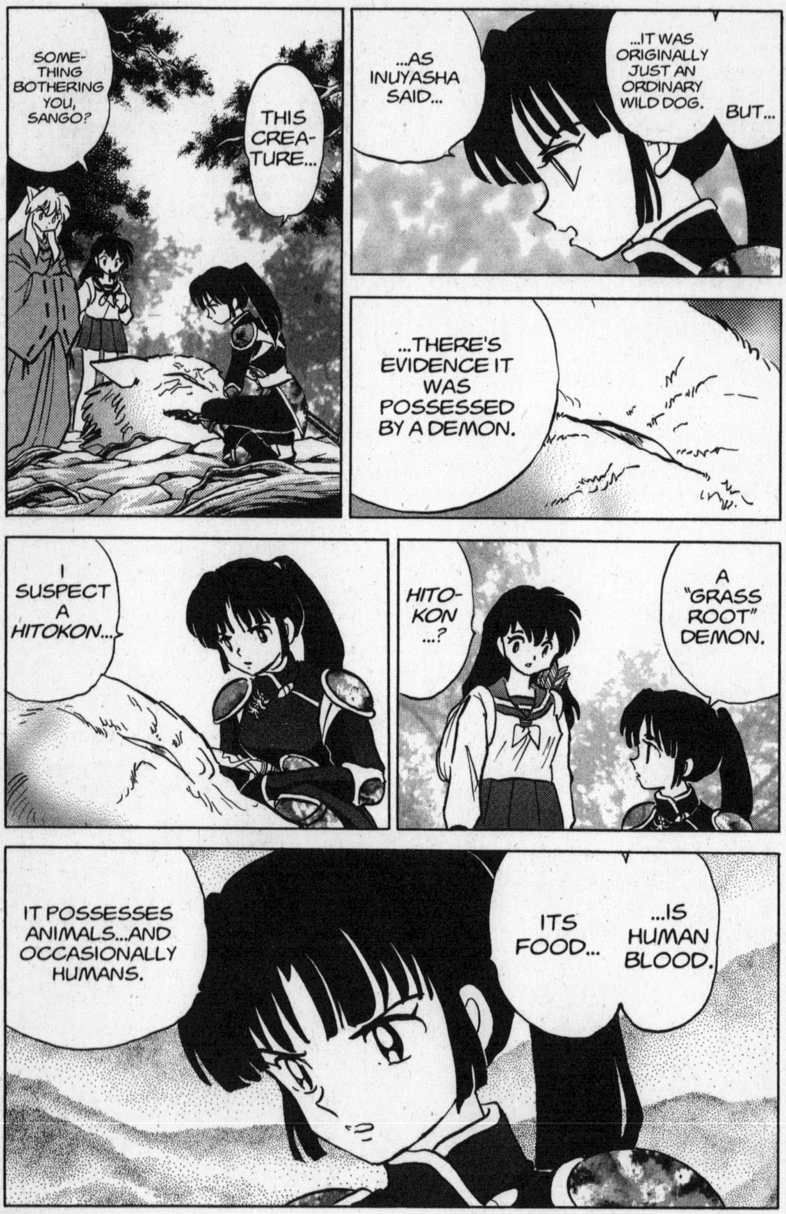
SOME-THING BOTHERING YOU, SANGO?
THIS CREA-TURE...
...AS INUYASHA SAID...
...IT WAS ORIGINALLY JUST AN ORDINARY WILD DOG.
BUT...
...THERE'S EVIDENCE IT WAS POSSESSED BY A DEMON.
I SUSPECT A HITOKON...
HITO-KON ...?
A "GRASS ROOT" DEMON.
IT POSSESSES ANIMALS...AND OCCASIONALLY HUMANS.
ITS FOOD...
...IS HUMAN BLOOD.

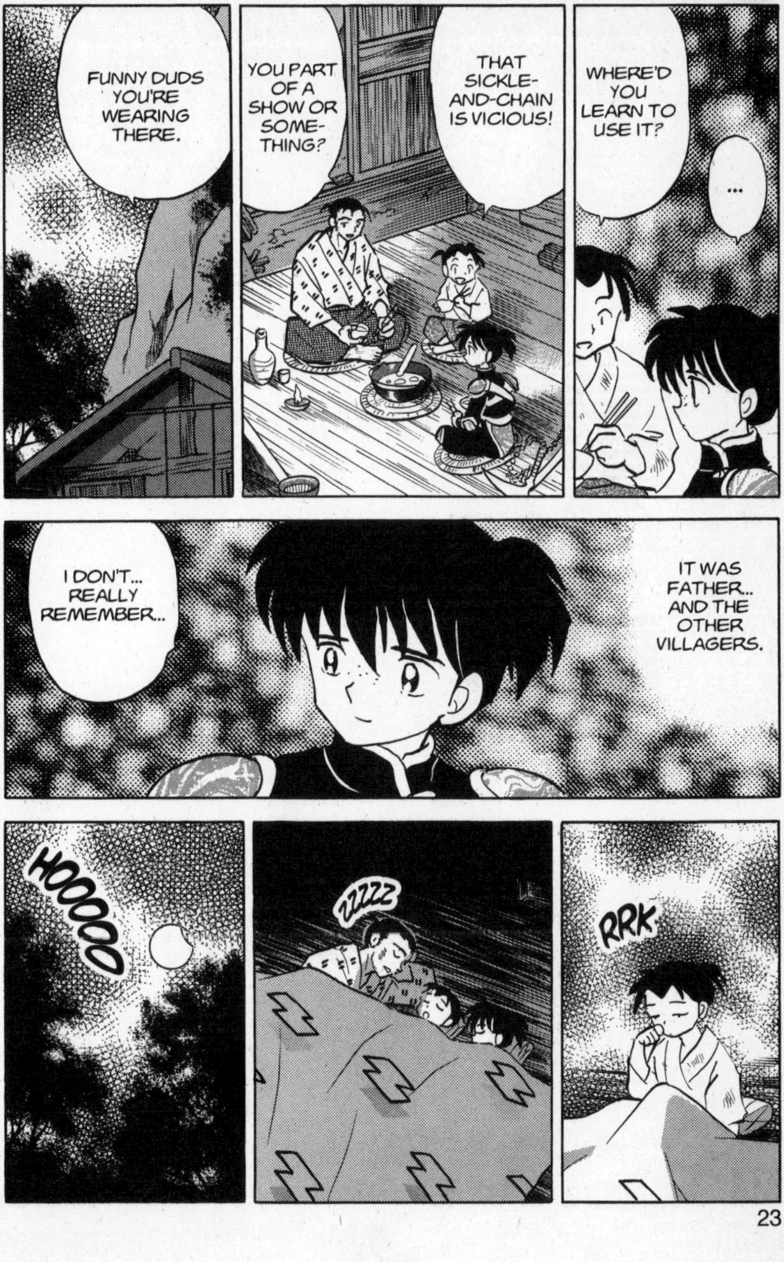
FUNNY DUDS YOU'RE WEARING THERE.
YOU PART OF A SHOW OR SOME-THING?
THAT SICKLE-AND-CHAIN IS VICIOUS!
WHERE'D YOU LEARN TO USE IT?
...
I DON'T... REALLY REMEMBER...
IT WAS FATHER... AND THE OTHER VILLAGERS.
HOOOOOO
ZZZZZ
RRK

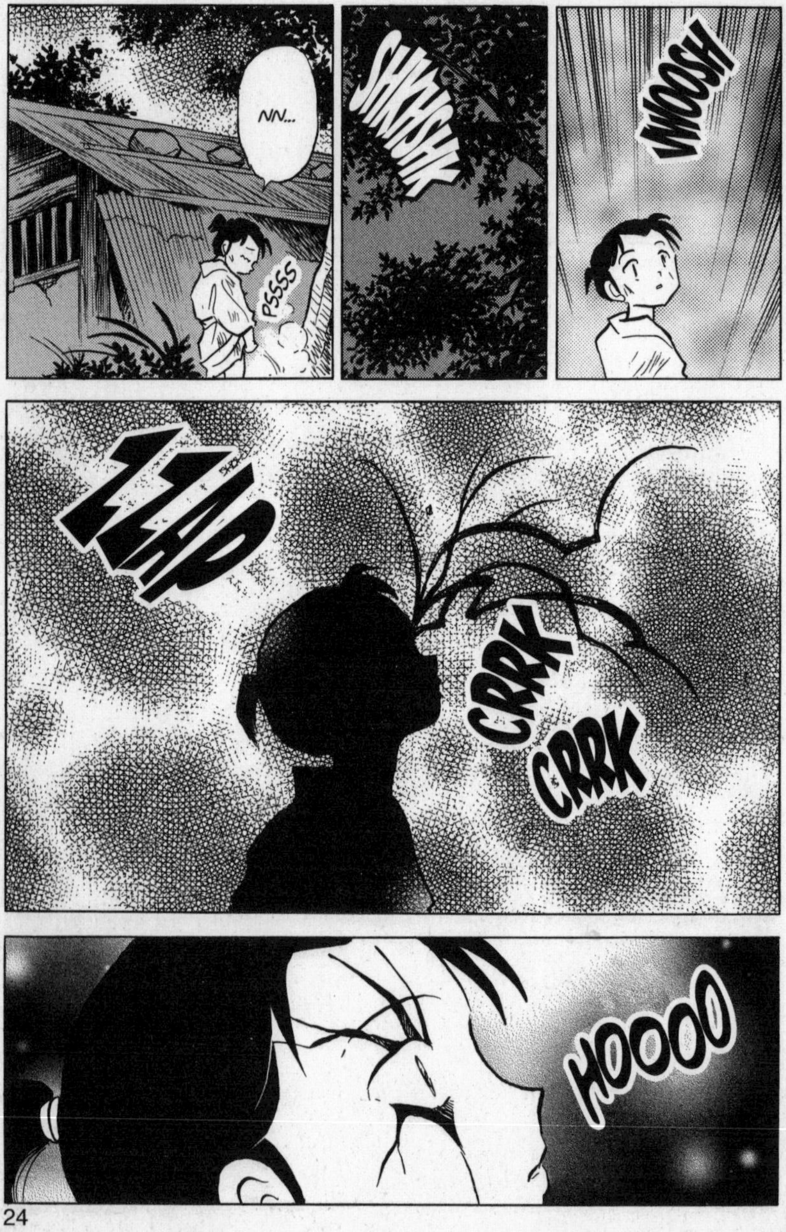
NN...
PSSSS
SHKSHK
WOOSH
ZZAP
CRRK
CRRK
HOOOO

SCROLL 2
MEMORIES

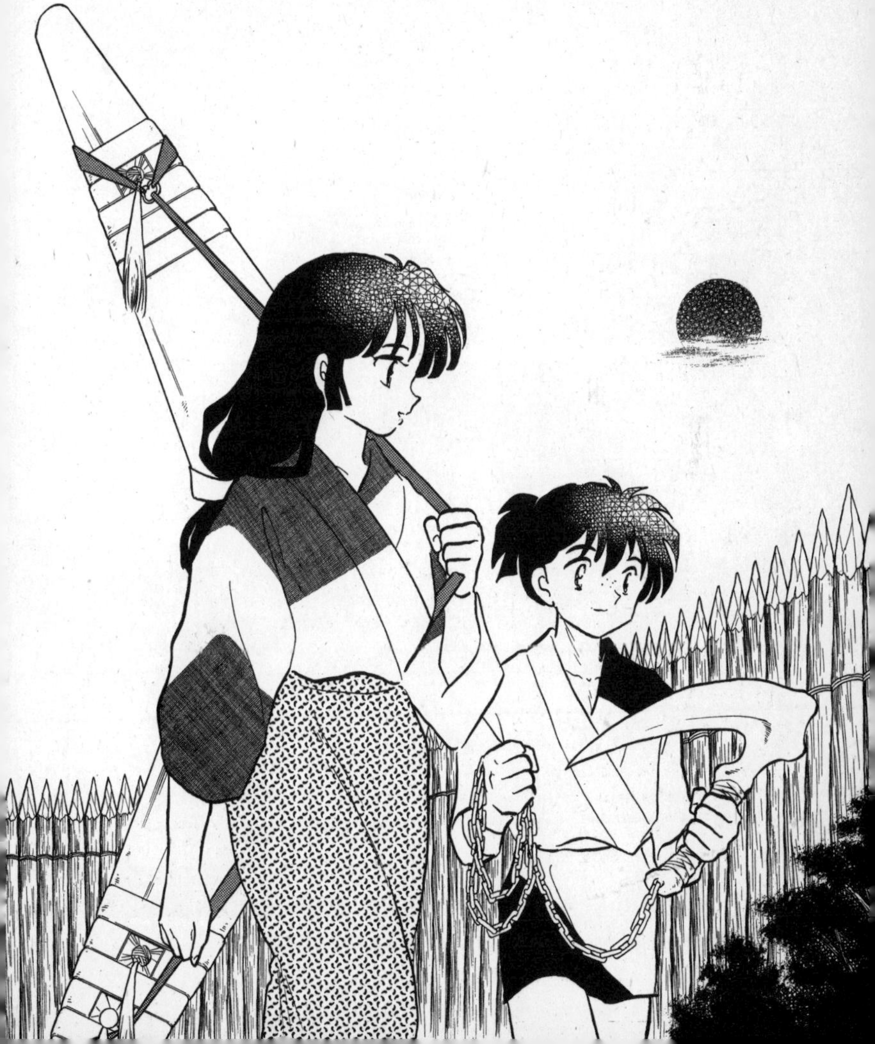

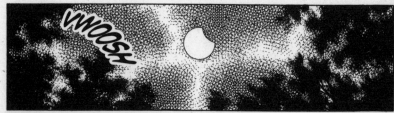

I SENSE A SHIKON SHARD.

KOHAKU'S NEARBY!

HE'S NOT ALONE.

I SMELL OTHER HUMANS...

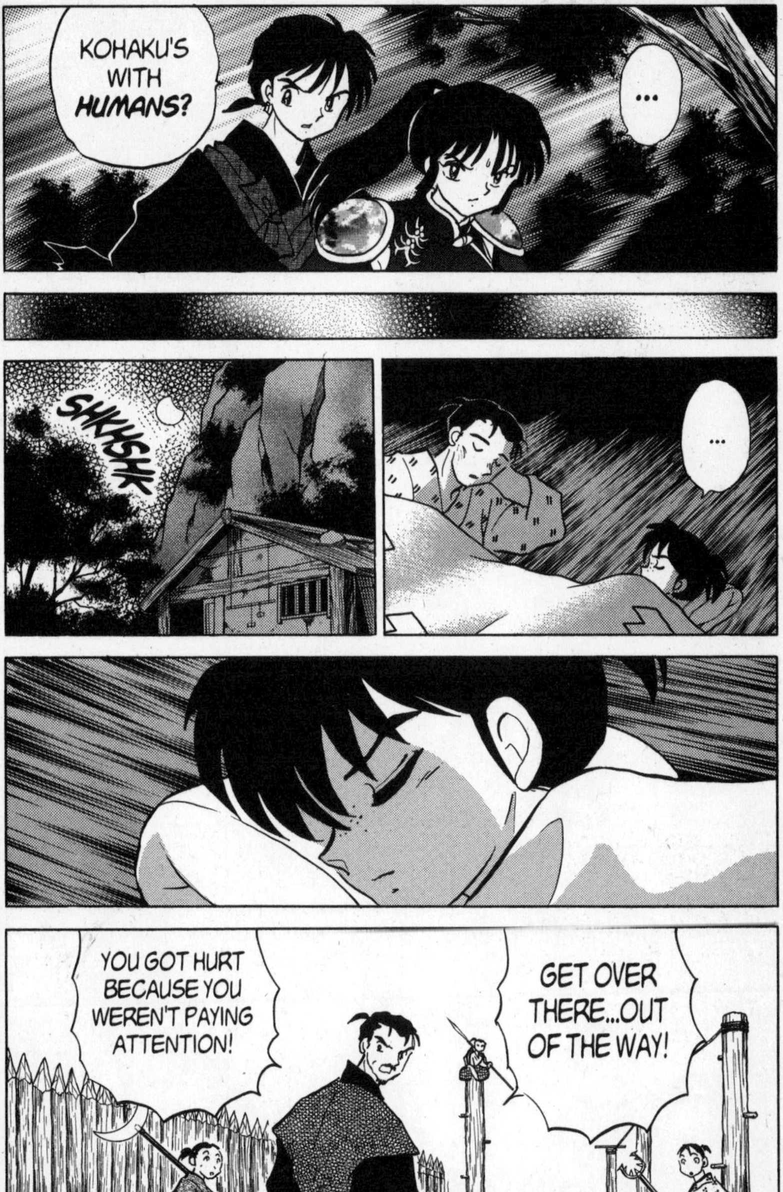
KOHAKU'S WITH HUMANS?
...
SHKKSHK
...
YOU GOT HURT BECAUSE YOU WEREN'T PAYING ATTENTION!
GET OVER THERE...OUT OF THE WAY!

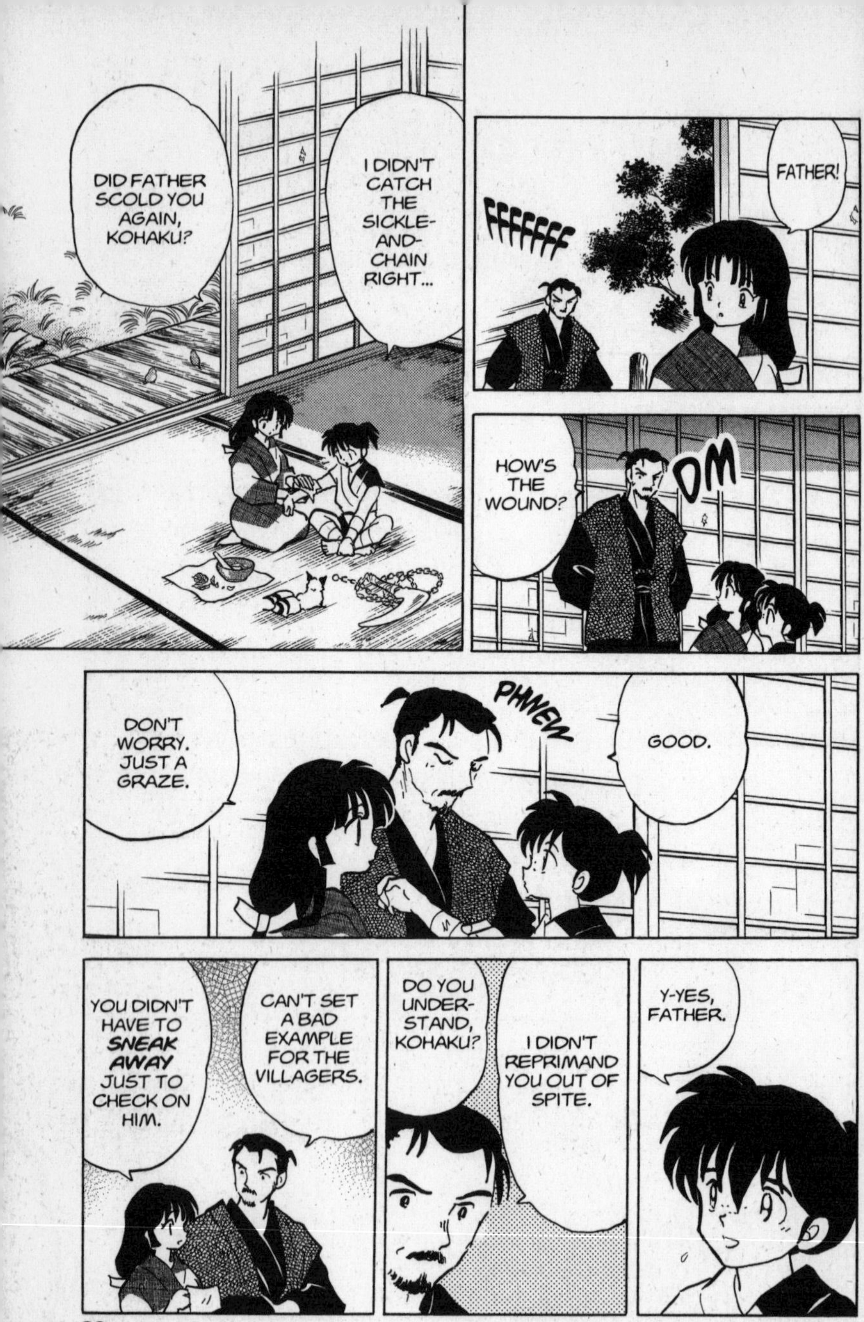
DID FATHER SCOLD YOU AGAIN, KOHAKU?
I DIDN'T CATCH THE SICKLE-AND-CHAIN RIGHT...
FATHER!
FFFFFFF
HOW'S THE WOUND?
DM
DON'T WORRY. JUST A GRAZE.
PHWEW
GOOD.
YOU DIDN'T HAVE TO **SNEAK AWAY** JUST TO CHECK ON HIM.
CAN'T SET A BAD EXAMPLE FOR THE VILLAGERS.
DO YOU UNDERSTAND, KOHAKU?
I DIDN'T REPRIMAND YOU OUT OF SPITE.
Y-YES, FATHER.

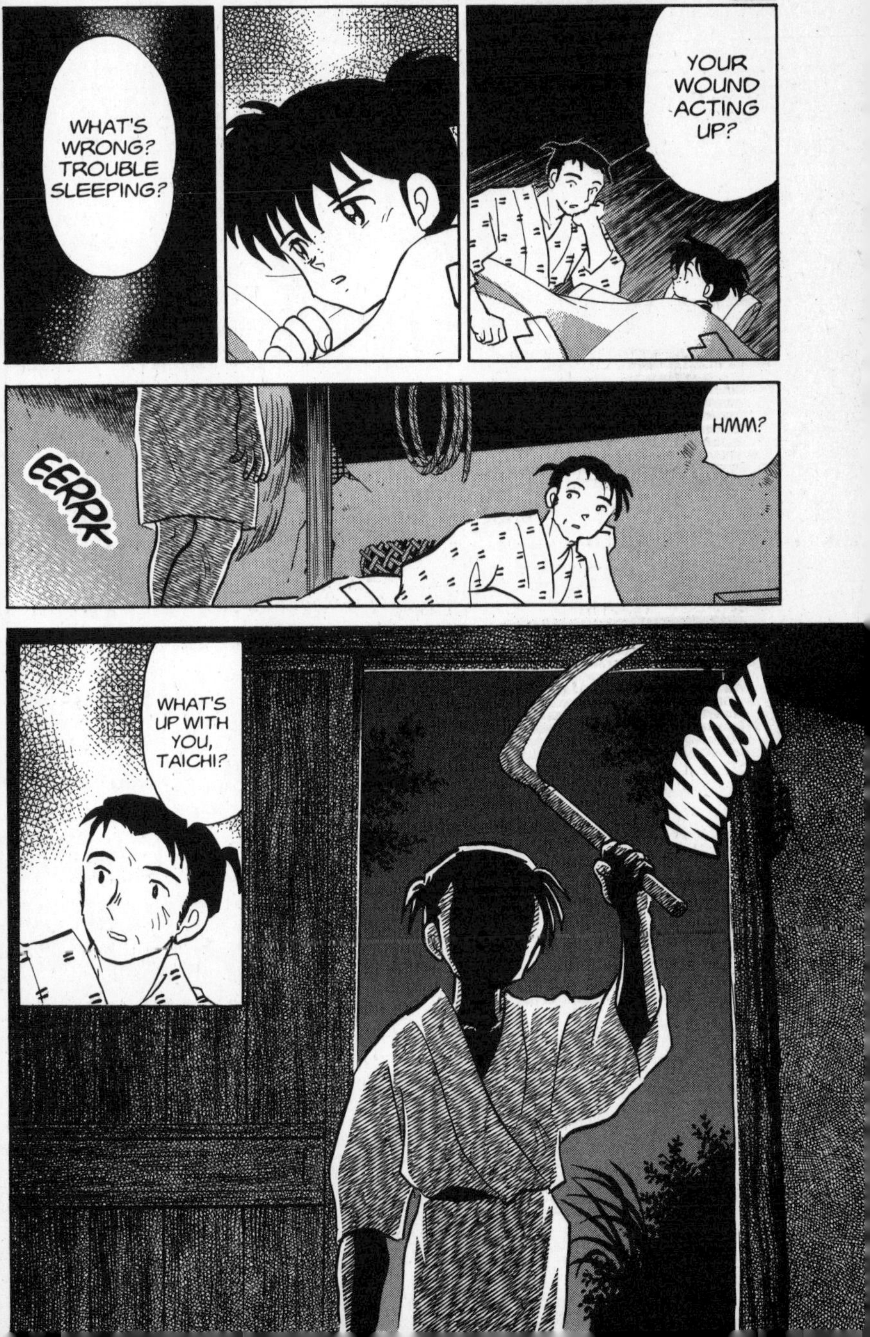
WHAT'S WRONG? TROUBLE SLEEPING?
YOUR WOUND ACTING UP?
EERRK
HMM?
WHAT'S UP WITH YOU, TAICHI?
WHOOSH

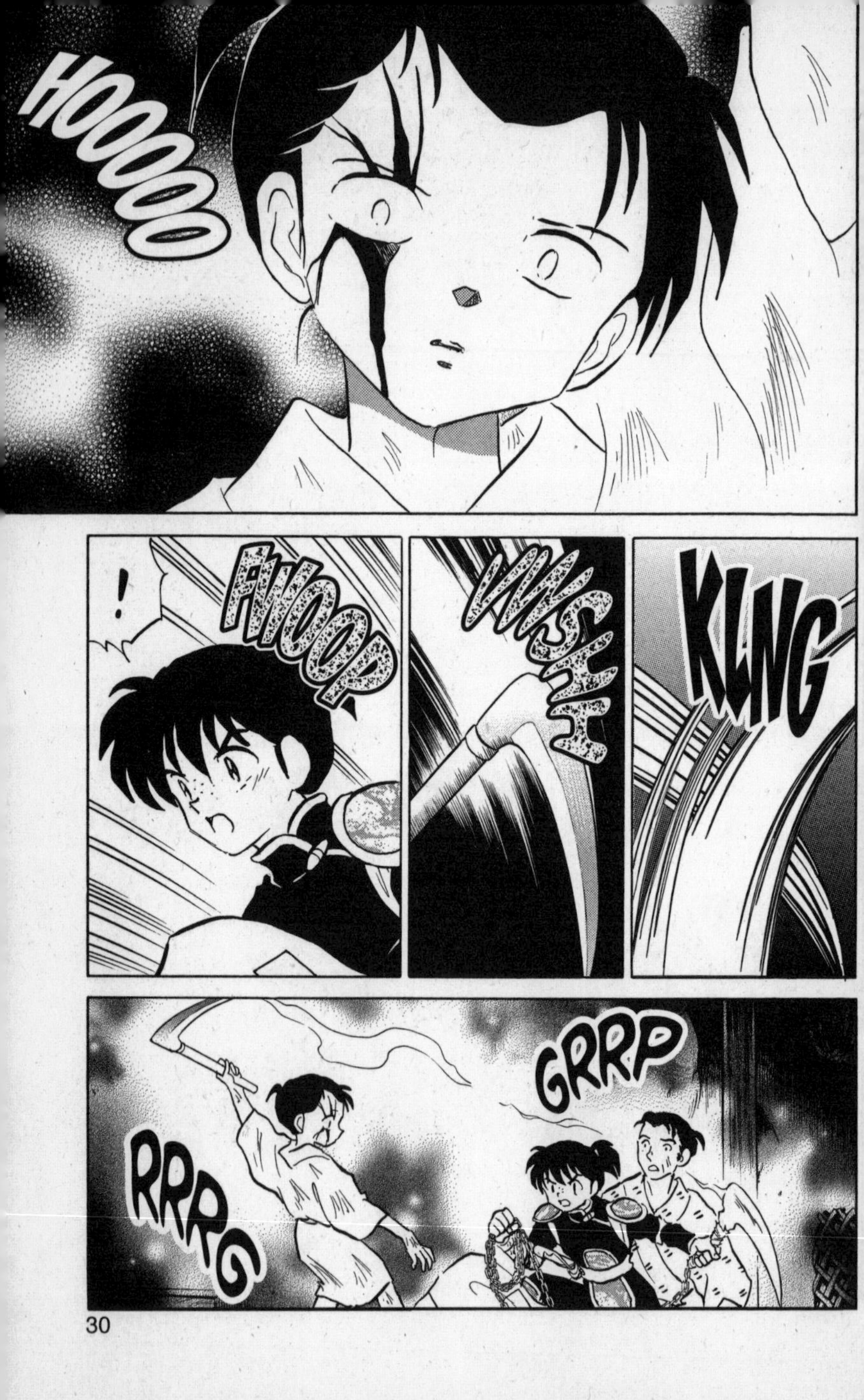
HOOOOO
!
FWOOP
WISHH
KLING
RRRG
GRRP

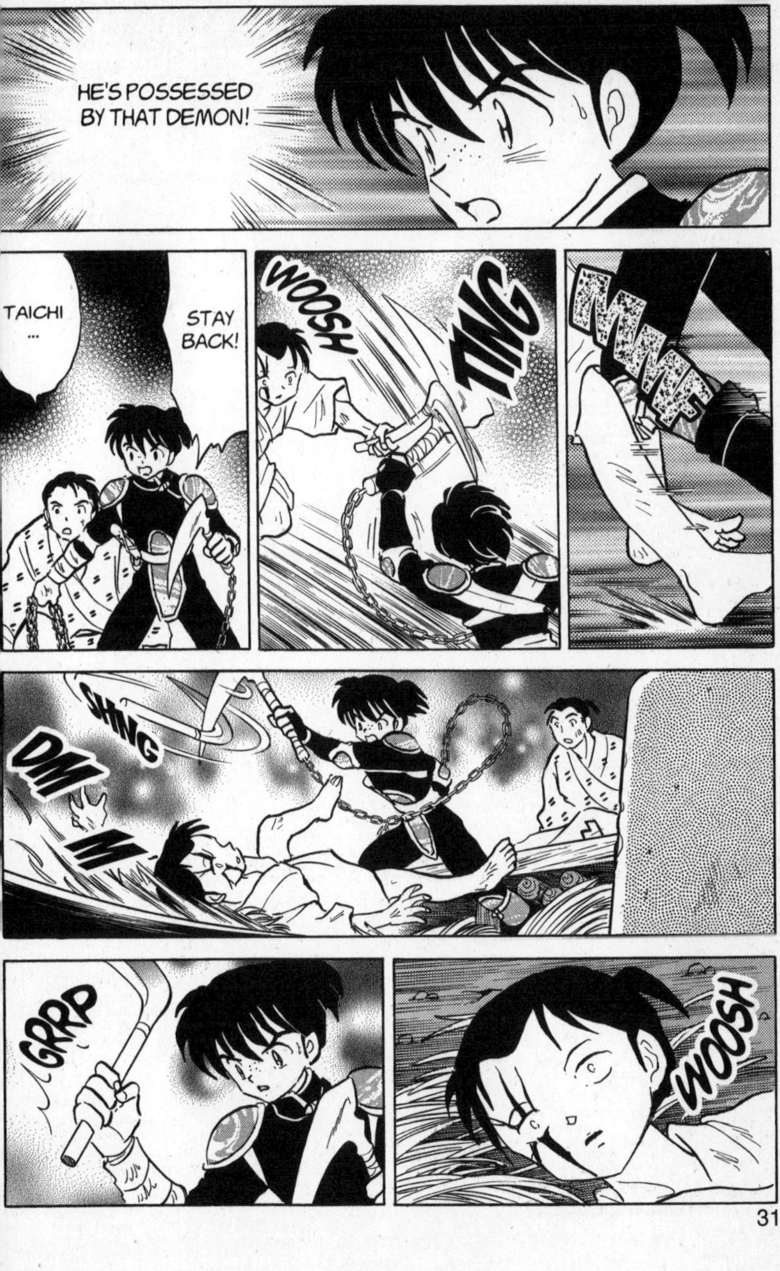
HE'S POSSESSED BY THAT DEMON!
TAICHI ...
STAY BACK!
WOOSH
TING
MMF
SHING
DMM
GRRP
WOOSH

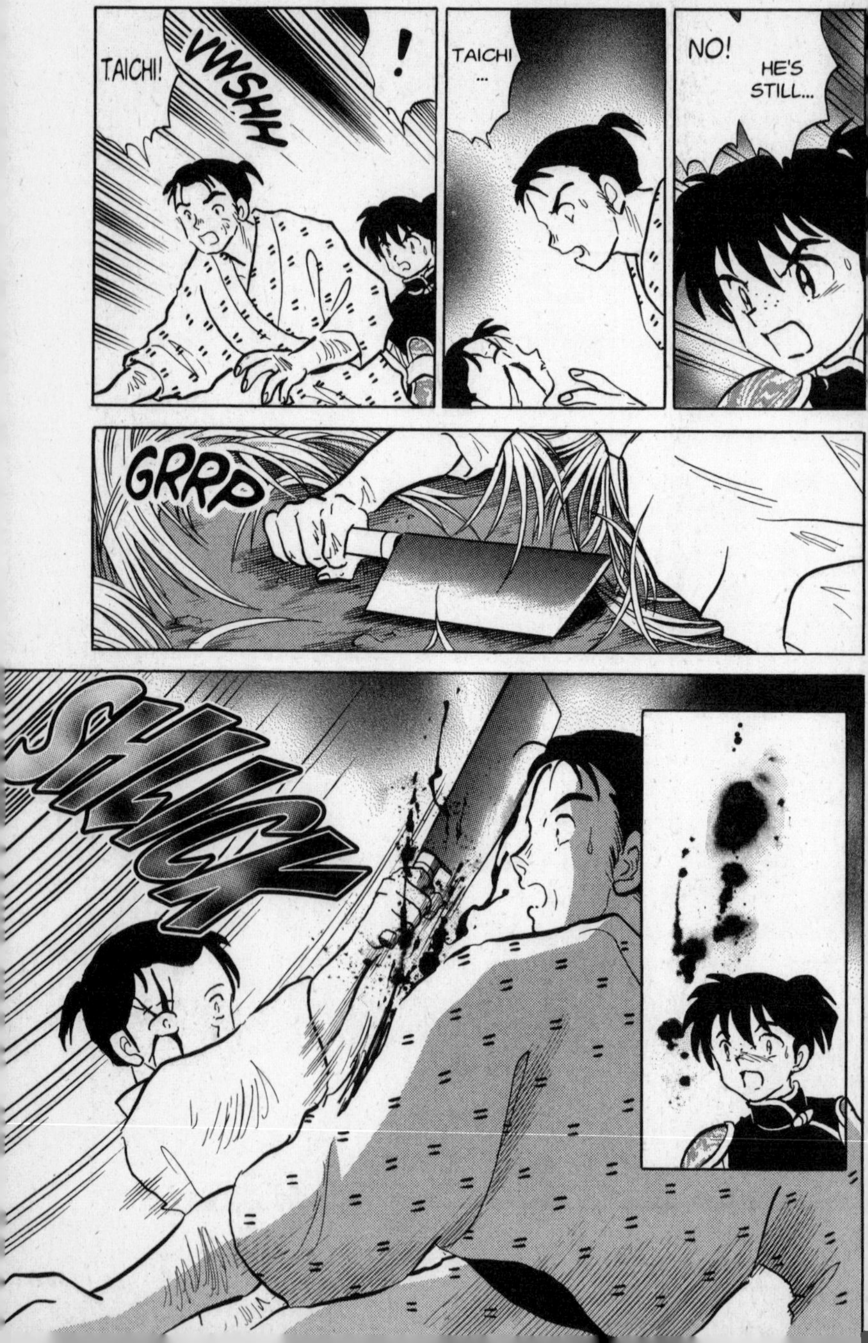
TAICHI!
VWSHH
!
TAICHI ...
NO!
HE'S STILL...
GRRP
SHICK

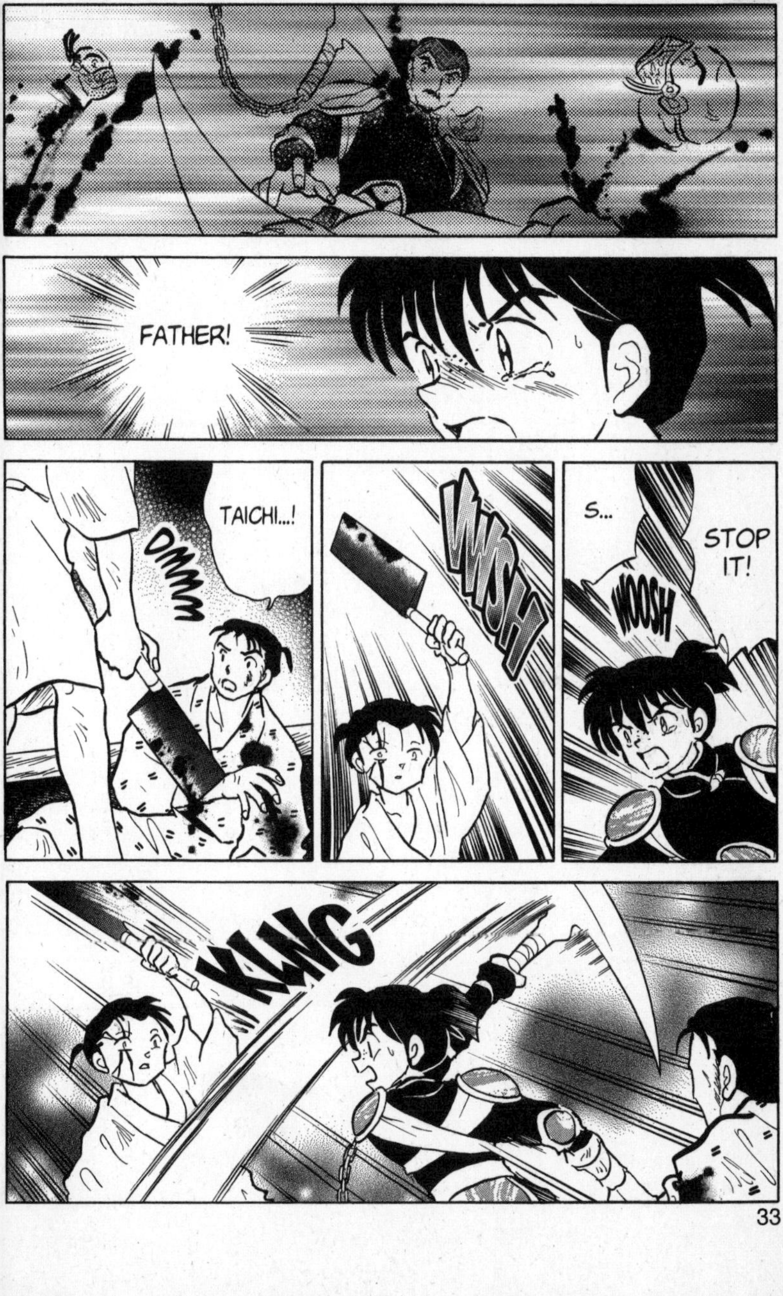
FATHER!
TAICHI...!
DMMM
VWISH
S...
STOP IT!
WOOSH
KLING

TAICHI...

WHY...?

HE'S BEING MANIPULATED!

HE'S POSSESSED!

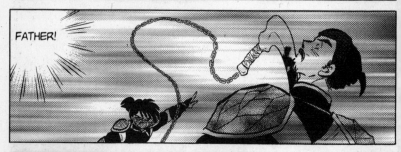

FATHER!

WOOSH

WHAT DO I DO?!

HOW DO I DRIVE THAT DEMON OUT?!

34

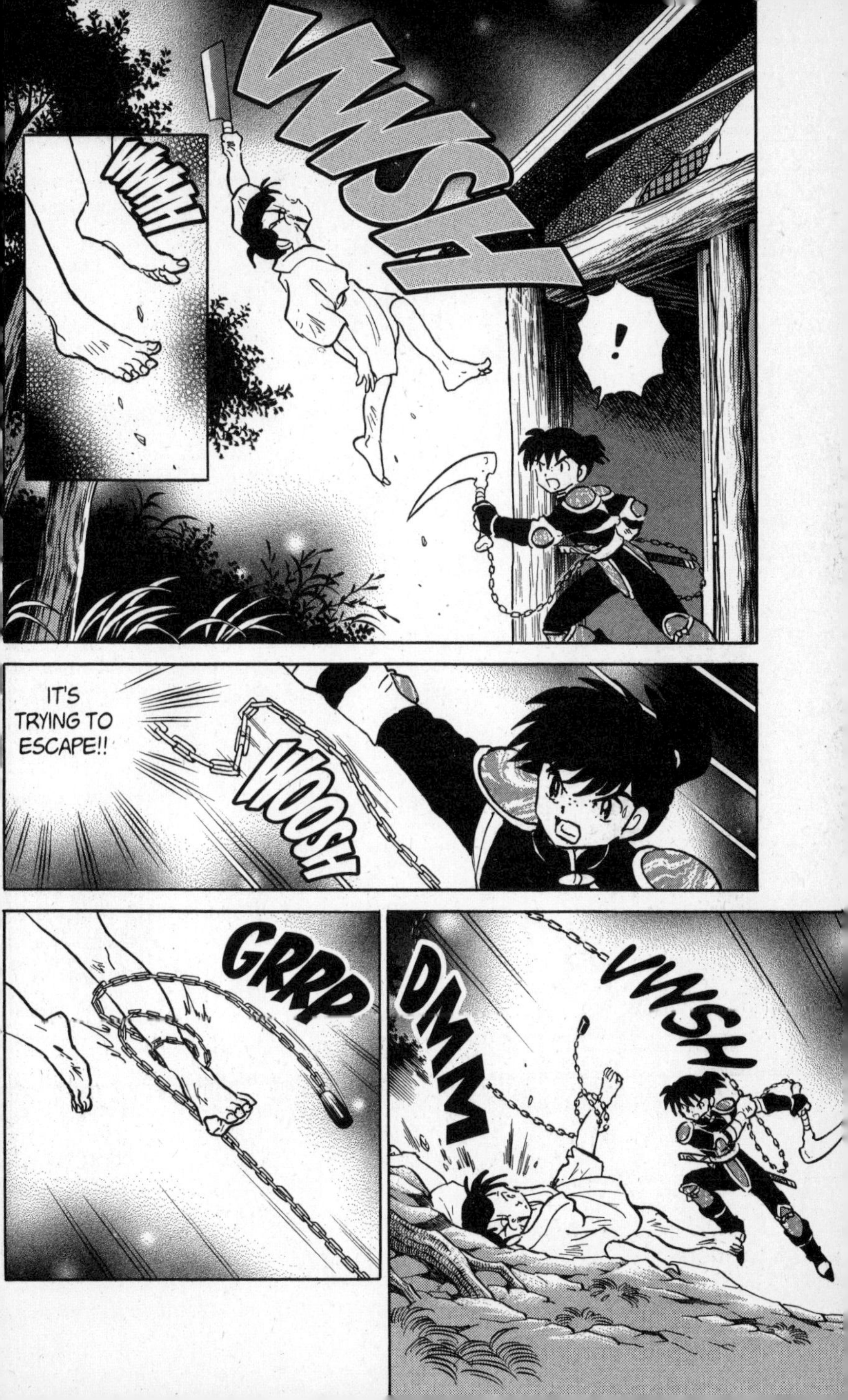
WHH
VWSH
!
IT'S TRYING TO ESCAPE!!
WOOSH
GRRP
DMM
VWSH

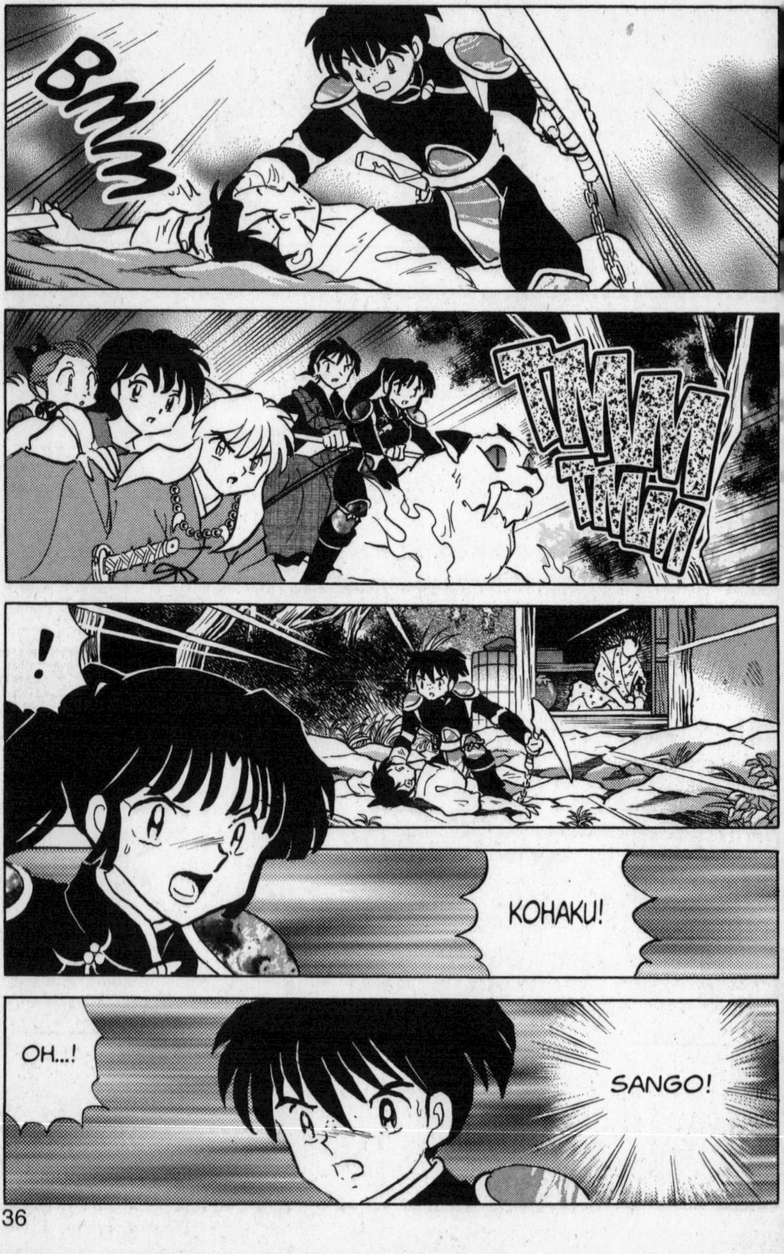
BMM
TMMM TMMM
!
KOHAKU!
OH...!
SANGO!

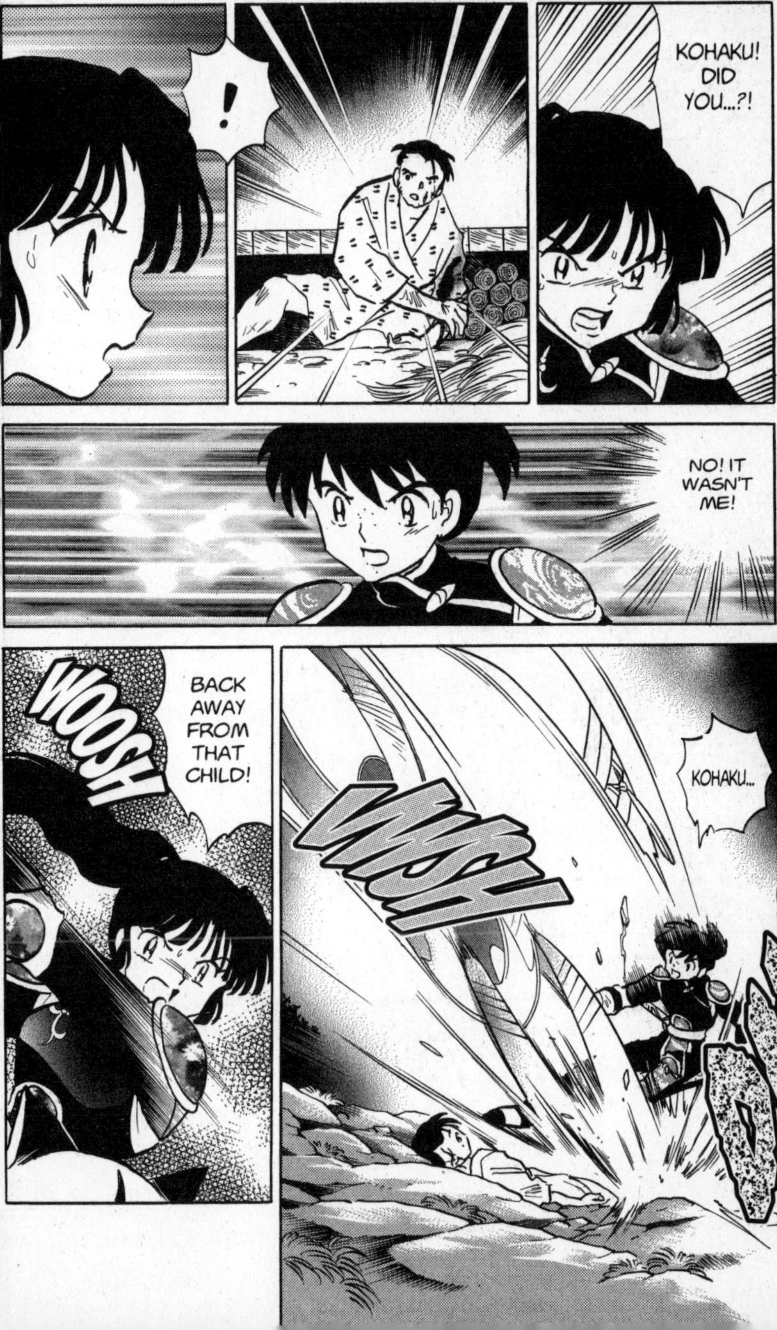
!
KOHAKU! DID YOU...?!
NO! IT WASN'T ME!
WOOSH
BACK AWAY FROM THAT CHILD!
KOHAKU...

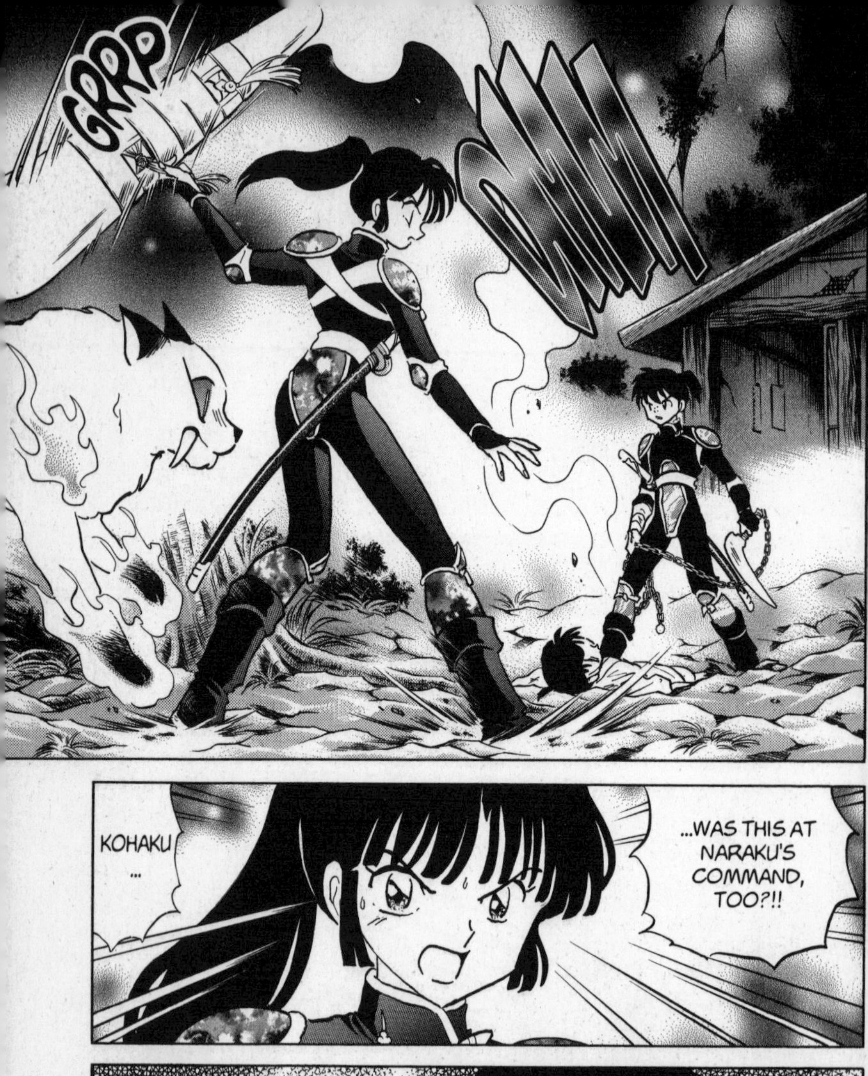
GRRP
KOHAKU ...
...WAS THIS AT NARAKU'S COMMAND, TOO?!!
...

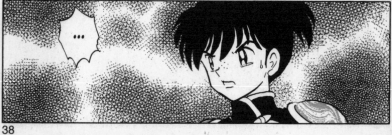

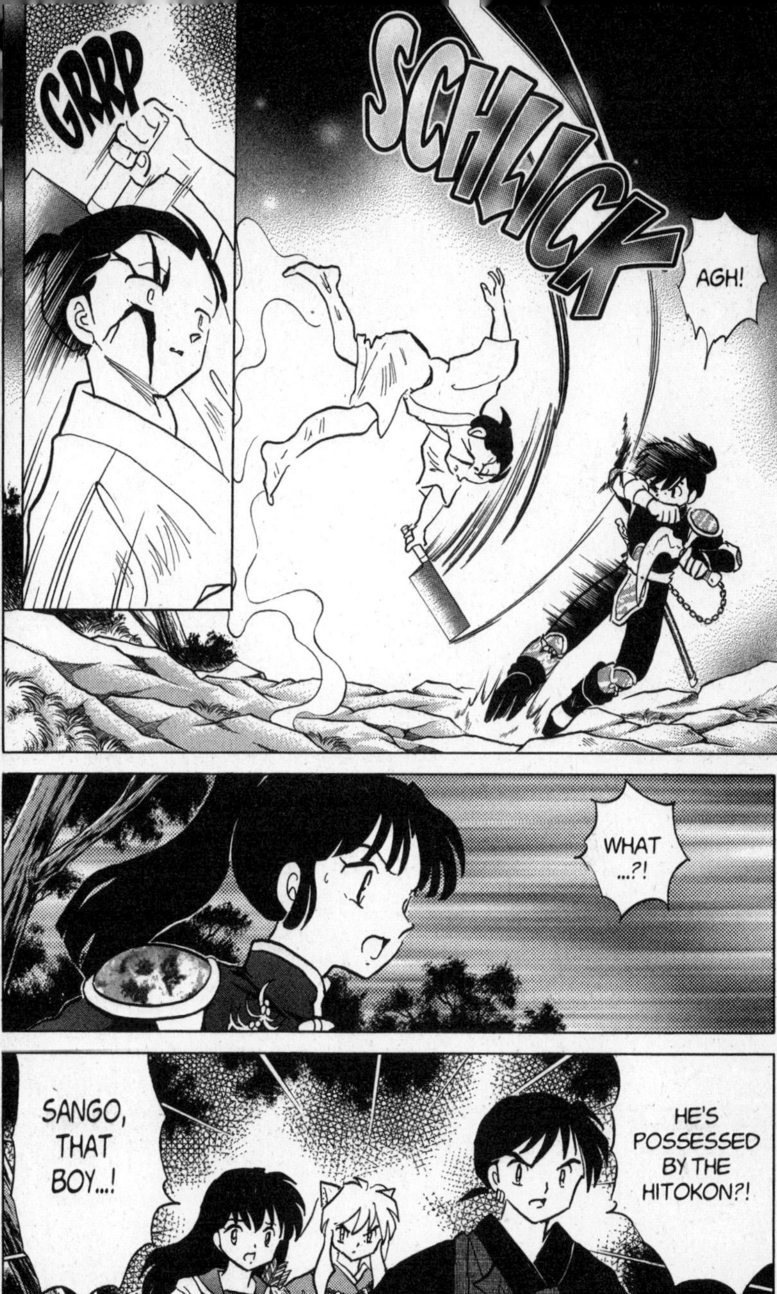
GRRP
SCHLICK
AGH!
WHAT ...?!
SANGO, THAT BOY...!
HE'S POSSESSED BY THE HITOKON?!

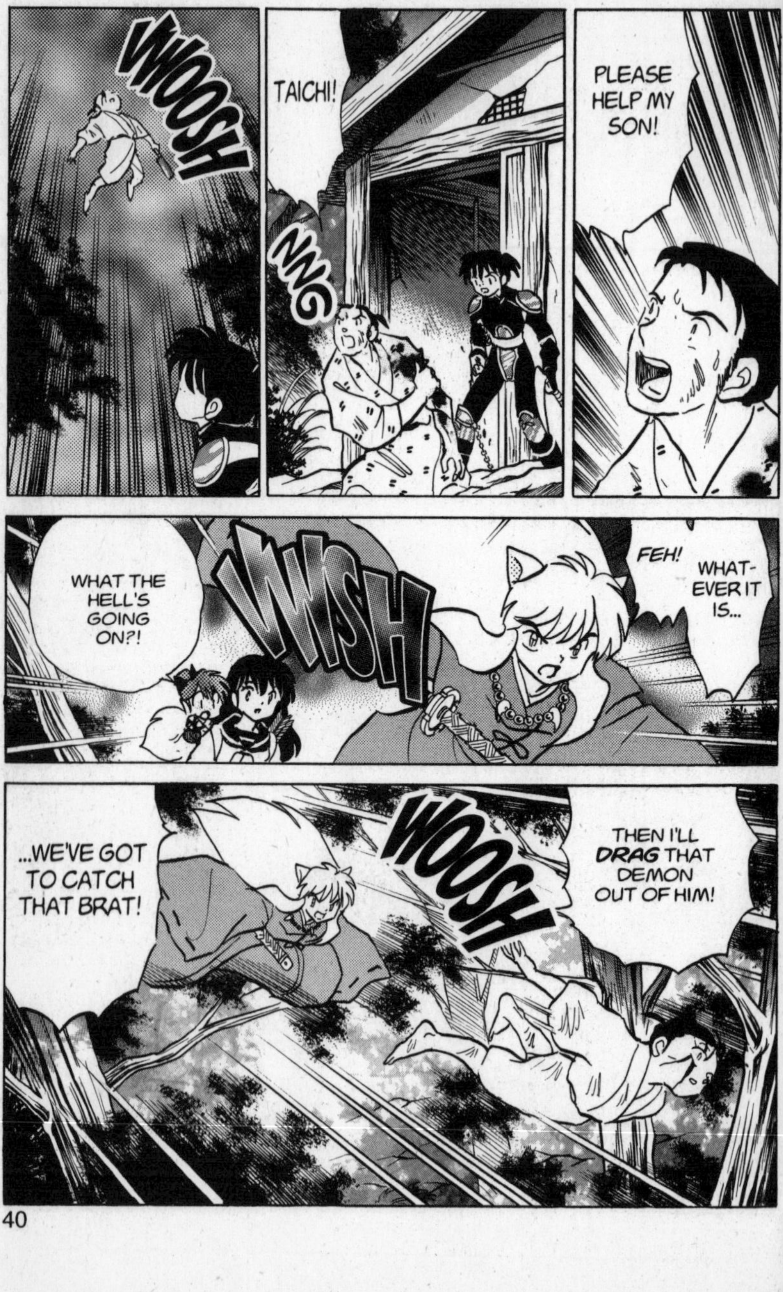
PLEASE HELP MY SON!
TAICHI!
NNG
WHOOSH
FEH!
WHAT-EVER IT IS...
WHOOSH
WHAT THE HELL'S GOING ON?!
THEN I'LL **DRAG** THAT DEMON OUT OF HIM!
WOOSH
...WE'VE GOT TO CATCH THAT BRAT!

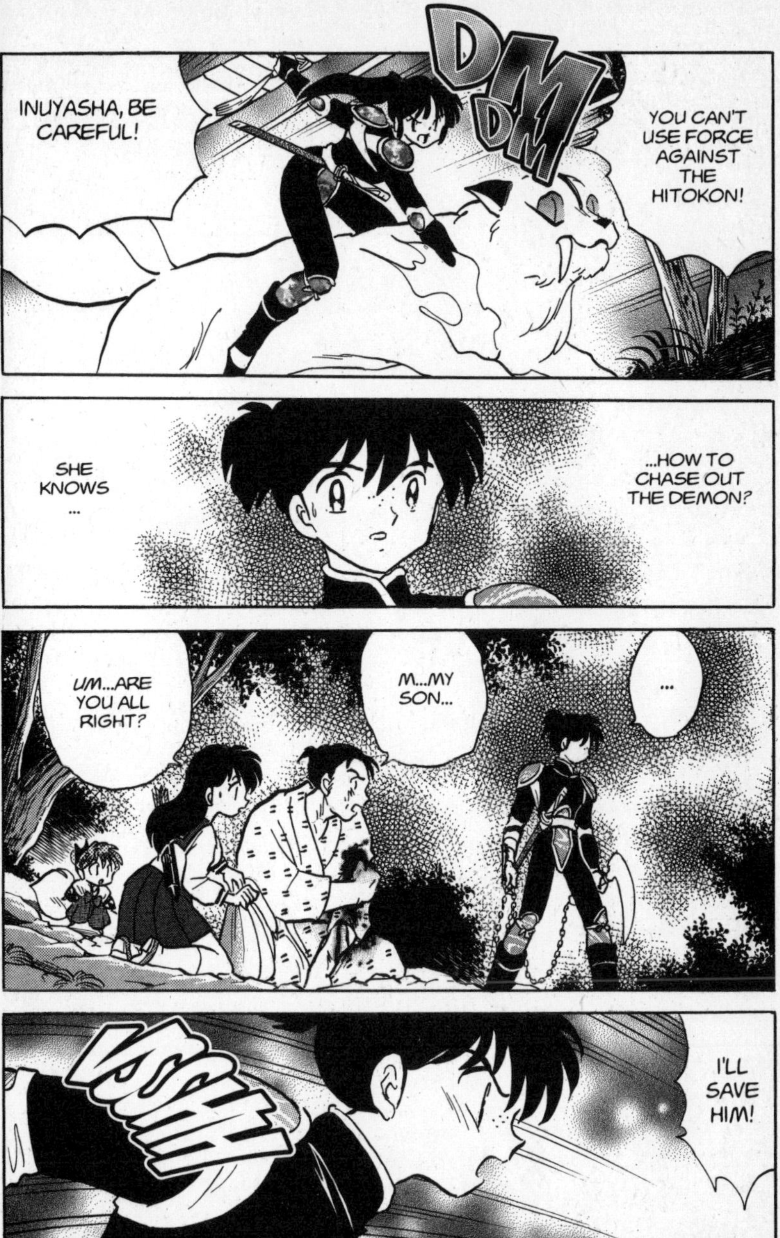
DM DM
INUYASHA, BE CAREFUL!
YOU CAN'T USE FORCE AGAINST THE HITOKON!
SHE KNOWS ...
...HOW TO CHASE OUT THE DEMON?
UM...ARE YOU ALL RIGHT?
M...MY SON...
...
VSSH!
I'LL SAVE HIM!

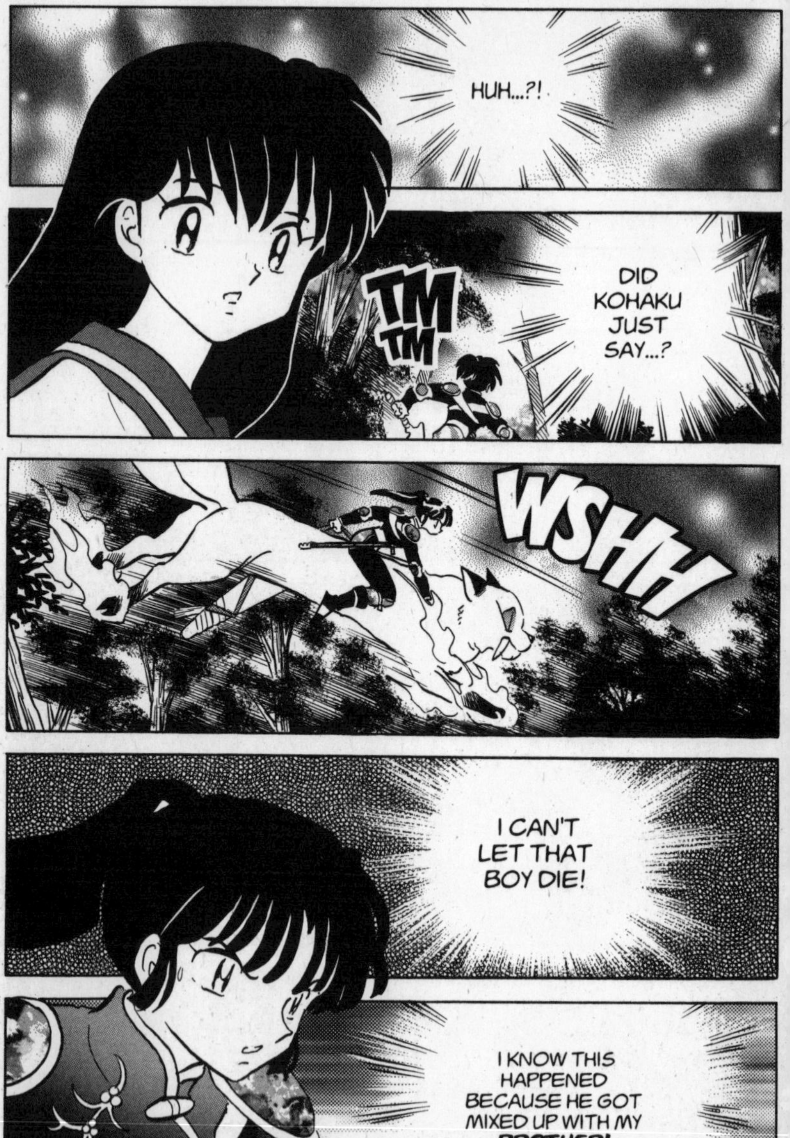
HUH...?!
TM TM
DID KOHAKU JUST SAY...?
WSHH
I CAN'T LET THAT BOY DIE!
I KNOW THIS HAPPENED BECAUSE HE GOT MIXED UP WITH MY ***BROTHER!***

SCROLL 3
SECRETS

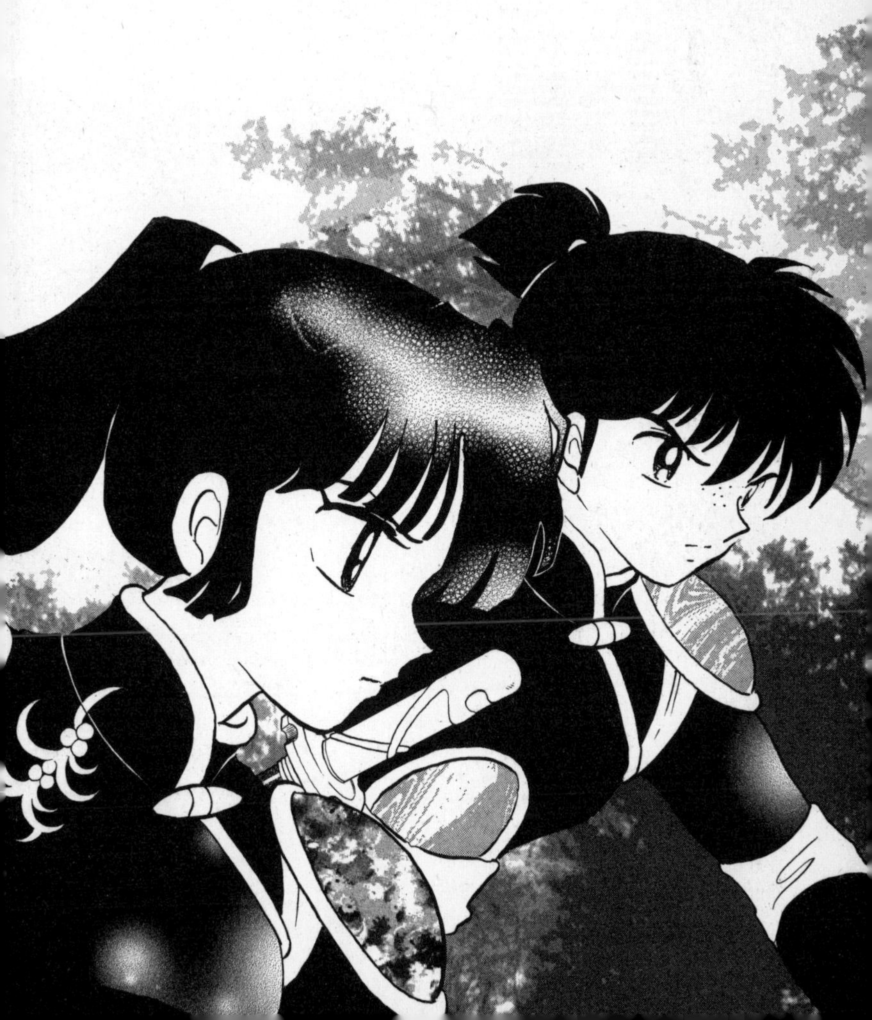

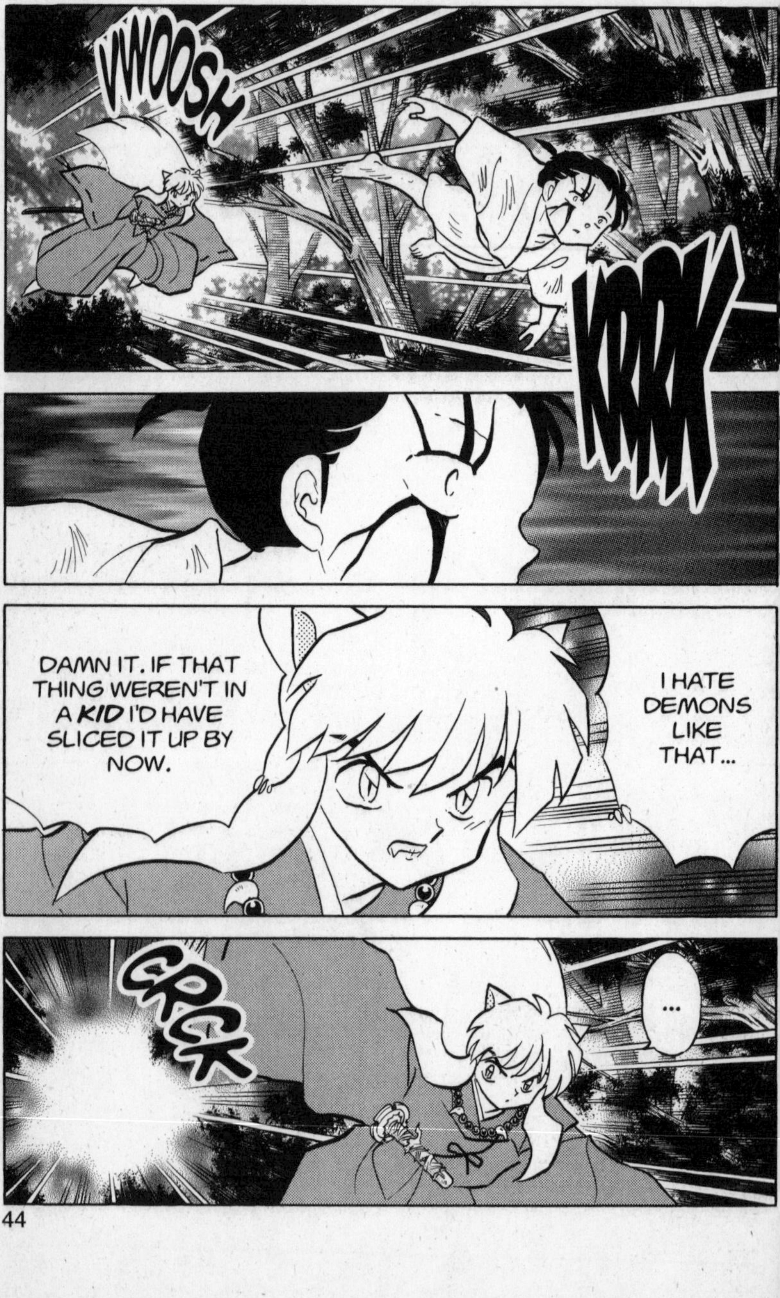
VWOOSH
KRAK
DAMN IT. IF THAT THING WEREN'T IN A KID I'D HAVE SLICED IT UP BY NOW.
I HATE DEMONS LIKE THAT...
CRCK
...

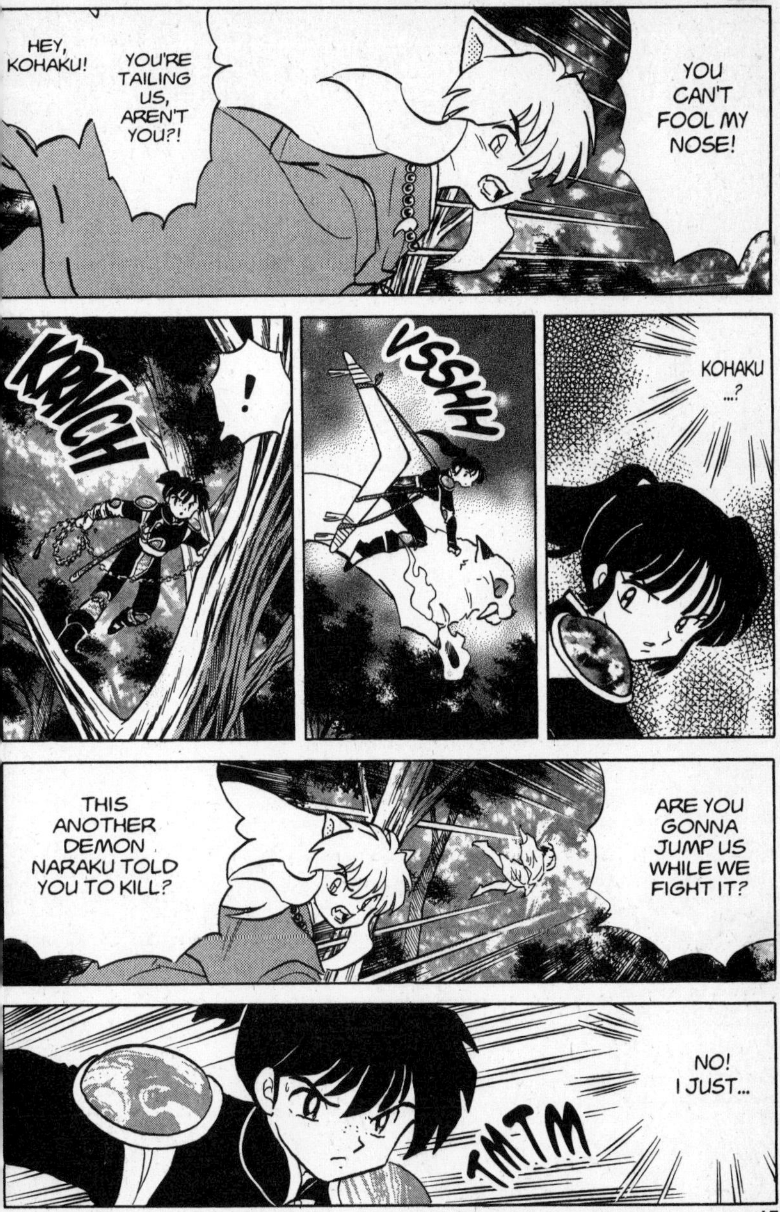
HEY, KOHAKU!
YOU'RE TAILING US, AREN'T YOU?!
YOU CAN'T FOOL MY NOSE!
KRNCH
!
VSSHH
KOHAKU ...?
THIS ANOTHER DEMON NARAKU TOLD YOU TO KILL?
ARE YOU GONNA JUMP US WHILE WE FIGHT IT?
TMTM
NO! I JUST...

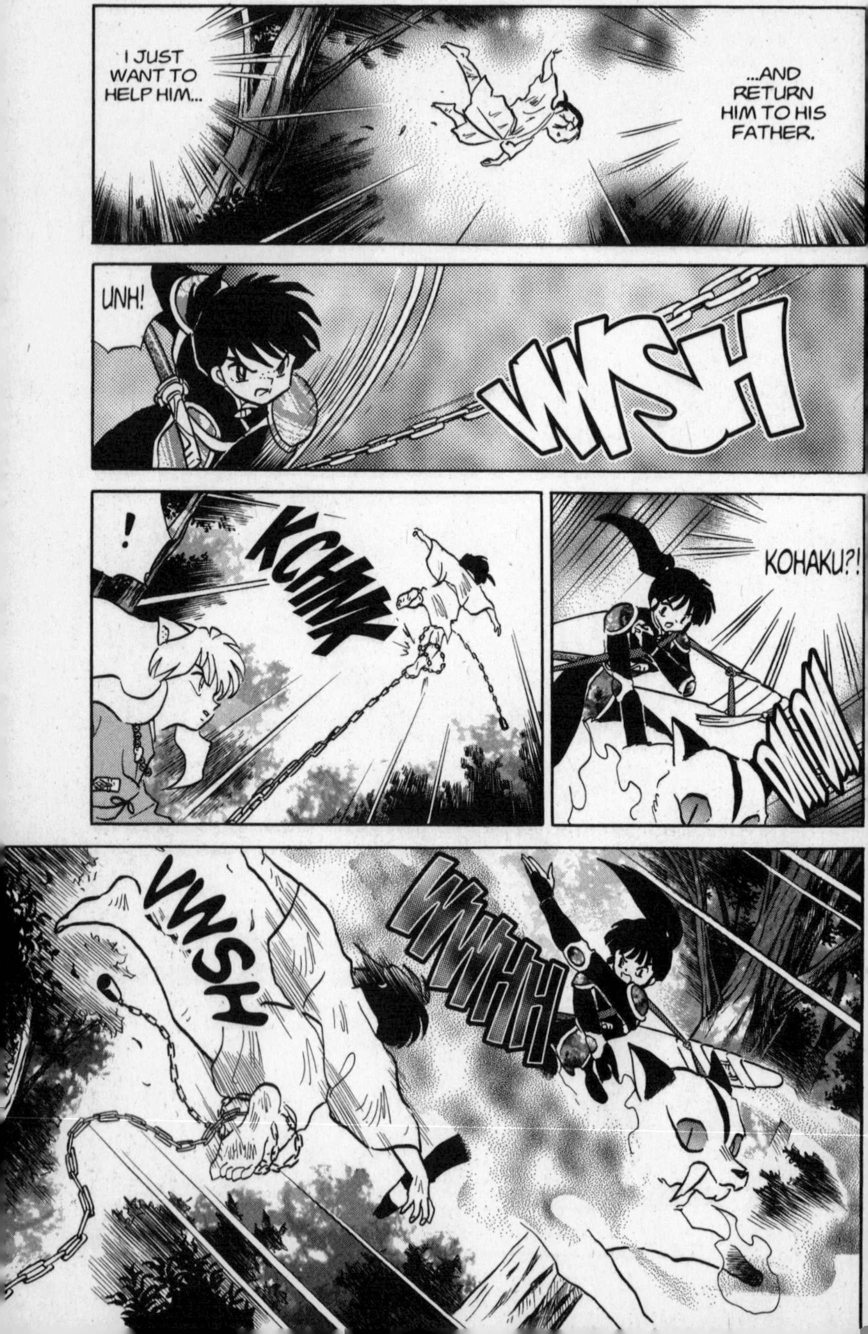
I JUST WANT TO HELP HIM...
...AND RETURN HIM TO HIS FATHER.
UNH!
WISH
!
KCHNK
KOHAKU?!
VWSH
WHHH

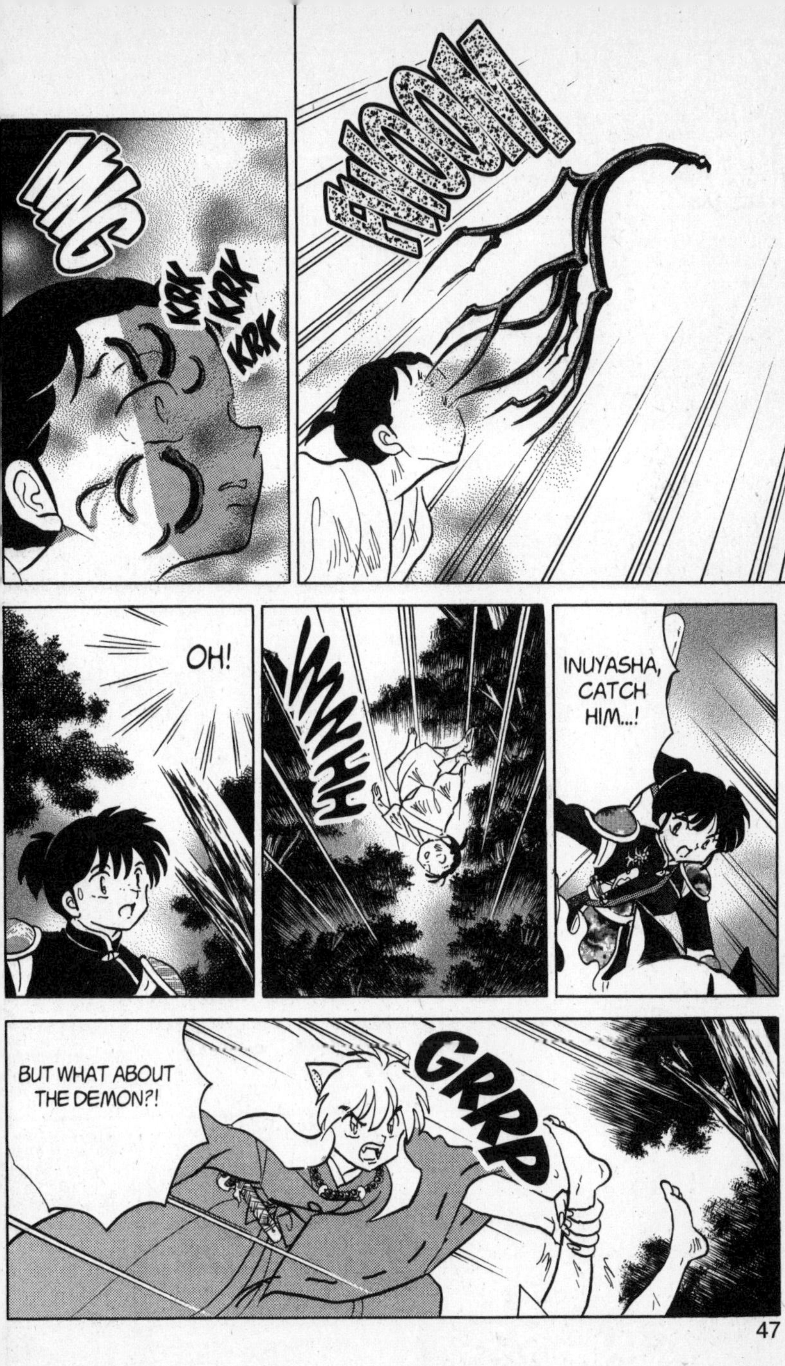
MNG
KRK
KRK
KRK
WOOOM!
OH!
WHHHH
INUYASHA, CATCH HIM...!
BUT WHAT ABOUT THE DEMON?!
GRRP

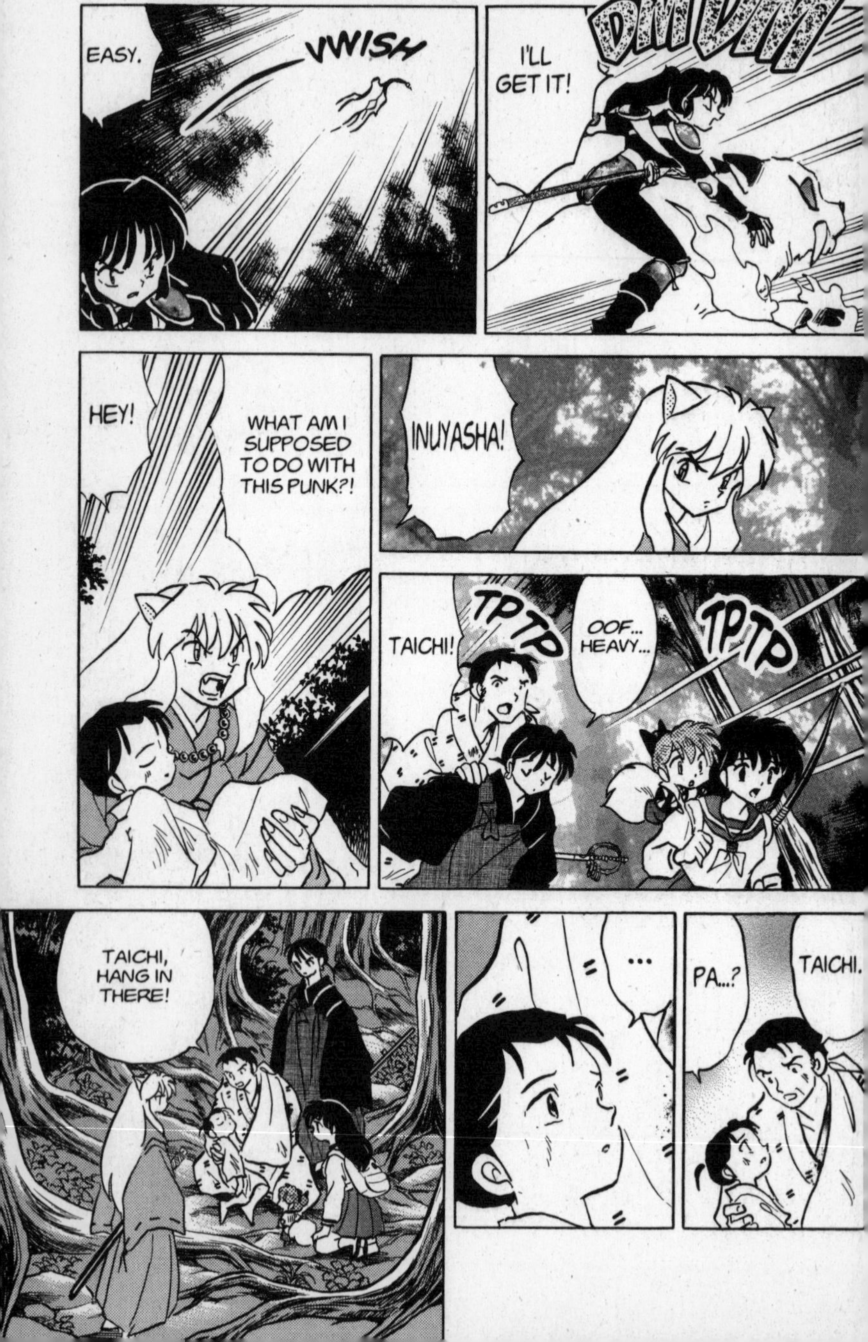
EASY.
VWISH
I'LL GET IT!
DM DM
HEY!
WHAT AM I SUPPOSED TO DO WITH THIS PUNK?!
INUYASHA!
TAICHI!
TP TP
OOF... HEAVY...
TP TP
TAICHI, HANG IN THERE!
...
PA...?
TAICHI.

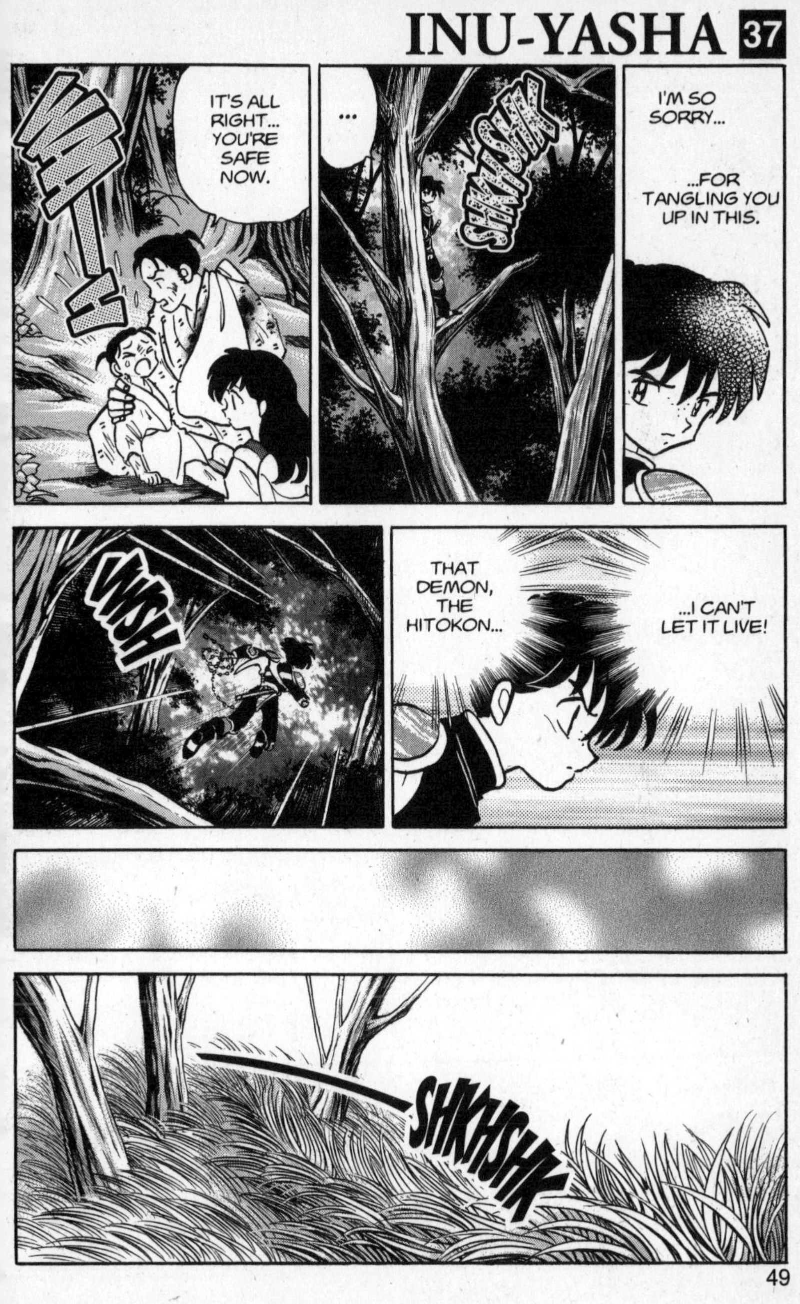
IT'S ALL RIGHT... YOU'RE SAFE NOW.
...
SHKSHK
I'M SO SORRY...
...FOR TANGLING YOU UP IN THIS.
WSH
THAT DEMON, THE HITOKON...
...I CAN'T LET IT LIVE!
SHKHSHK

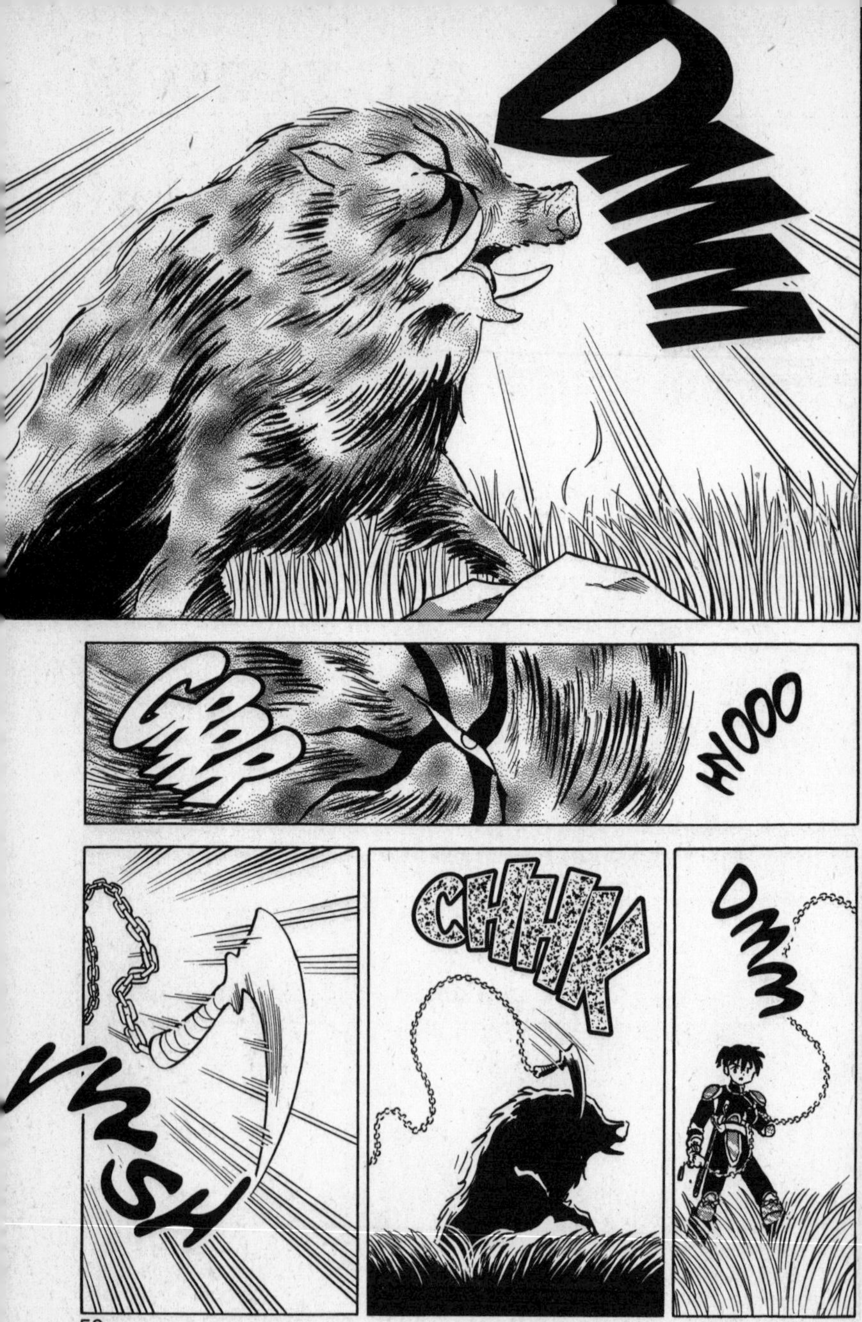
DMMM
GRRR
HYOOO
VMSH
CHHK
DMM

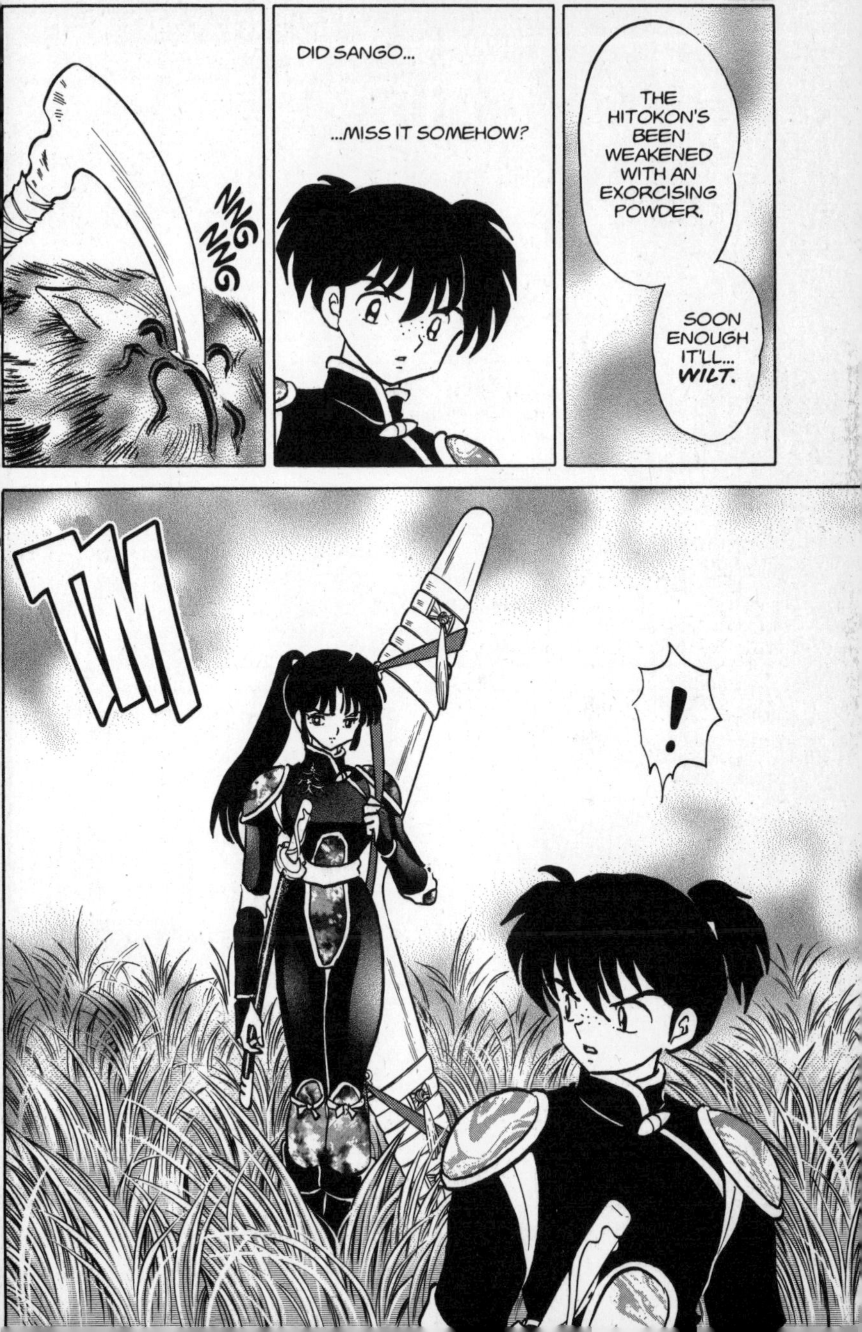
NNG NNG NNG
DID SANGO...
...MISS IT SOMEHOW?
THE HITOKON'S BEEN WEAKENED WITH AN EXORCISING POWDER.
SOON ENOUGH IT'LL... *WILT*.
TM
!

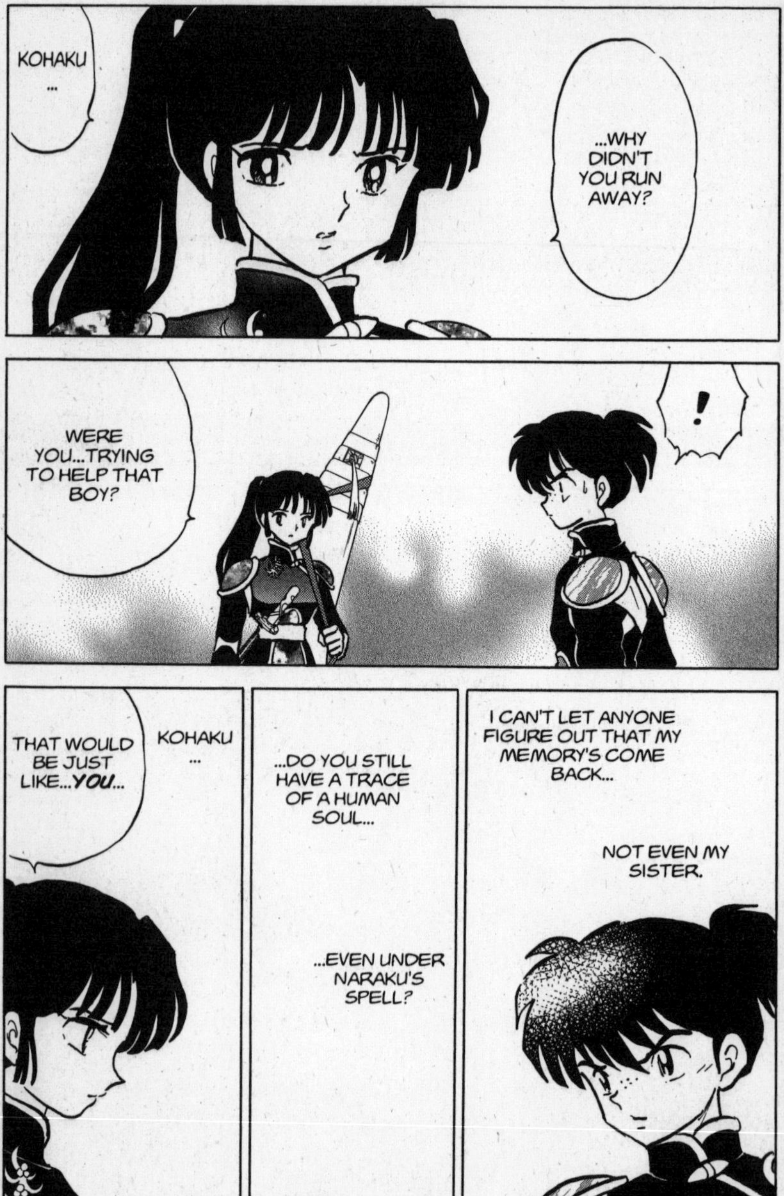
KOHAKU ...
...WHY DIDN'T YOU RUN AWAY?
WERE YOU...TRYING TO HELP THAT BOY?
!
THAT WOULD BE JUST LIKE...*YOU*...
KOHAKU ...
...DO YOU STILL HAVE A TRACE OF A HUMAN SOUL...
...EVEN UNDER NARAKU'S SPELL?
I CAN'T LET ANYONE FIGURE OUT THAT MY MEMORY'S COME BACK...
NOT EVEN MY SISTER.

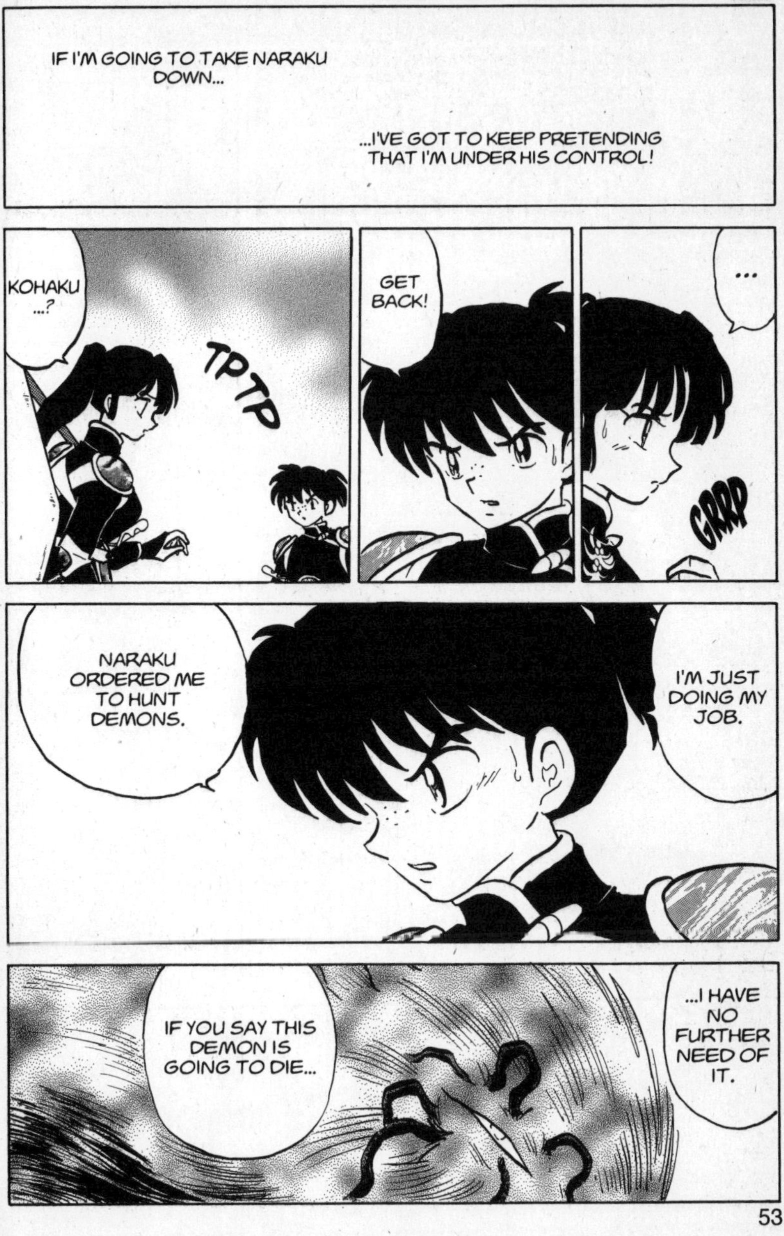
IF I'M GOING TO TAKE NARAKU DOWN...
...I'VE GOT TO KEEP PRETENDING THAT I'M UNDER HIS CONTROL!
KOHAKU ...?
TP TP
GET BACK!
...
GRRP
NARAKU ORDERED ME TO HUNT DEMONS.
I'M JUST DOING MY JOB.
IF YOU SAY THIS DEMON IS GOING TO DIE...
...I HAVE NO FURTHER NEED OF IT.

KOHAKU!

DNDN!!

FWOOSH

DON'T FOLLOW ME!

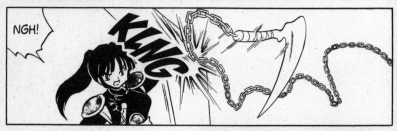

NGH!

KLNG

KOHAKU!

COME BACK!

TM TM

KOHAKU
...

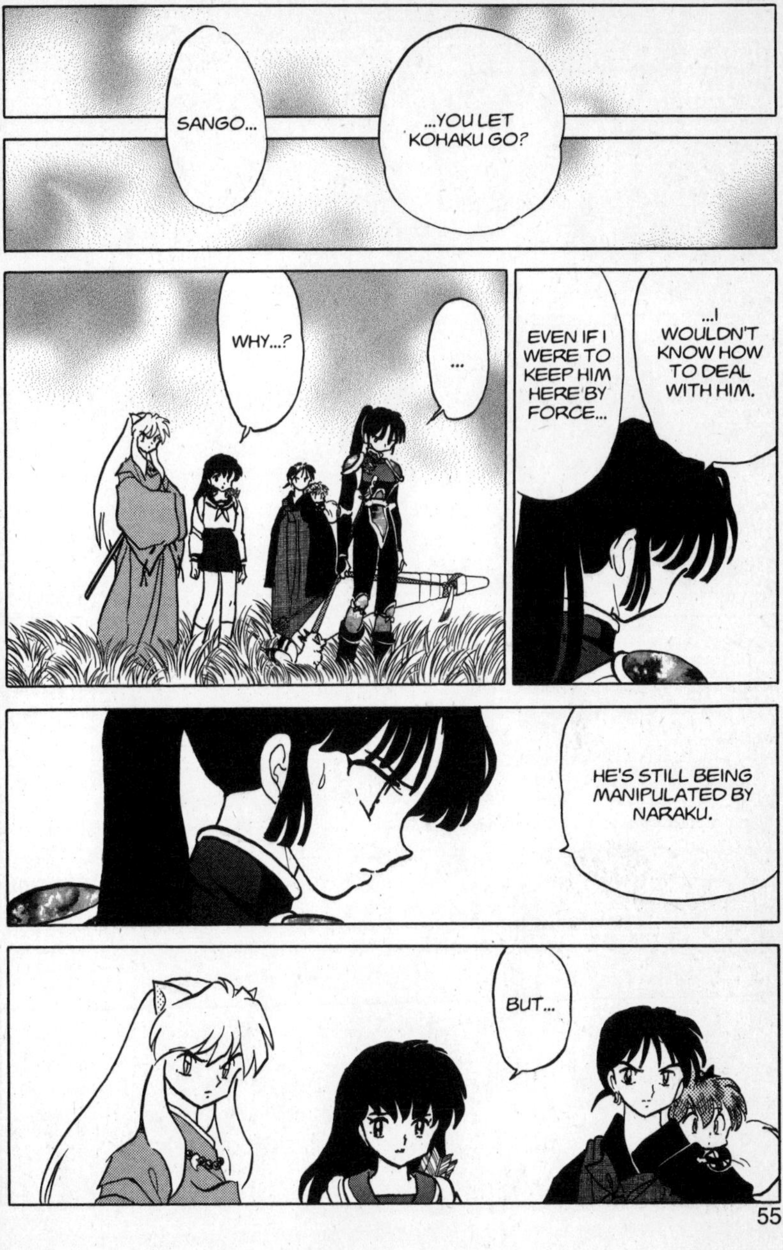
SANGO...
...YOU LET KOHAKU GO?
WHY...?
...
EVEN IF I WERE TO KEEP HIM HERE BY FORCE...
...I WOULDN'T KNOW HOW TO DEAL WITH HIM.
HE'S STILL BEING MANIPULATED BY NARAKU.
BUT...

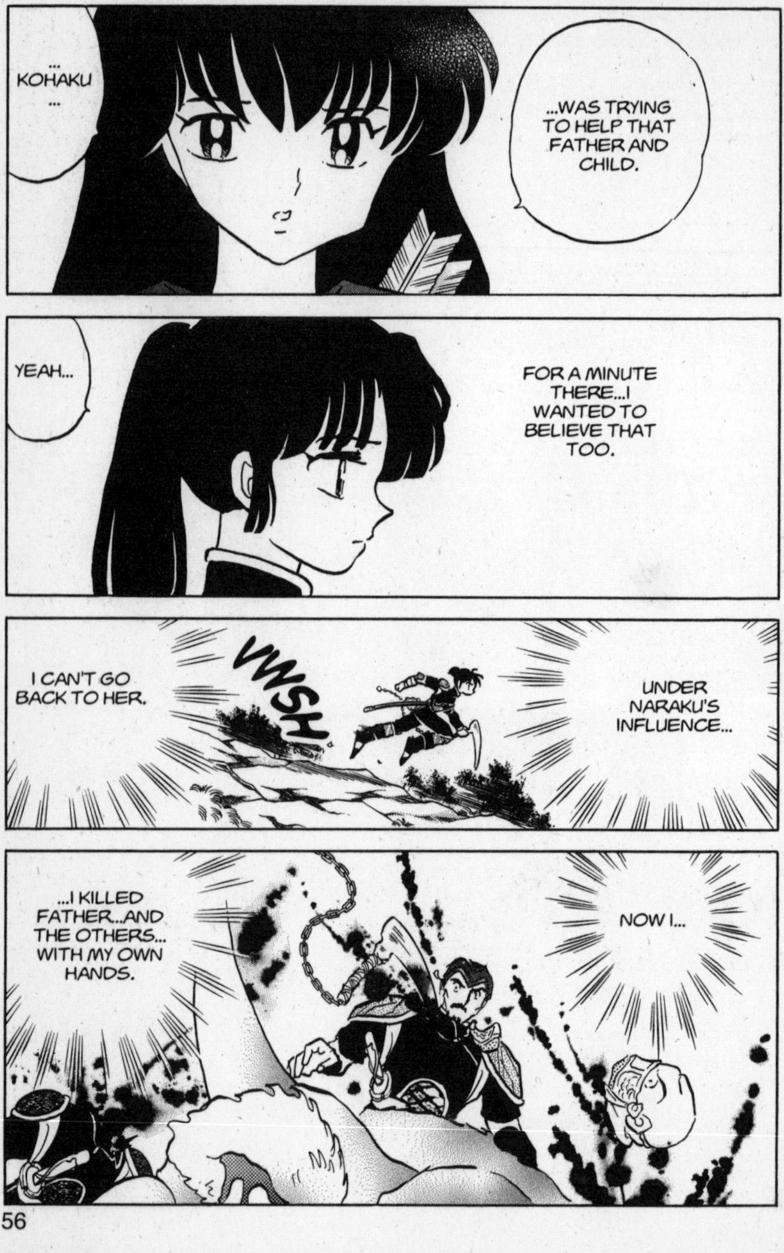

... KOHAKU ...
...WAS TRYING TO HELP THAT FATHER AND CHILD.
YEAH...
FOR A MINUTE THERE...I WANTED TO BELIEVE THAT TOO.
I CAN'T GO BACK TO HER.
VWSH
UNDER NARAKU'S INFLUENCE...
...I KILLED FATHER...AND THE OTHERS... WITH MY OWN HANDS.
NOW I...

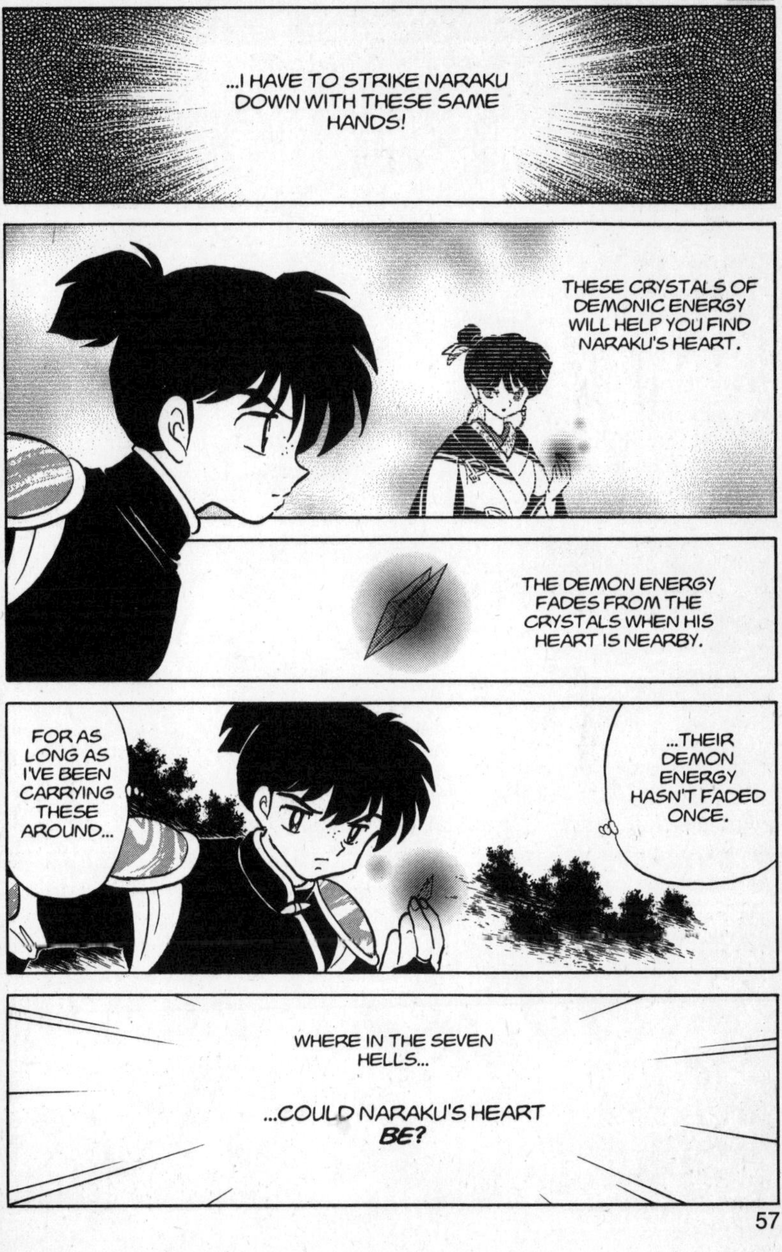
...I HAVE TO STRIKE NARAKU DOWN WITH THESE SAME HANDS!
THESE CRYSTALS OF DEMONIC ENERGY WILL HELP YOU FIND NARAKU'S HEART.
THE DEMON ENERGY FADES FROM THE CRYSTALS WHEN HIS HEART IS NEARBY.
FOR AS LONG AS I'VE BEEN CARRYING THESE AROUND...
...THEIR DEMON ENERGY HASN'T FADED ONCE.
WHERE IN THE SEVEN HELLS...
...COULD NARAKU'S HEART *BE?*

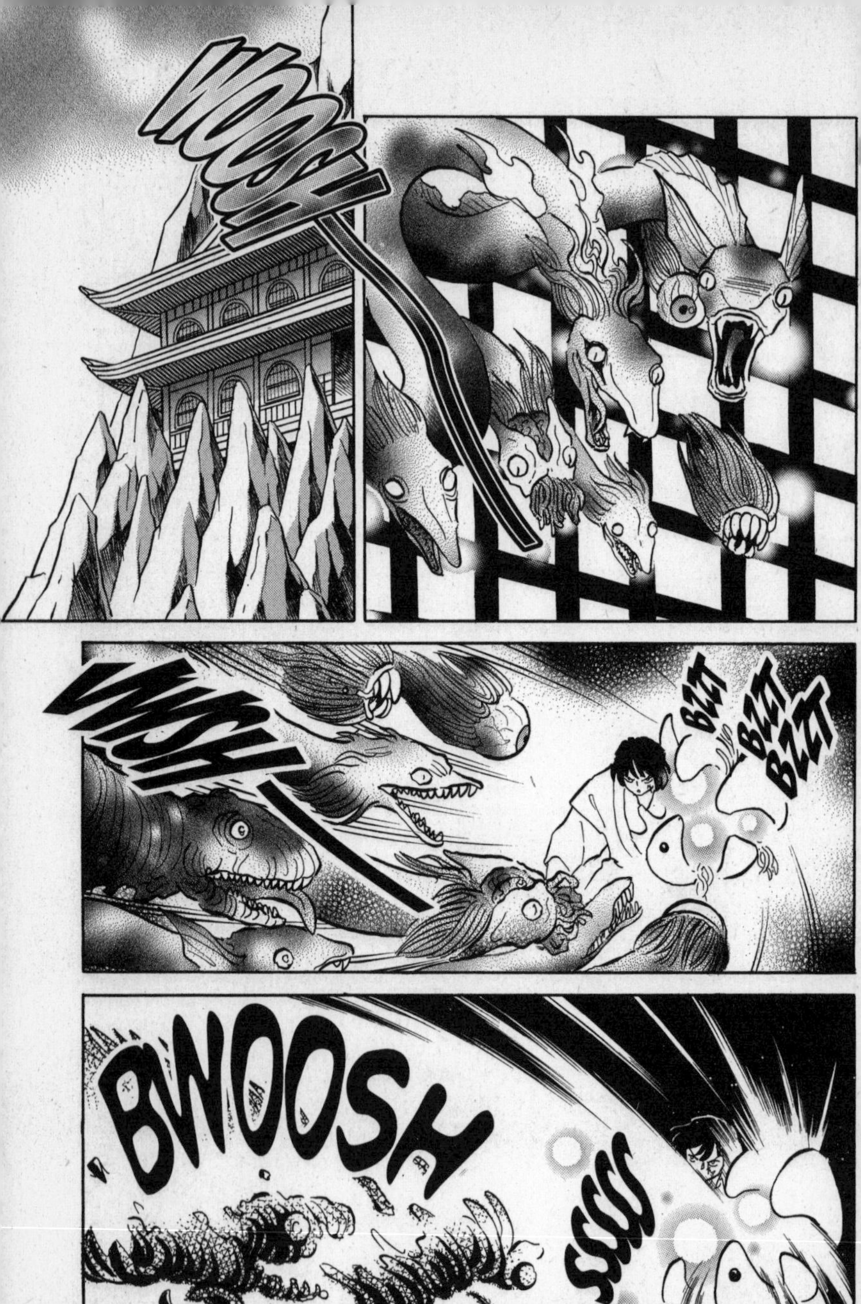
WOOSH!
VWSH
BZZT
BZZT
BZZT
BWOOSH
SSSS

BLOORP
GRRP GRRP
BLORP
...
RRRG
HE'S ABSORBING THE DEMONS!
HEY, GORYOMARU.
JUST WHAT **ARE** YOU?

WHY IS NARAKU KEEPING YOU LOCKED UP?

AND WHY IS HE THROWING CAPTURED DEMONS AT HIM...

...ONE AFTER ANOTHER, FOR HIM TO...

...ABSORB ...?

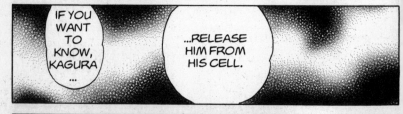

IF YOU WANT TO KNOW, KAGURA...

...RELEASE HIM FROM HIS CELL.

HAKUDOSHI ?!...!

SCROLL 4
ESCAPE

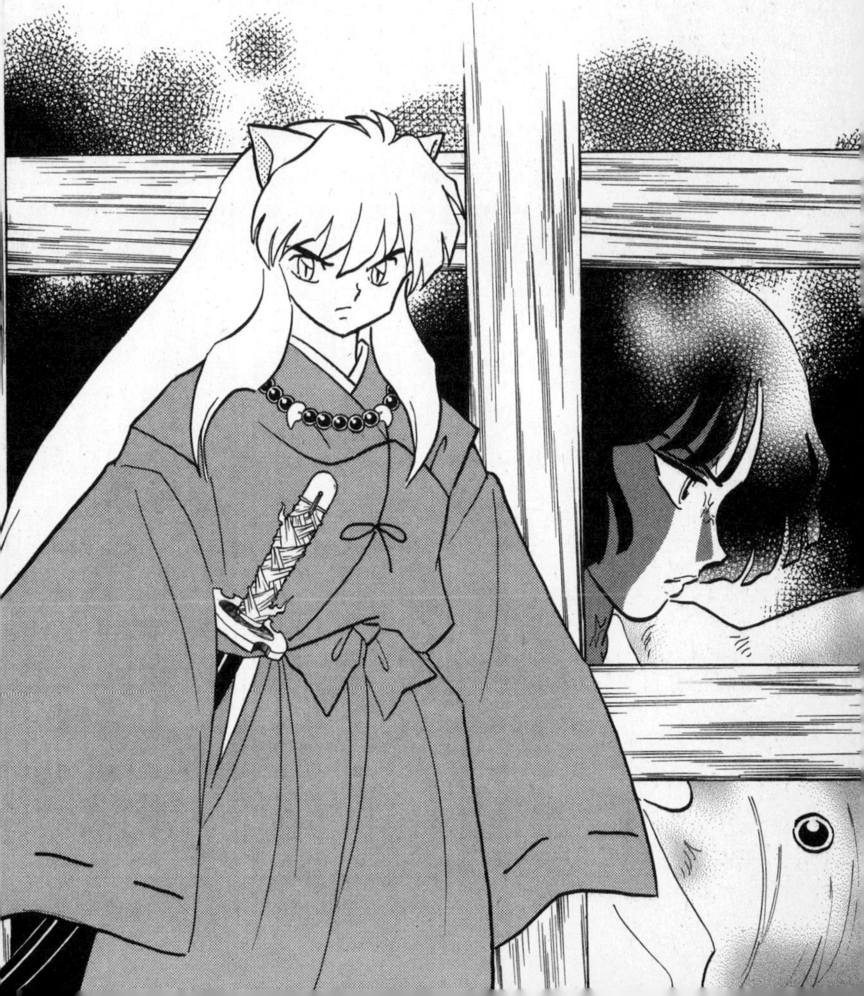

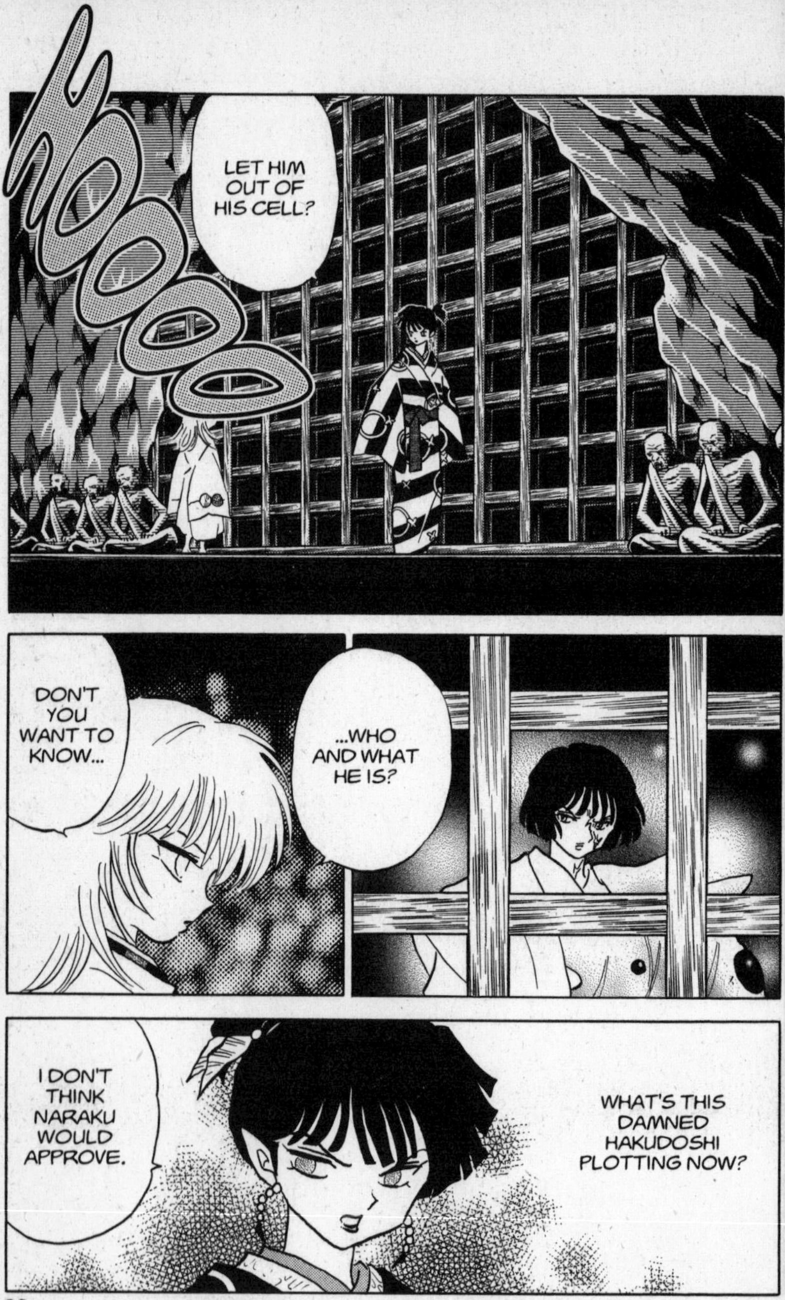
HOOOOO
LET HIM OUT OF HIS CELL?
...WHO AND WHAT HE IS?
DON'T YOU WANT TO KNOW...
WHAT'S THIS DAMNED HAKUDOSHI PLOTTING NOW?
I DON'T THINK NARAKU WOULD APPROVE.

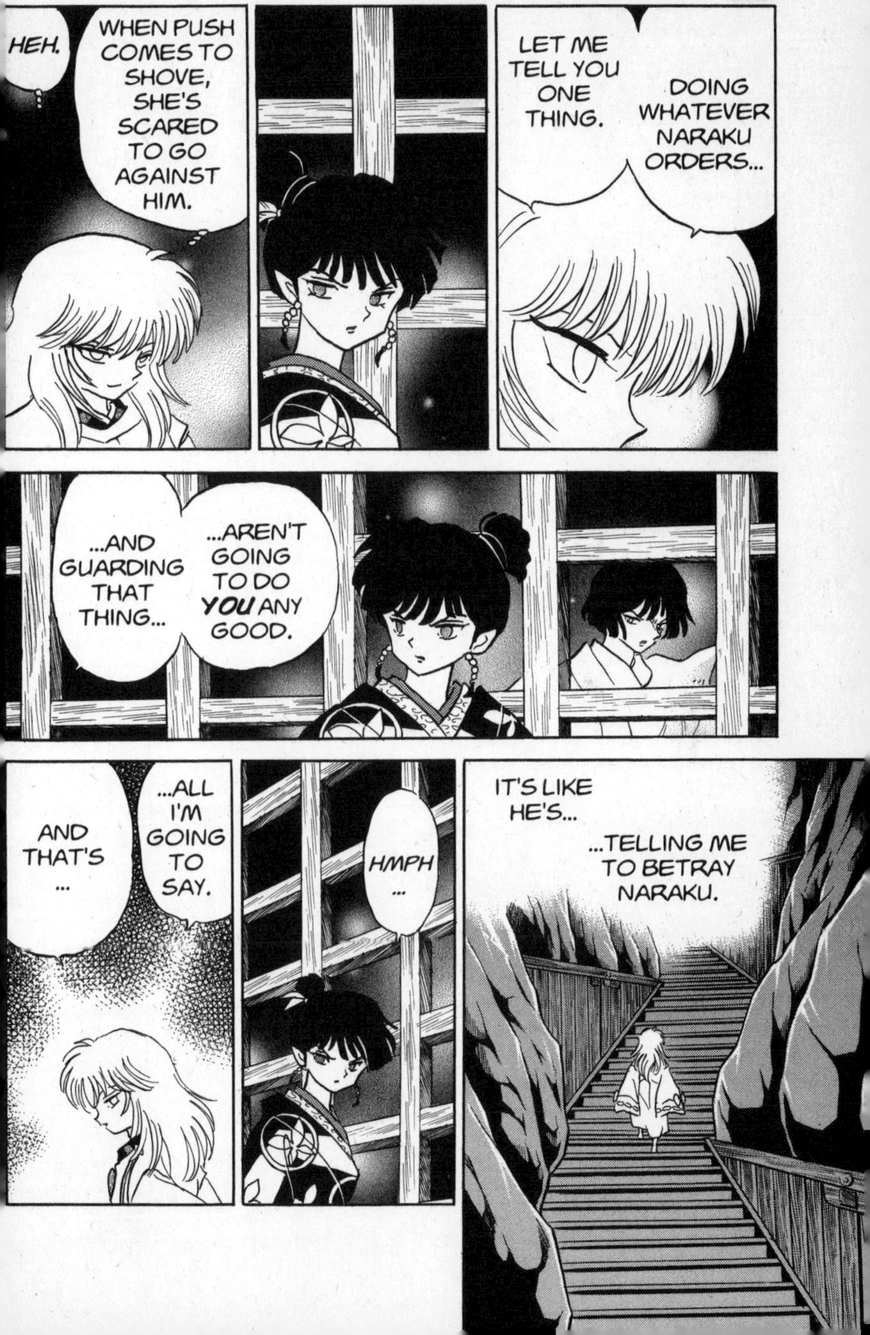
HEH.
WHEN PUSH COMES TO SHOVE, SHE'S SCARED TO GO AGAINST HIM.
LET ME TELL YOU ONE THING.
DOING WHATEVER NARAKU ORDERS...
...AND GUARDING THAT THING...
...AREN'T GOING TO DO YOU ANY GOOD.
AND THAT'S ...
...ALL I'M GOING TO SAY.
HMPH ...
IT'S LIKE HE'S...
...TELLING ME TO BETRAY NARAKU.

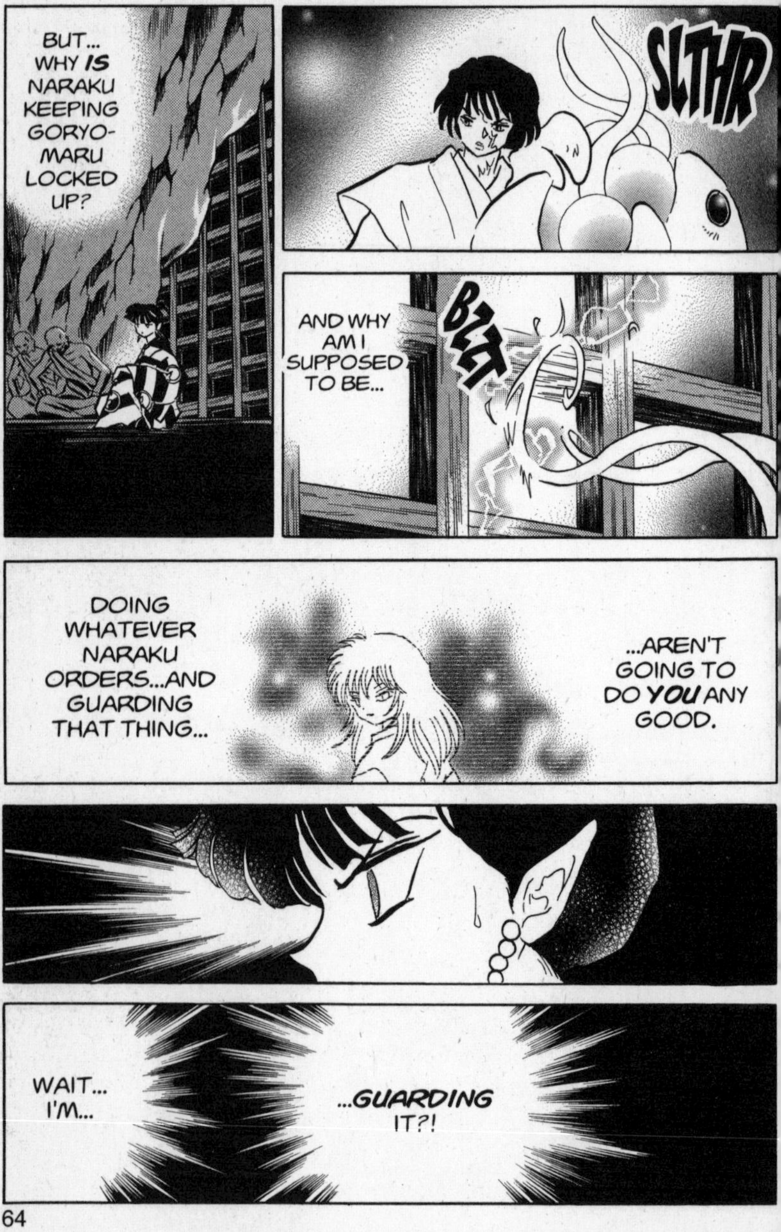
BUT... WHY IS NARAKU KEEPING GORYO-MARU LOCKED UP?
SLTHR
AND WHY AM I SUPPOSED TO BE...
BZZT
DOING WHATEVER NARAKU ORDERS...AND GUARDING THAT THING...
...AREN'T GOING TO DO YOU ANY GOOD.
WAIT... I'M...
...GUARDING IT?!

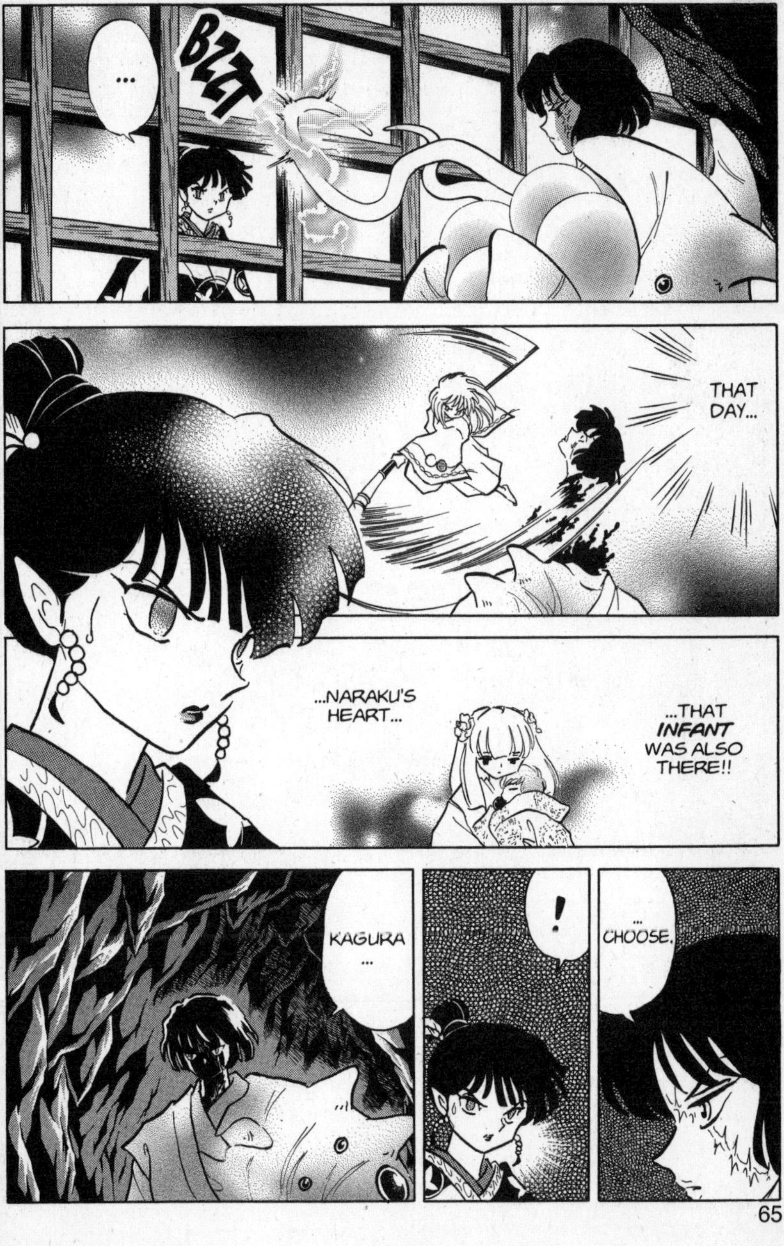
...
BZZT
THAT DAY...
...NARAKU'S HEART...
...THAT *INFANT* WAS ALSO THERE!!
KAGURA ...
!
... CHOOSE.

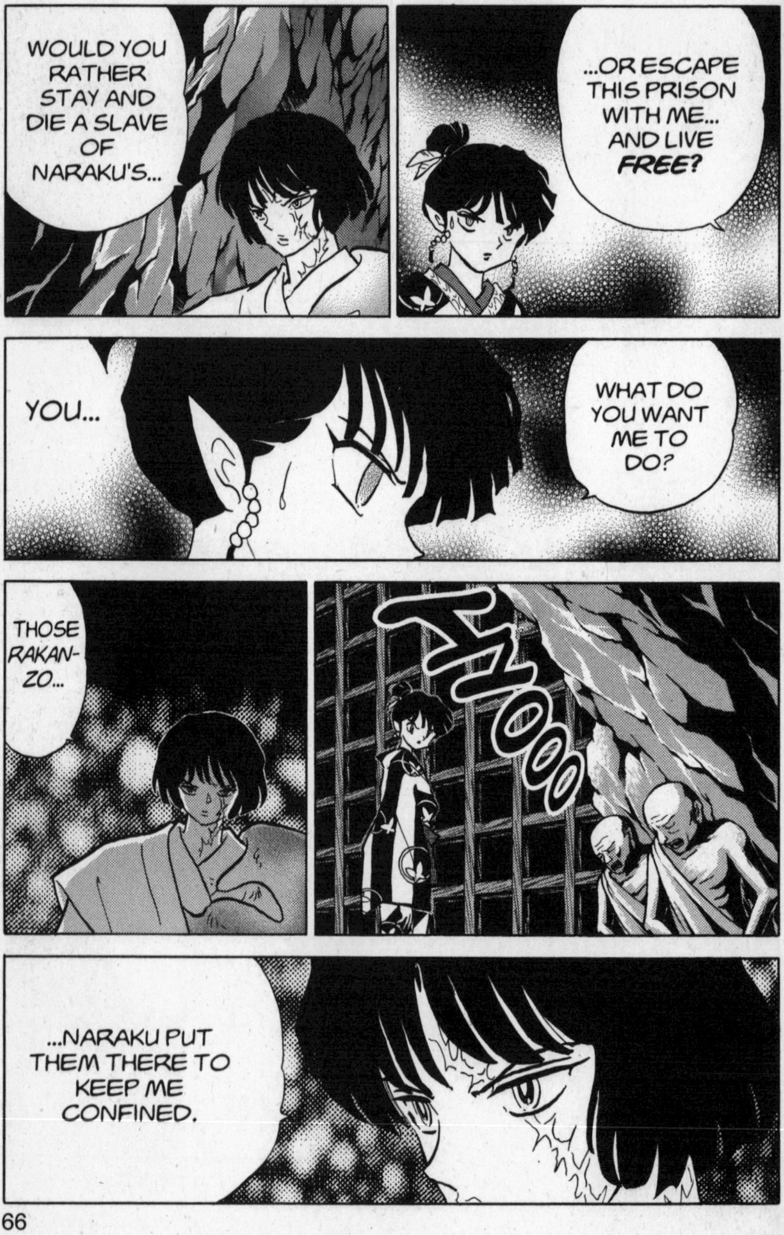
WOULD YOU RATHER STAY AND DIE A SLAVE OF NARAKU'S...
...OR ESCAPE THIS PRISON WITH ME... AND LIVE **FREE?**
YOU...
WHAT DO YOU WANT ME TO DO?
THOSE RAKAN-ZO...
FWOOOO
...NARAKU PUT THEM THERE TO KEEP ME CONFINED.

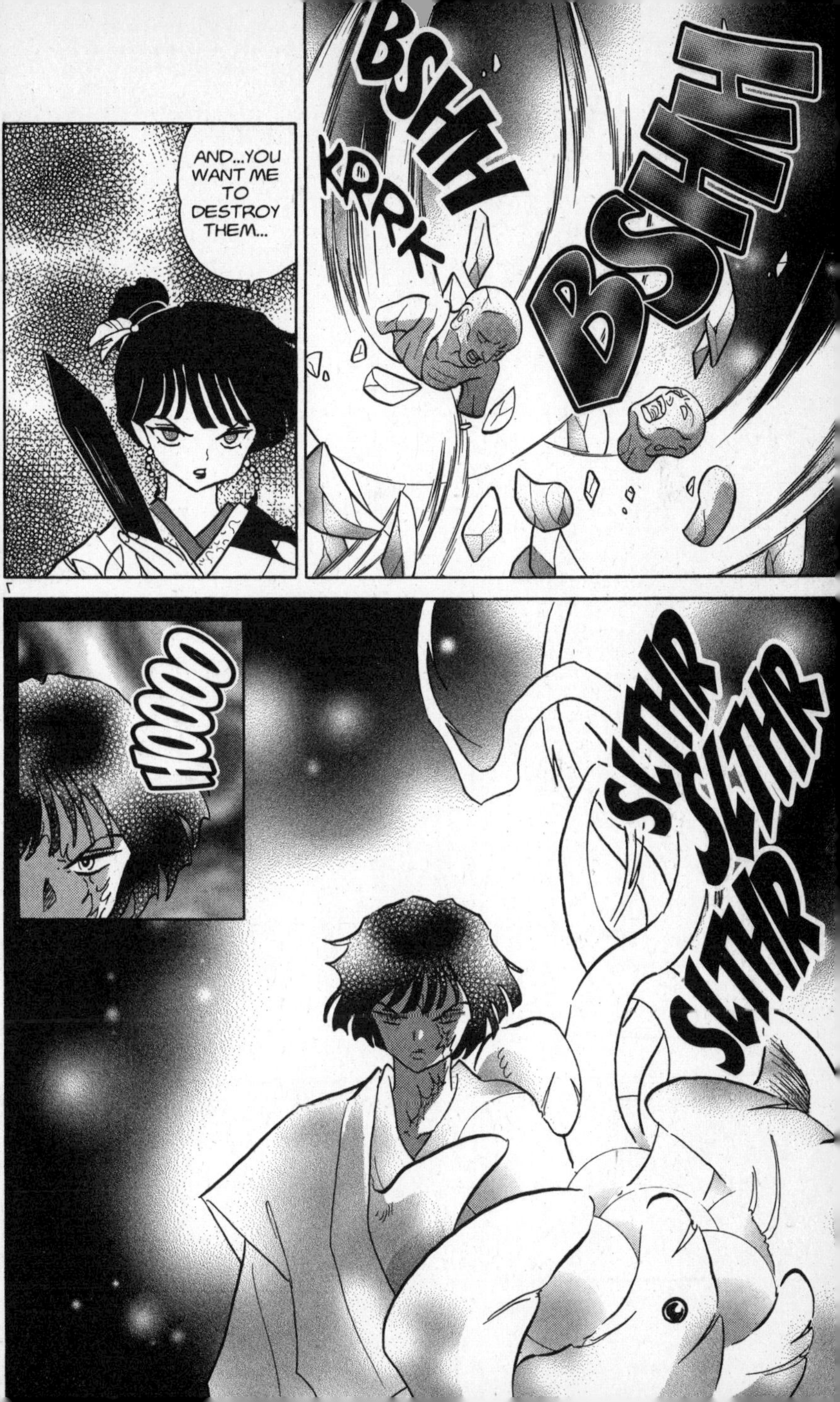
AND...YOU WANT ME TO DESTROY THEM...
BSHH
KRRK
BSHH
HOOOO
SLTHR
SLTHR
SLTHR

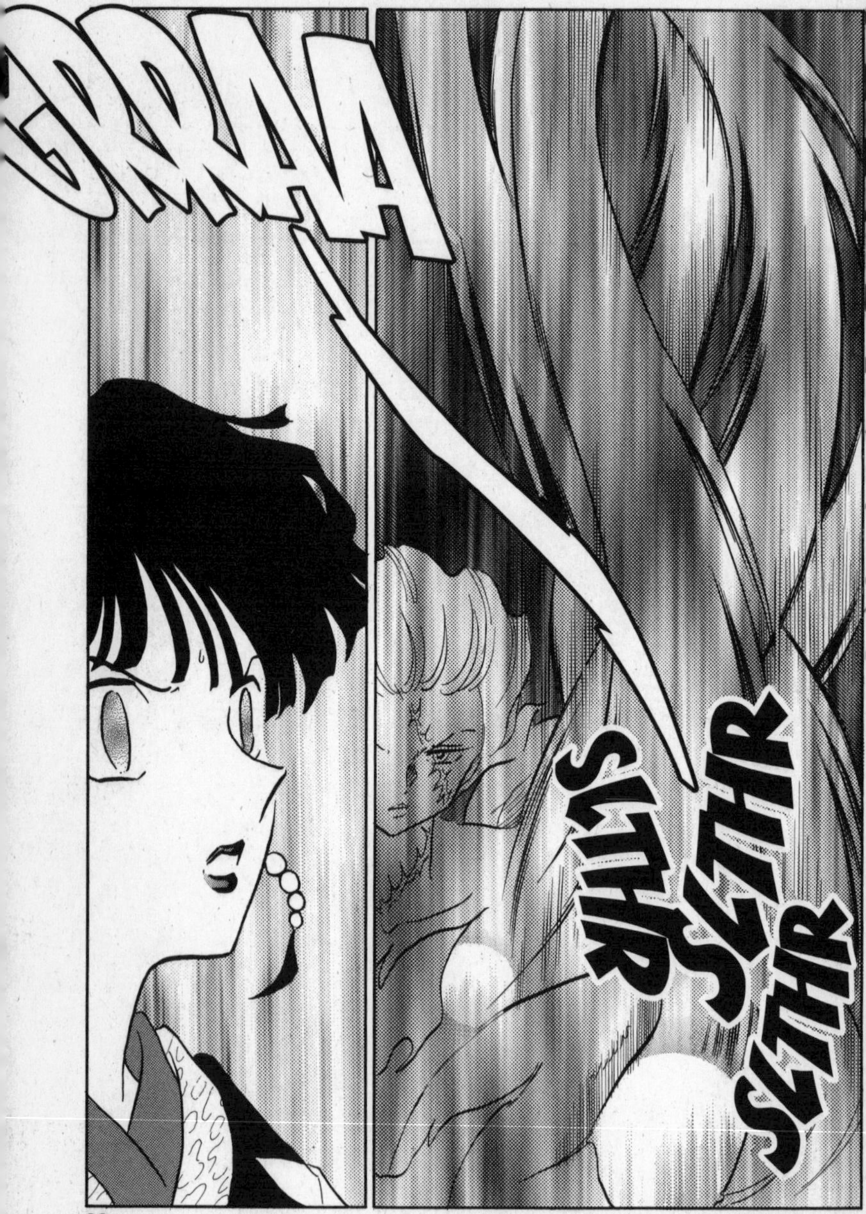
GRRAA
SLTHR
SLTHR
SLTHR

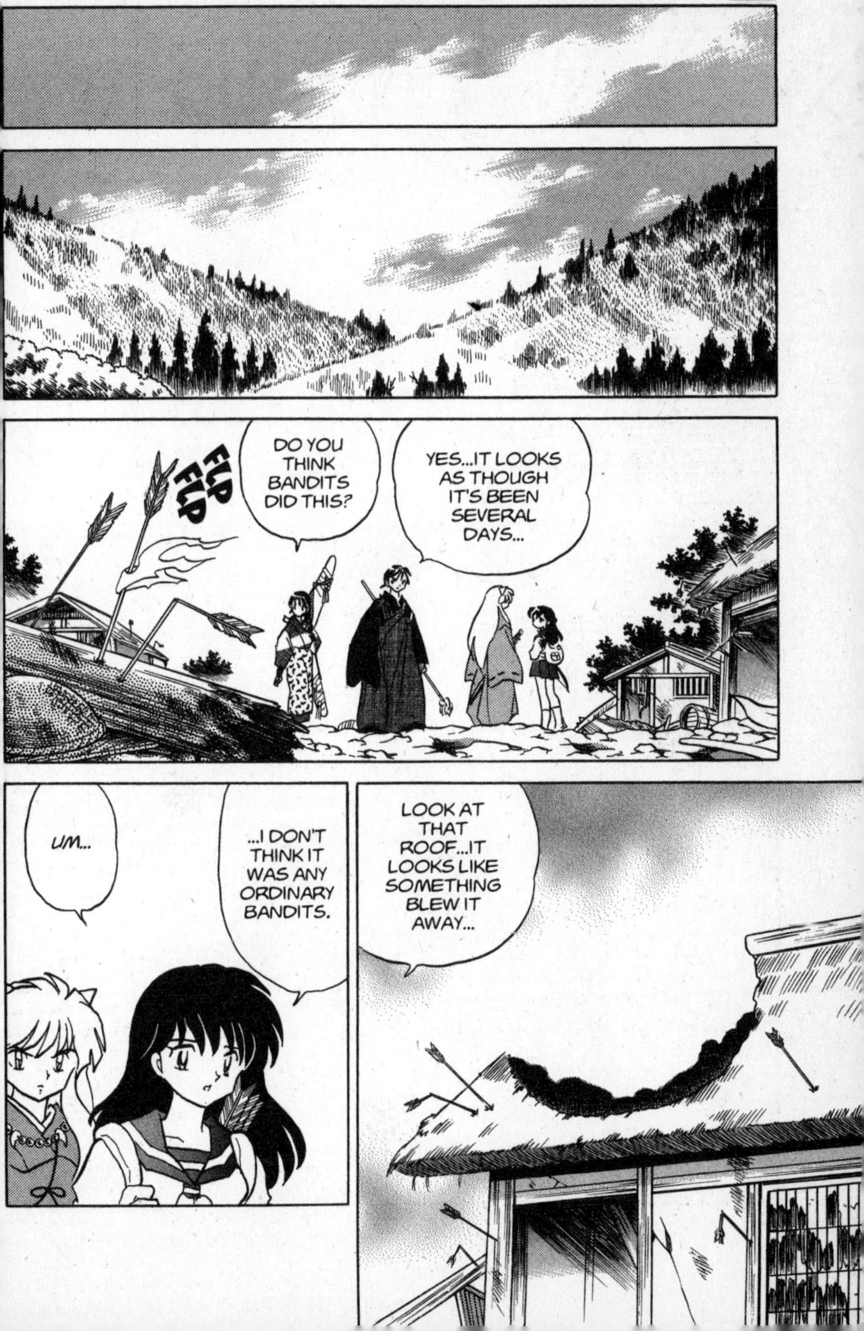
DO YOU THINK BANDITS DID THIS?
YES...IT LOOKS AS THOUGH IT'S BEEN SEVERAL DAYS...
FLP FLP
UM...
...I DON'T THINK IT WAS ANY ORDINARY BANDITS.
LOOK AT THAT ROOF...IT LOOKS LIKE SOMETHING BLEW IT AWAY...

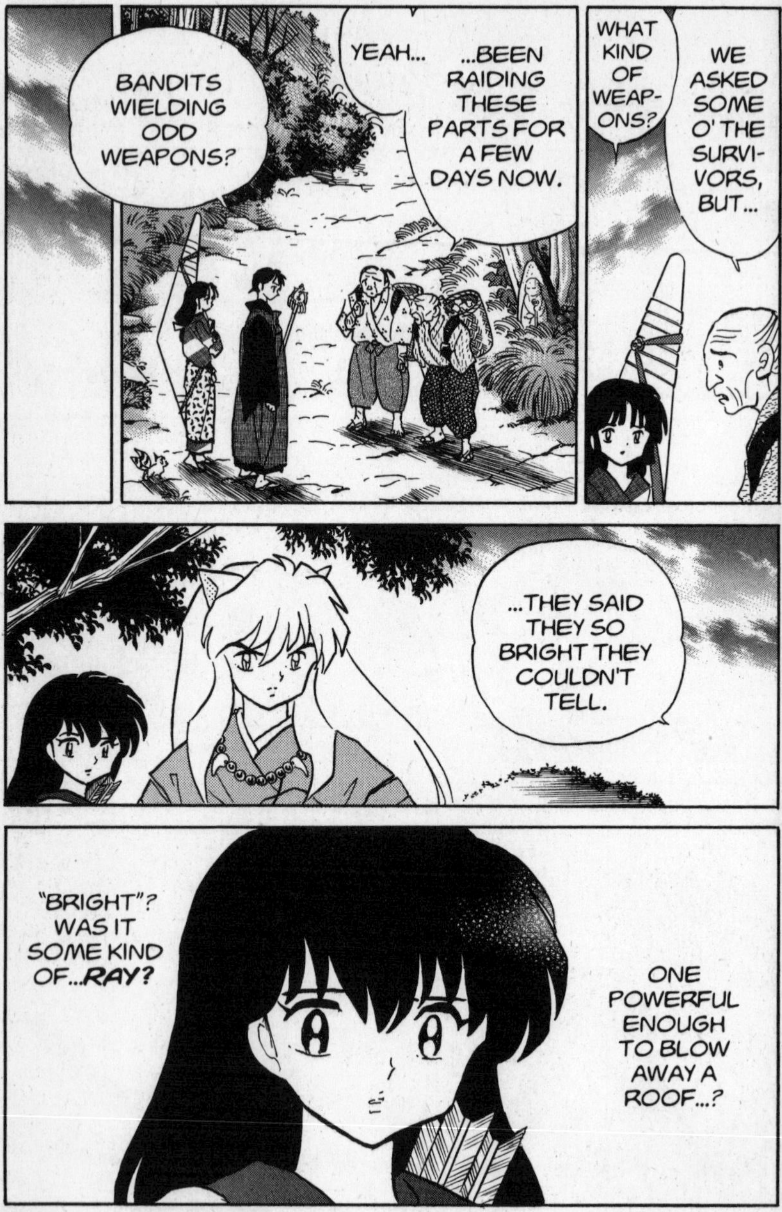
BANDITS WIELDING ODD WEAPONS?
YEAH...
...BEEN RAIDING THESE PARTS FOR A FEW DAYS NOW.
WHAT KIND OF WEAP-ONS?
WE ASKED SOME O' THE SURVI-VORS, BUT...
...THEY SAID THEY SO BRIGHT THEY COULDN'T TELL.
"BRIGHT"? WAS IT SOME KIND OF...*RAY?*
ONE POWERFUL ENOUGH TO BLOW AWAY A ROOF...?

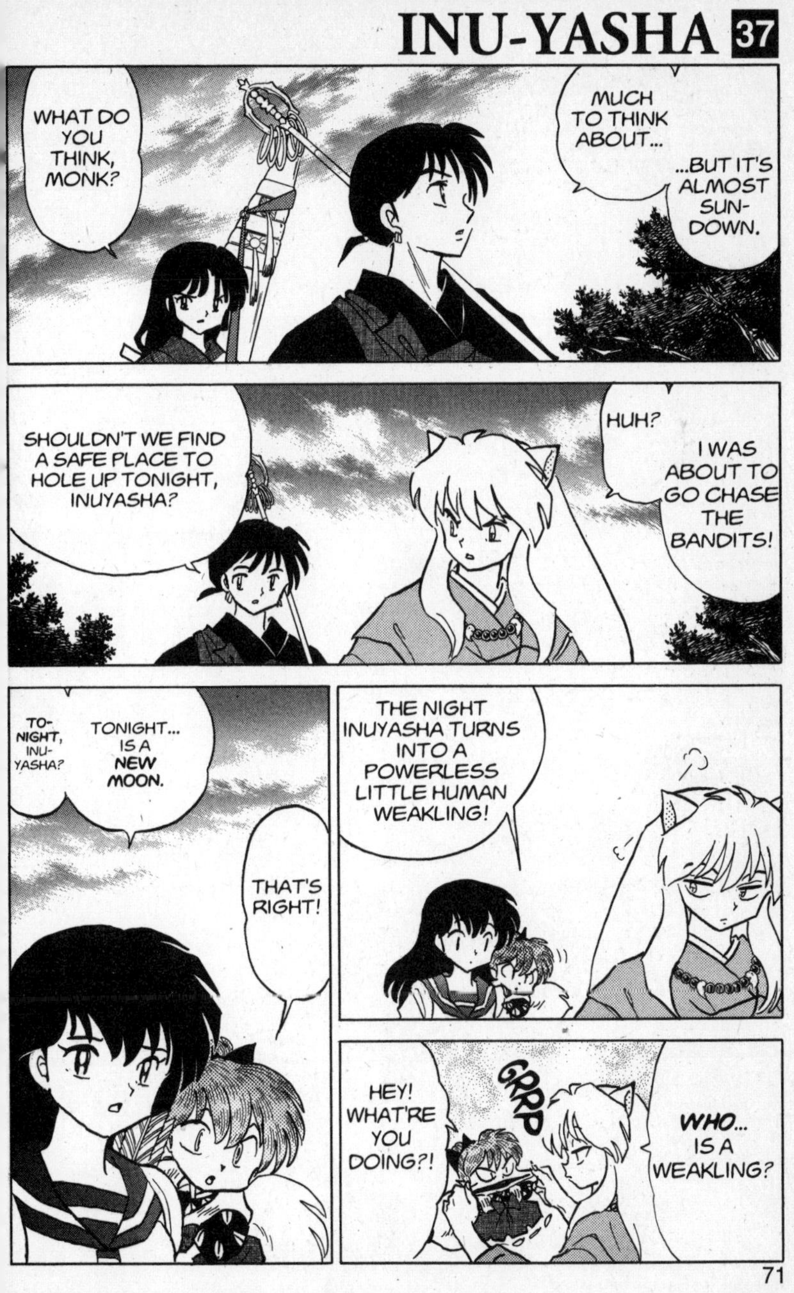
WHAT DO YOU THINK, MONK?
MUCH TO THINK ABOUT...
...BUT IT'S ALMOST SUN-DOWN.
SHOULDN'T WE FIND A SAFE PLACE TO HOLE UP TONIGHT, INUYASHA?
HUH?
I WAS ABOUT TO GO CHASE THE BANDITS!
TO-NIGHT, INU-YASHA?
TONIGHT... IS A **NEW MOON.**
THAT'S RIGHT!
THE NIGHT INUYASHA TURNS INTO A POWERLESS LITTLE HUMAN WEAKLING!
HEY! WHAT'RE YOU DOING?!
GRRP
WHO... IS A WEAKLING?

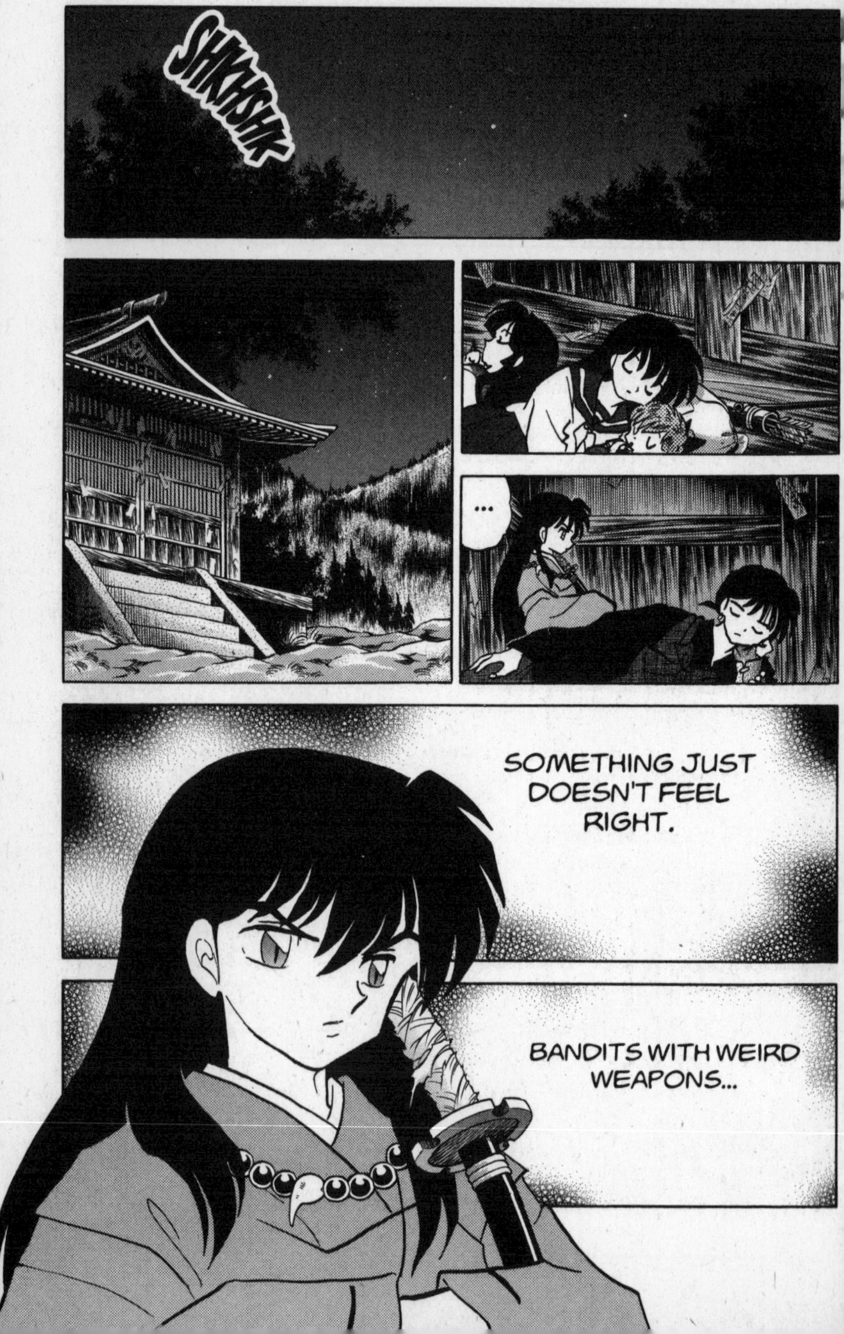
SHKSHK
...
SOMETHING JUST DOESN'T FEEL RIGHT.
BANDITS WITH WEIRD WEAPONS...

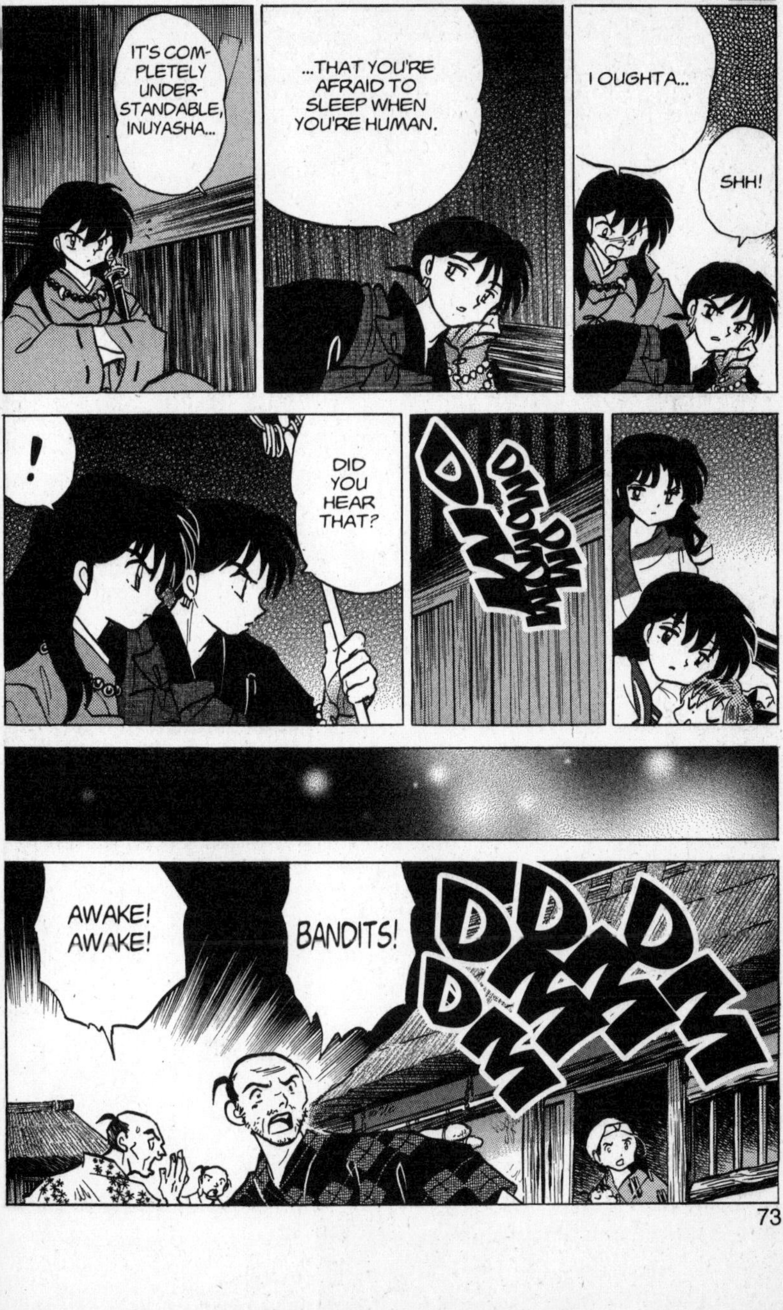
IT'S COMPLETELY UNDERSTANDABLE, INUYASHA...
...THAT YOU'RE AFRAID TO SLEEP WHEN YOU'RE HUMAN.
I OUGHTA...
SHH!
!
DID YOU HEAR THAT?
AWAKE! AWAKE!
BANDITS!

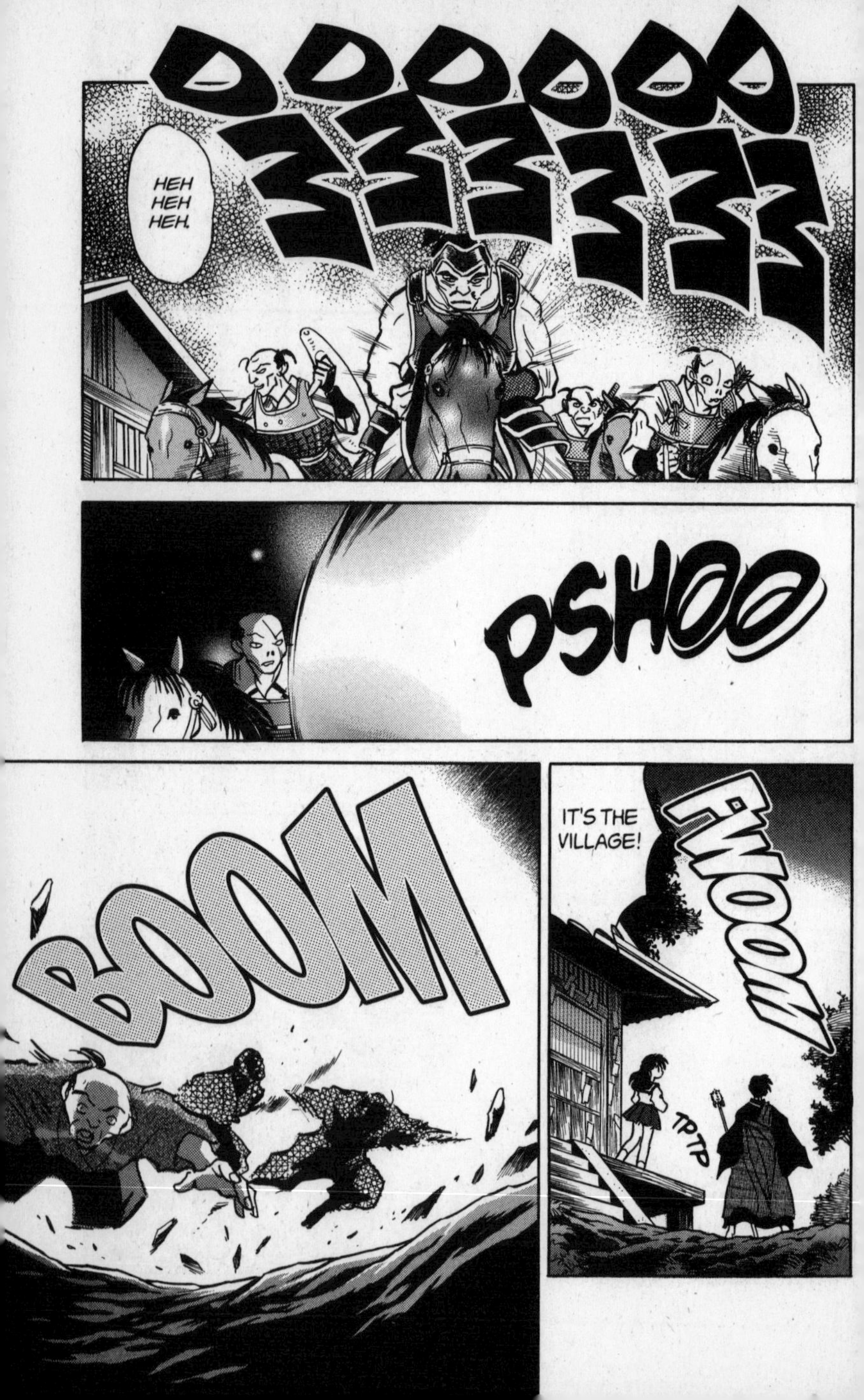
HEH HEH HEH.
DDDDDD ZZZZZZ
PSHOO
BOOM
IT'S THE VILLAGE!
FWOOM
TP TP

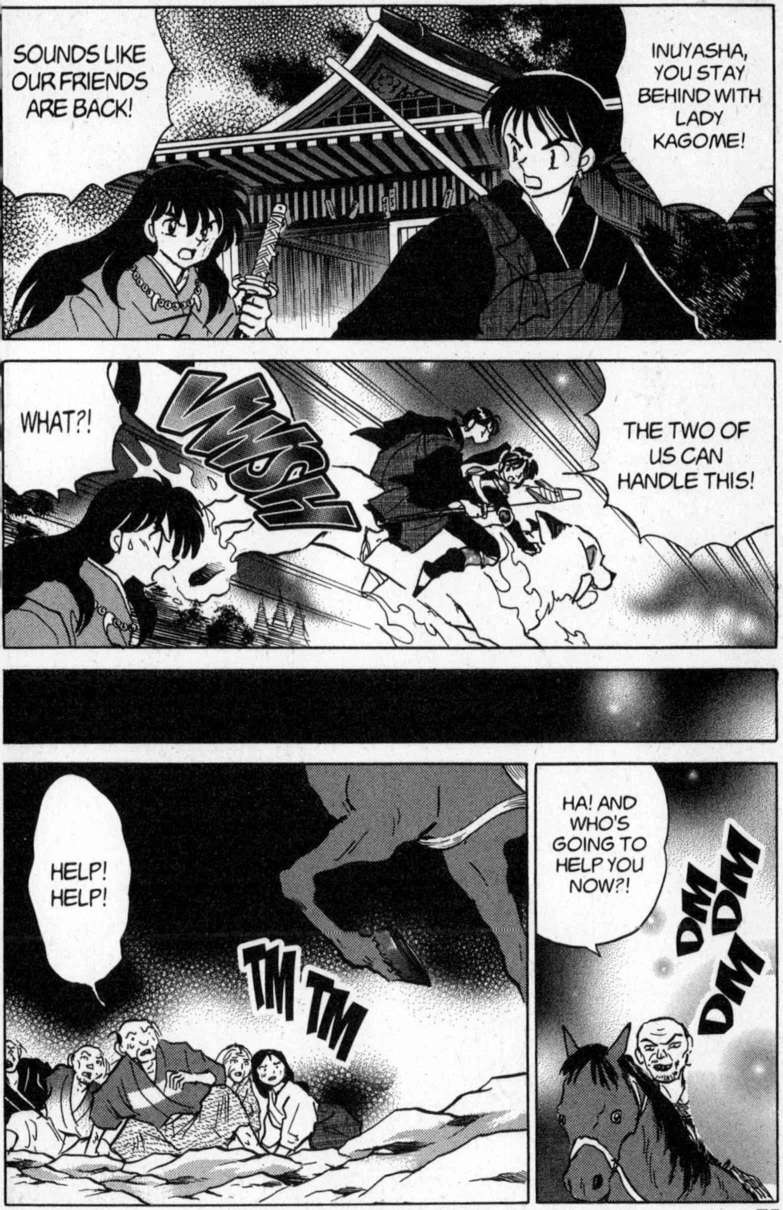
SOUNDS LIKE OUR FRIENDS ARE BACK!
INUYASHA, YOU STAY BEHIND WITH LADY KAGOME!
WHAT?!
VWSH!
THE TWO OF US CAN HANDLE THIS!
HELP! HELP!
TM TM
HA! AND WHO'S GOING TO HELP YOU NOW?!
DM DM DM

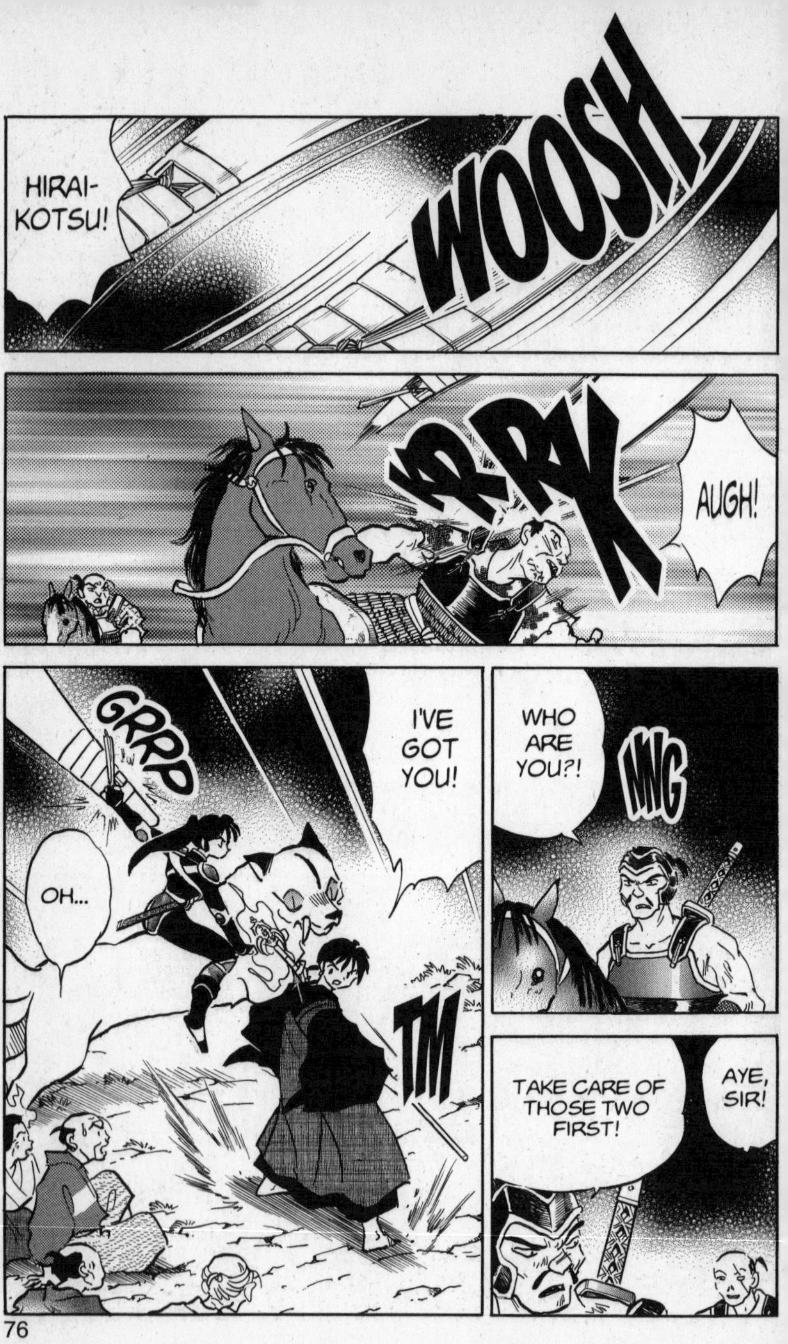
HIRAI-KOTSU!
WOOSH
KRRK
AUGH!
GRRRP
OH...
I'VE GOT YOU!
TM
WHO ARE YOU?!
MNG
TAKE CARE OF THOSE TWO FIRST!
AYE, SIR!

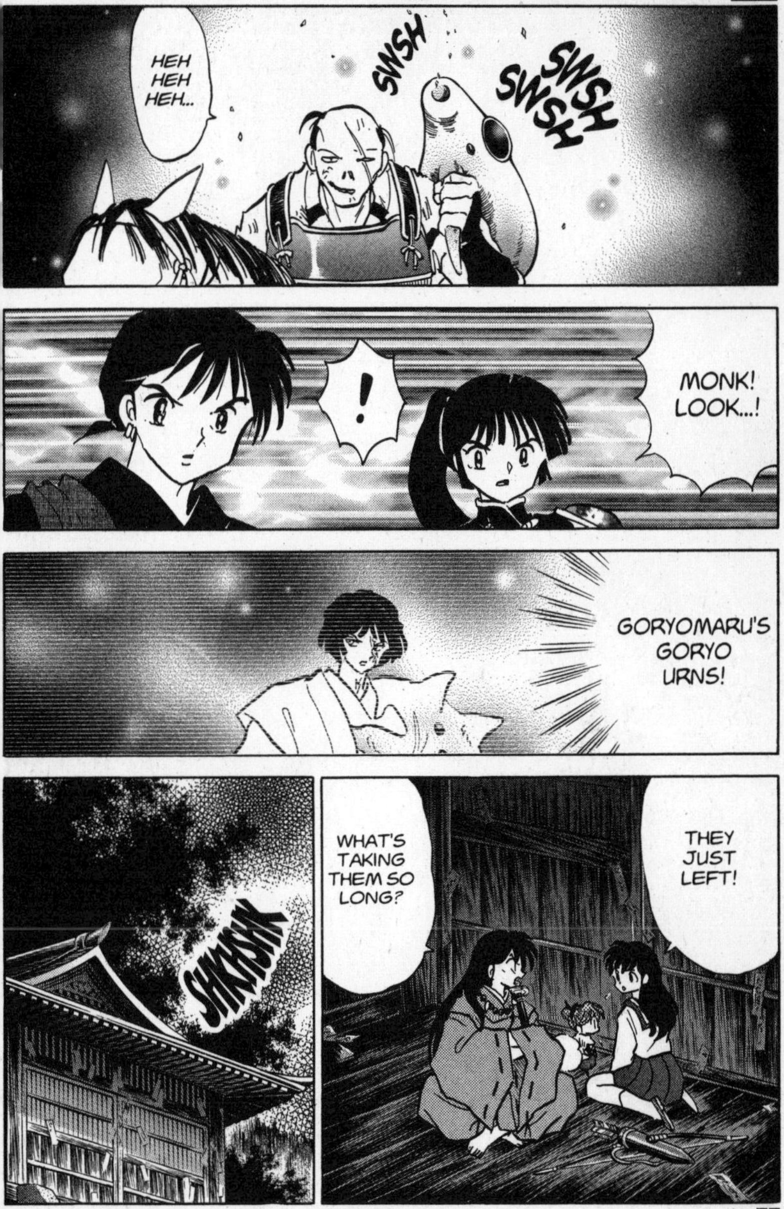
HEH HEH HEH...
SWSH
SWSH SWSH
!
MONK! LOOK...!
GORYOMARU'S GORYO URNS!
SHKSHK
WHAT'S TAKING THEM SO LONG?
THEY JUST LEFT!

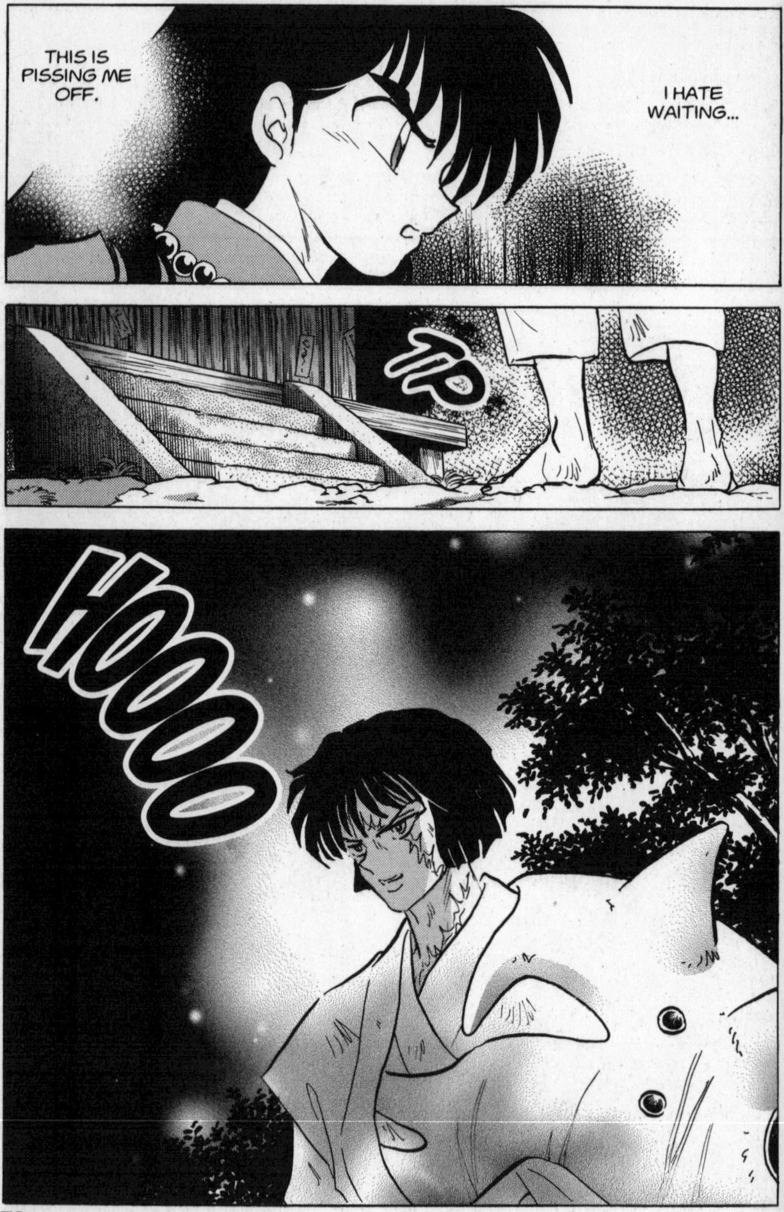
THIS IS PISSING ME OFF.
I HATE WAITING...
TIP
HOOOO

SCROLL 5
GORYOMARU'S IDENTITY

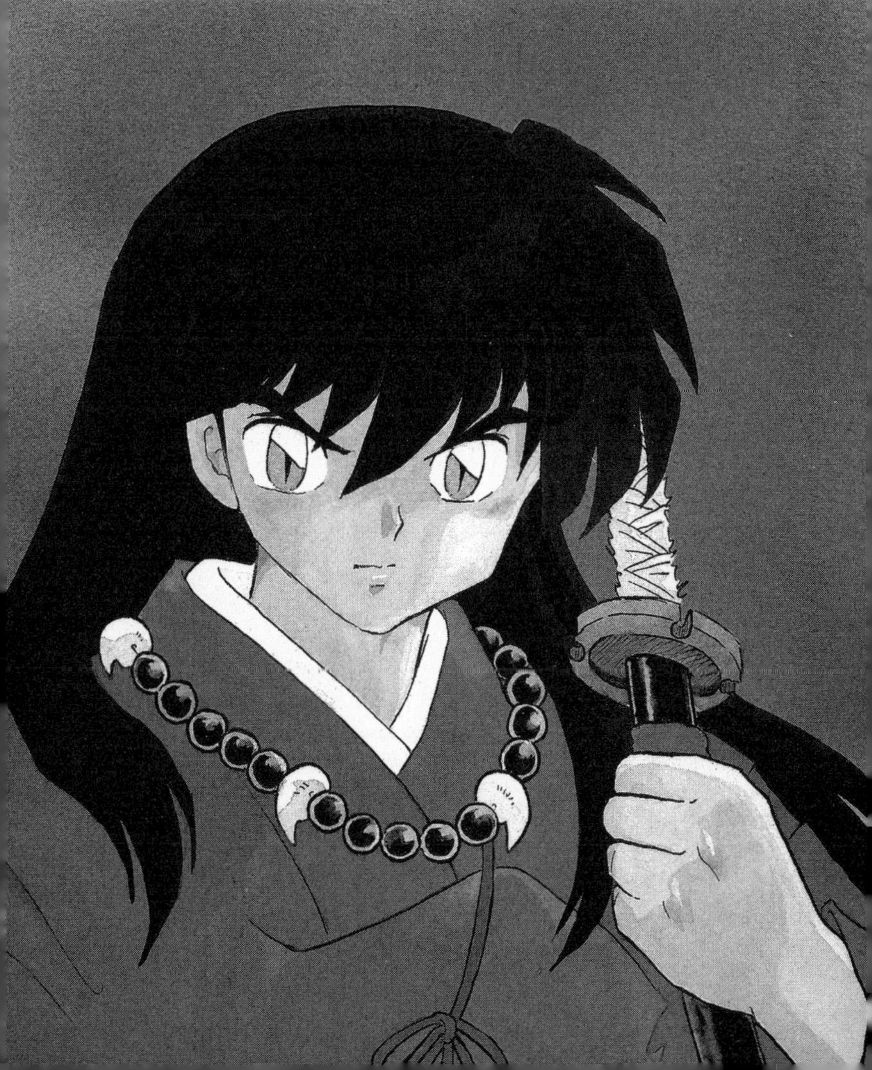

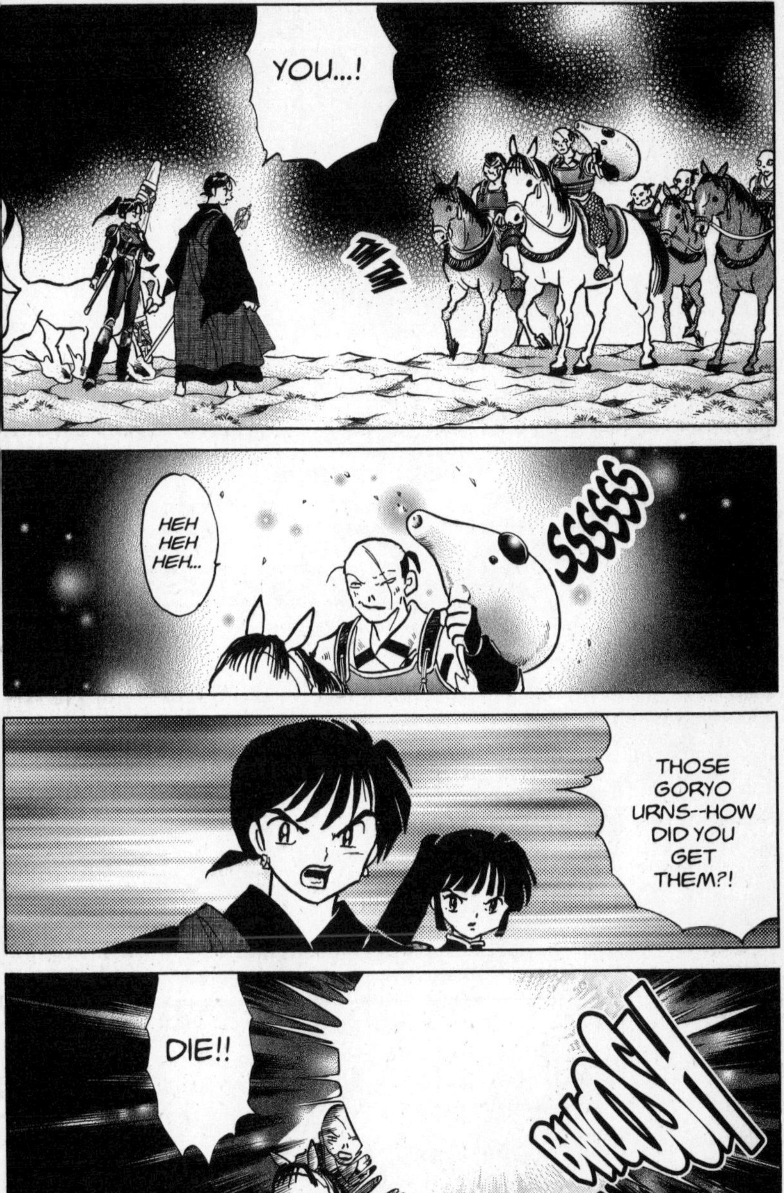
YOU...!
TM TM
HEH HEH HEH...
SSSSSS
THOSE GORYO URNS--HOW DID YOU GET THEM?!
DIE!!
BWOSH

WIND
TUNNEL!

CHK HCK

WISH

EH...?!

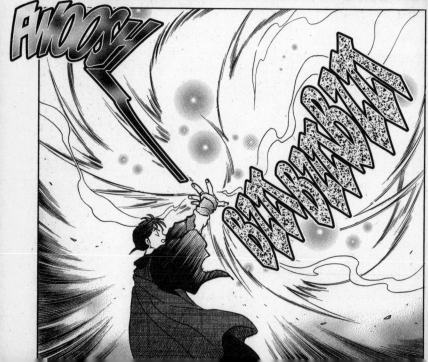

FWOOSH

SHADADADDT

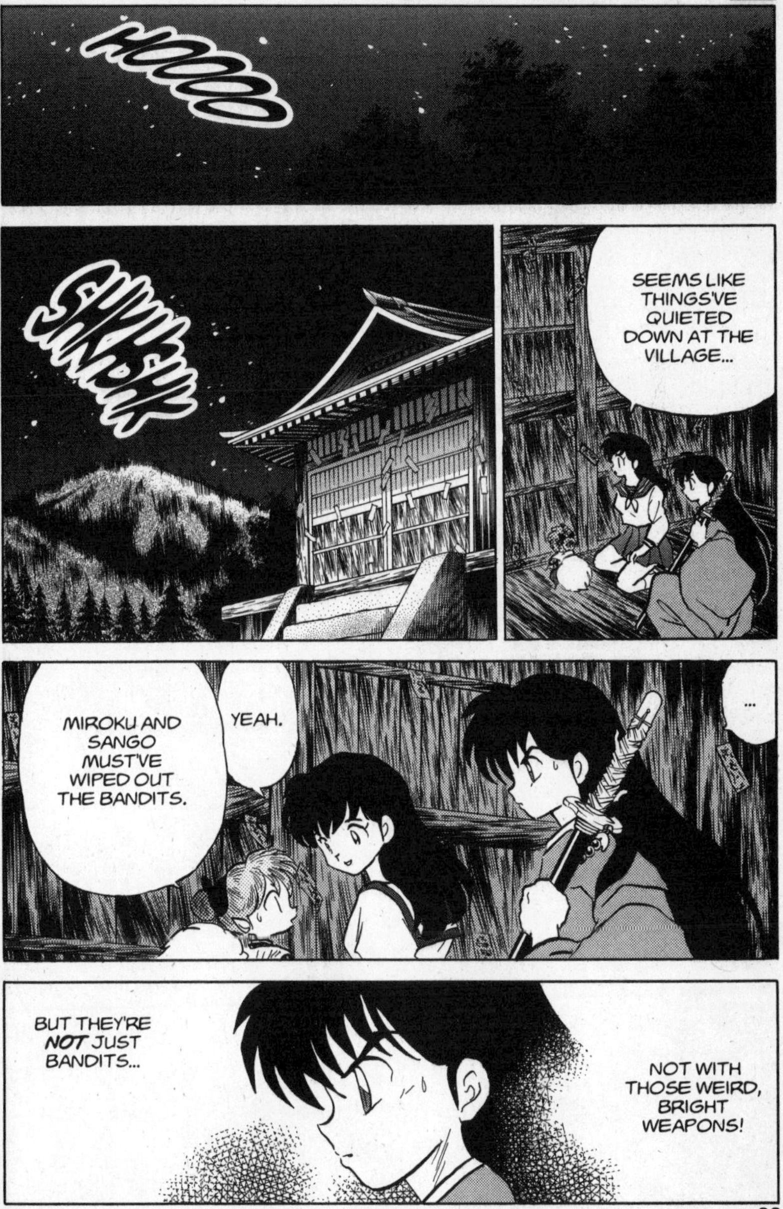
HOOOO
SEEMS LIKE THINGS'VE QUIETED DOWN AT THE VILLAGE...
MIROKU AND SANGO MUST'VE WIPED OUT THE BANDITS.
YEAH.
...
BUT THEY'RE *NOT* JUST BANDITS...
NOT WITH THOSE WEIRD, BRIGHT WEAPONS!

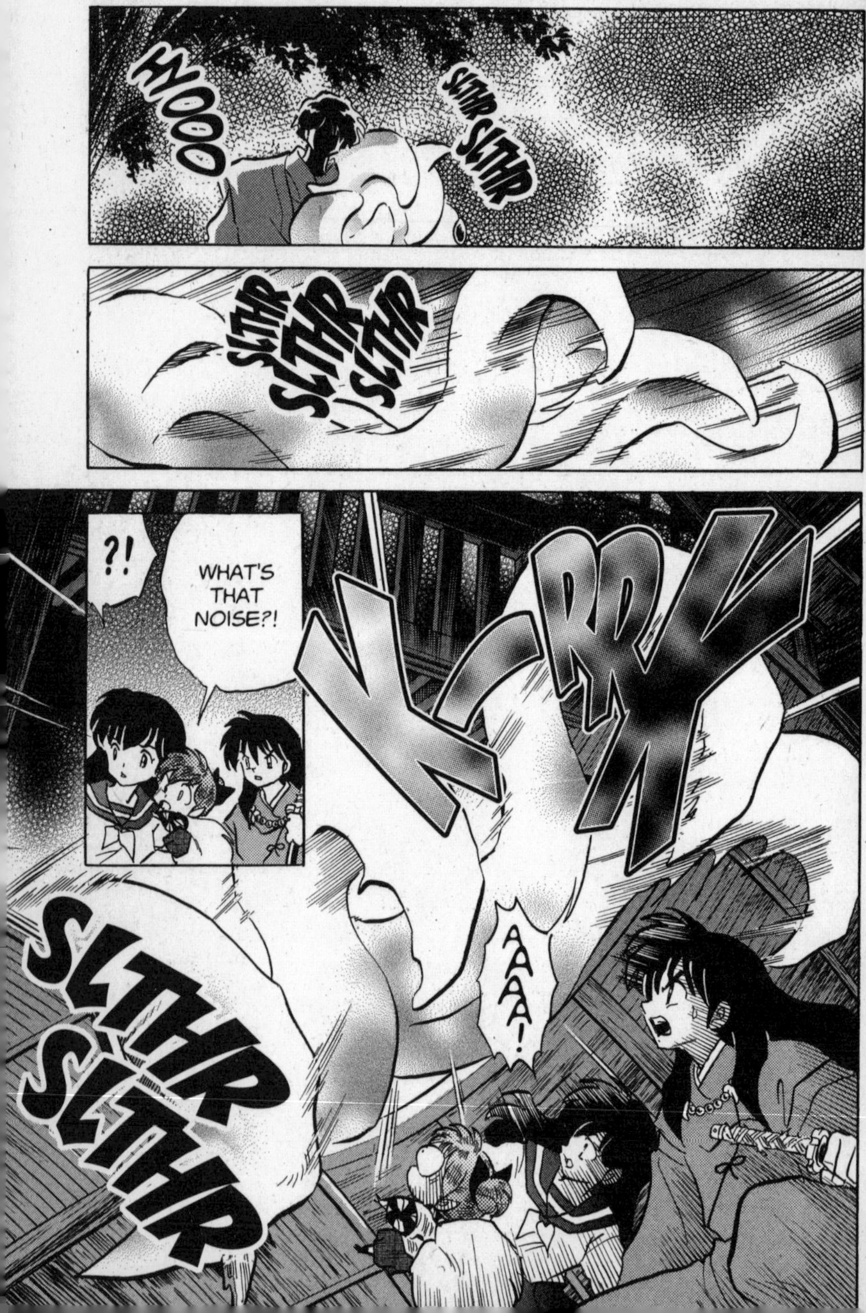
HYOOO
SLTHR SLTHR
SLTHR SLTHR SLTHR
?!
WHAT'S THAT NOISE?!
KRRK
AAAA!
SLTHR SLTHR

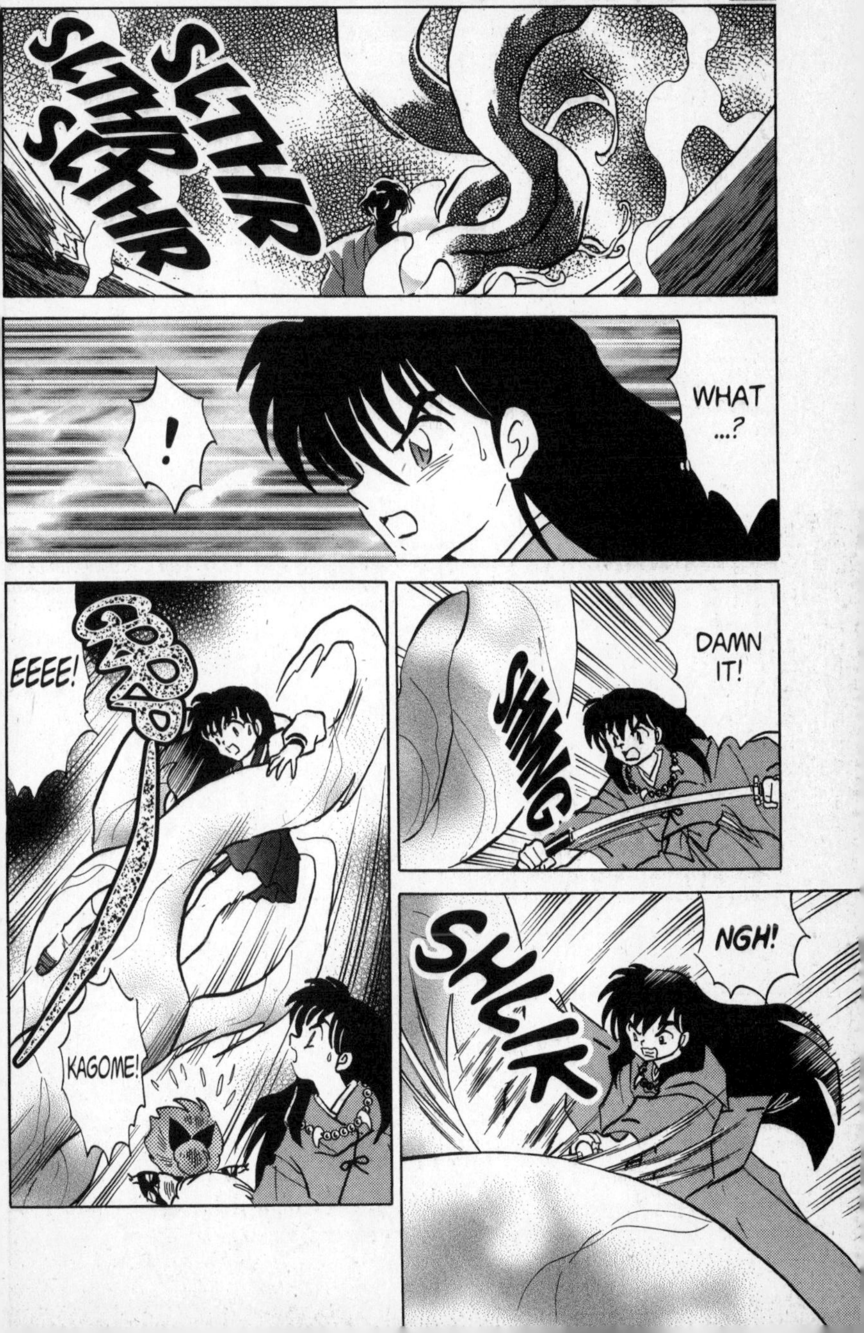
SLITHR
SLITHR
!
WHAT ...?
EEEE!
GRAB
KAGOME!
DAMN IT!
SHING
NGH!
SHLIK

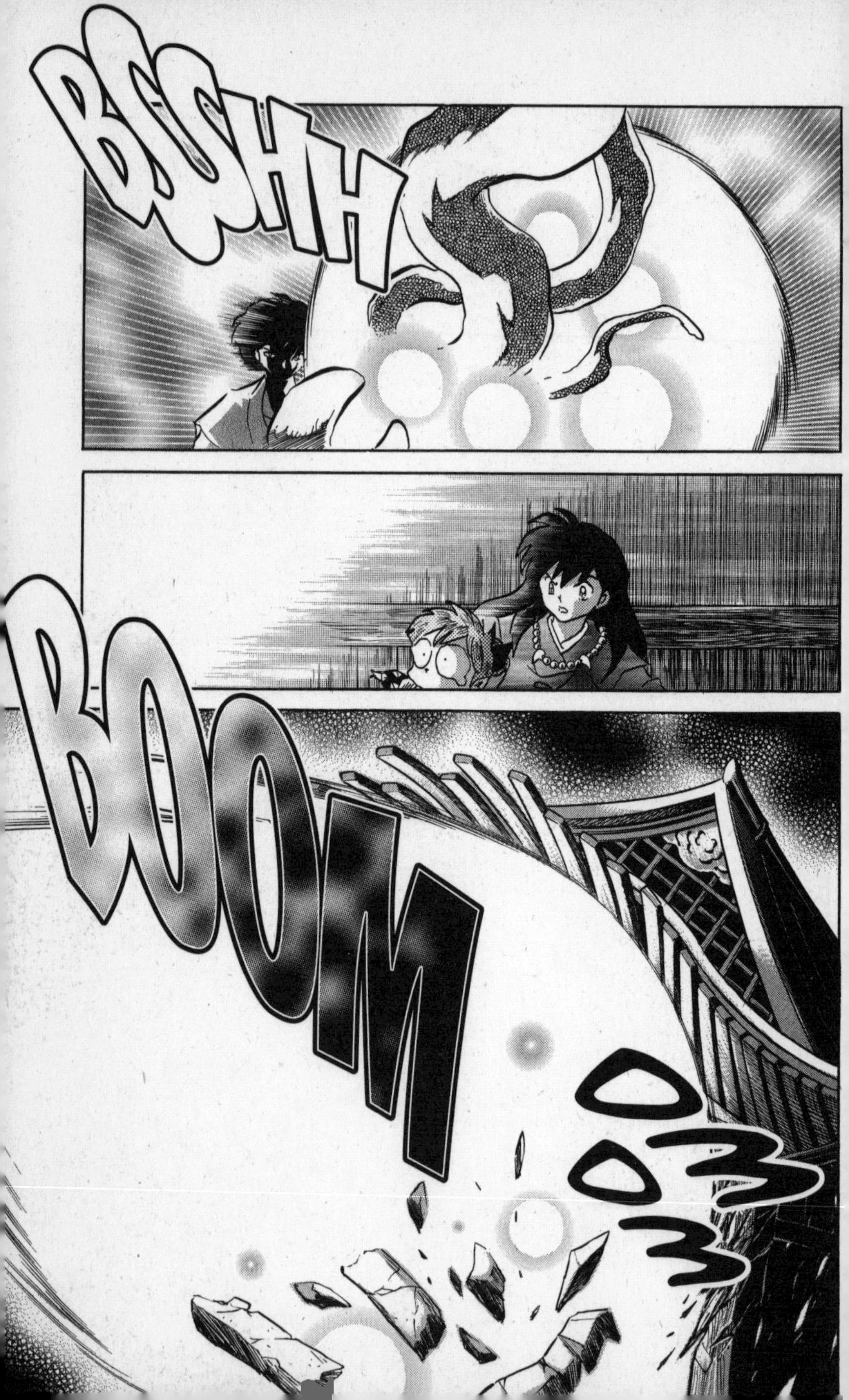
BSSHH
BOOM
OOMM

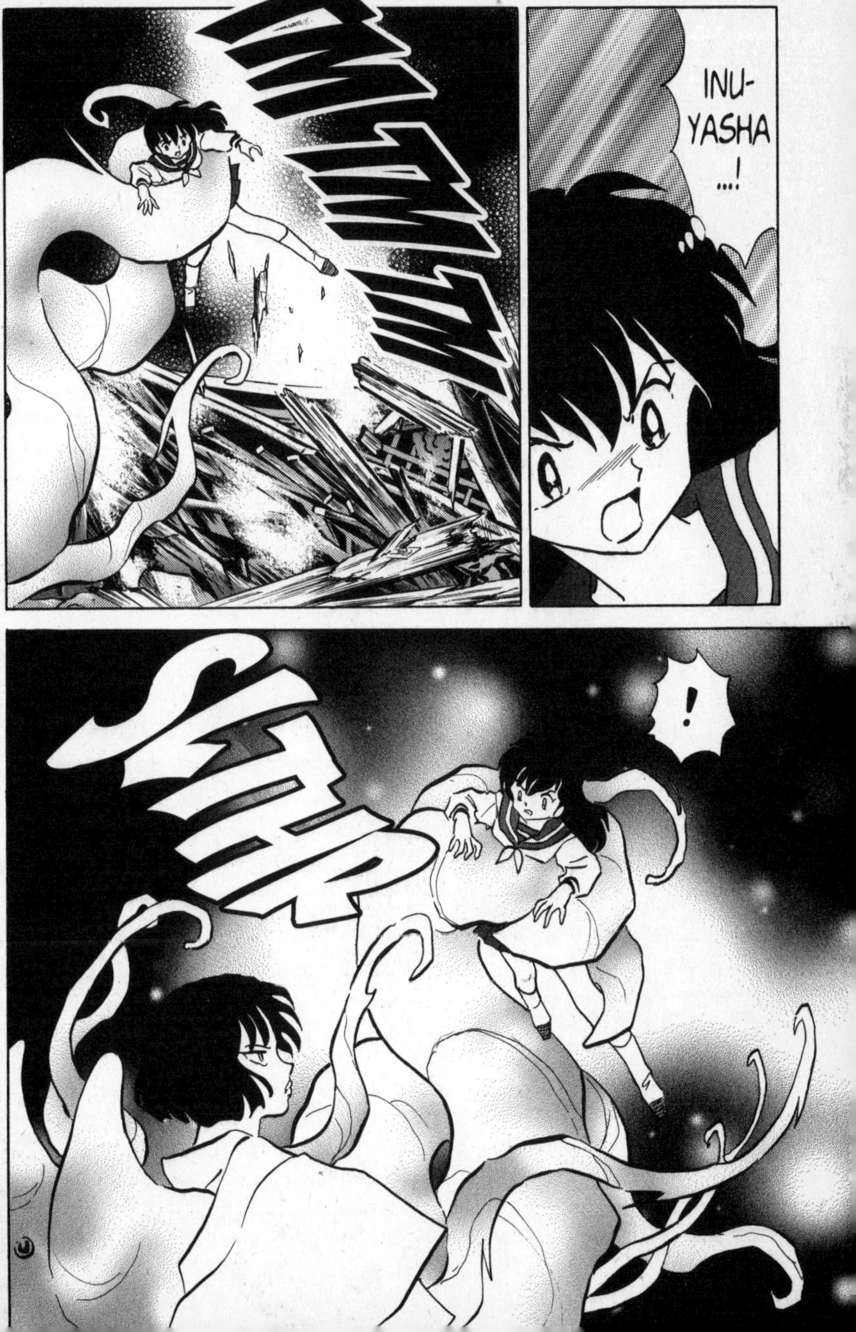
INU-YASHA ...!
!

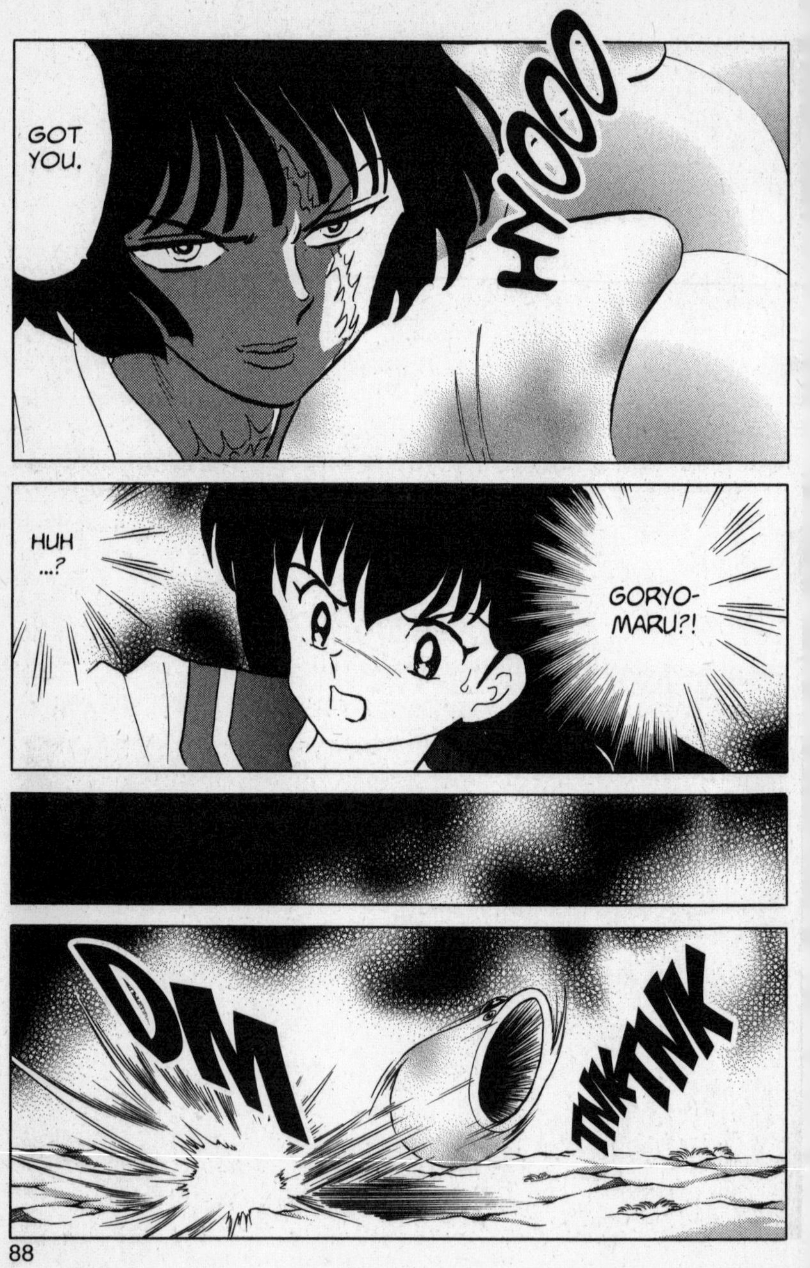
GOT YOU.
HYOOO
HUH ...?
GORYO-MARU?!
DM
TNKTNK

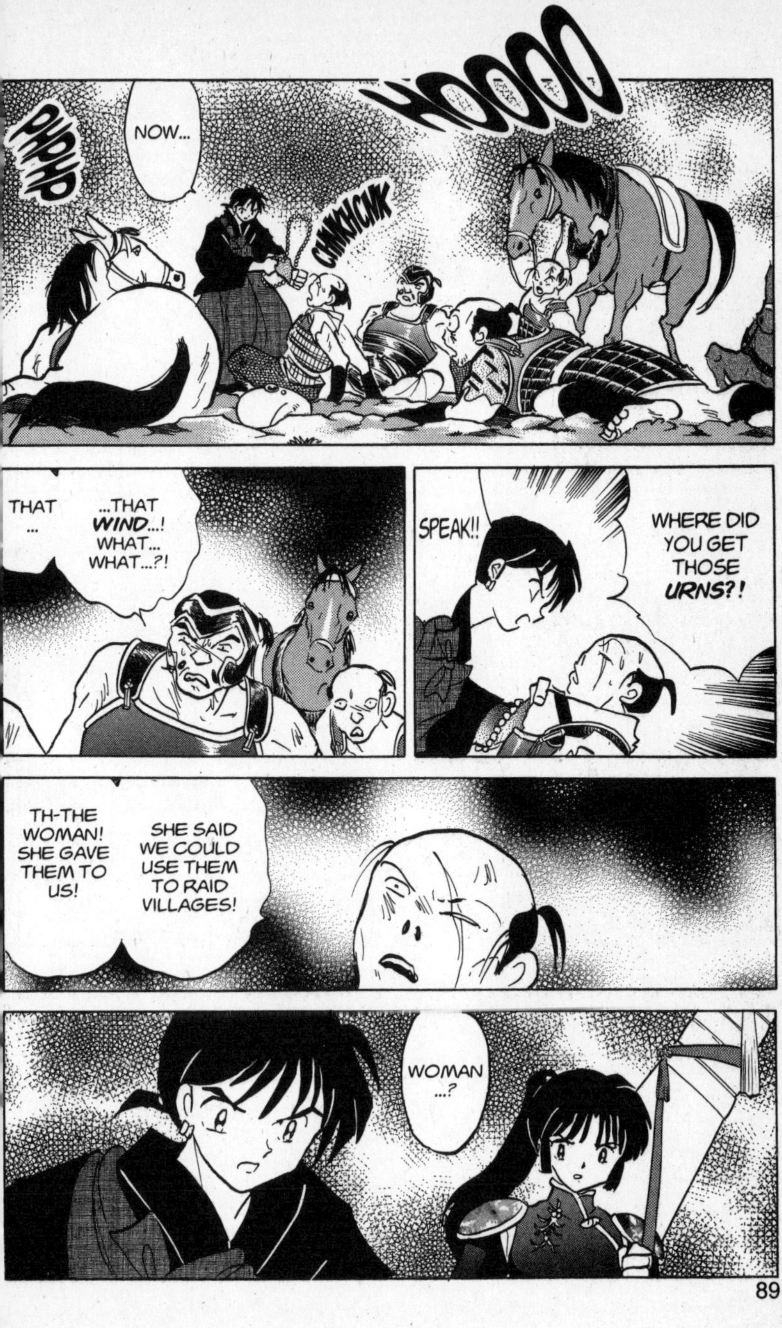
PHPHP
NOW...
CHKHCHK
HOOOO
THAT ...
...THAT WIND...! WHAT... WHAT...?!
SPEAK!!
WHERE DID YOU GET THOSE URNS?!
TH-THE WOMAN! SHE GAVE THEM TO US!
SHE SAID WE COULD USE THEM TO RAID VILLAGES!
WOMAN ...?

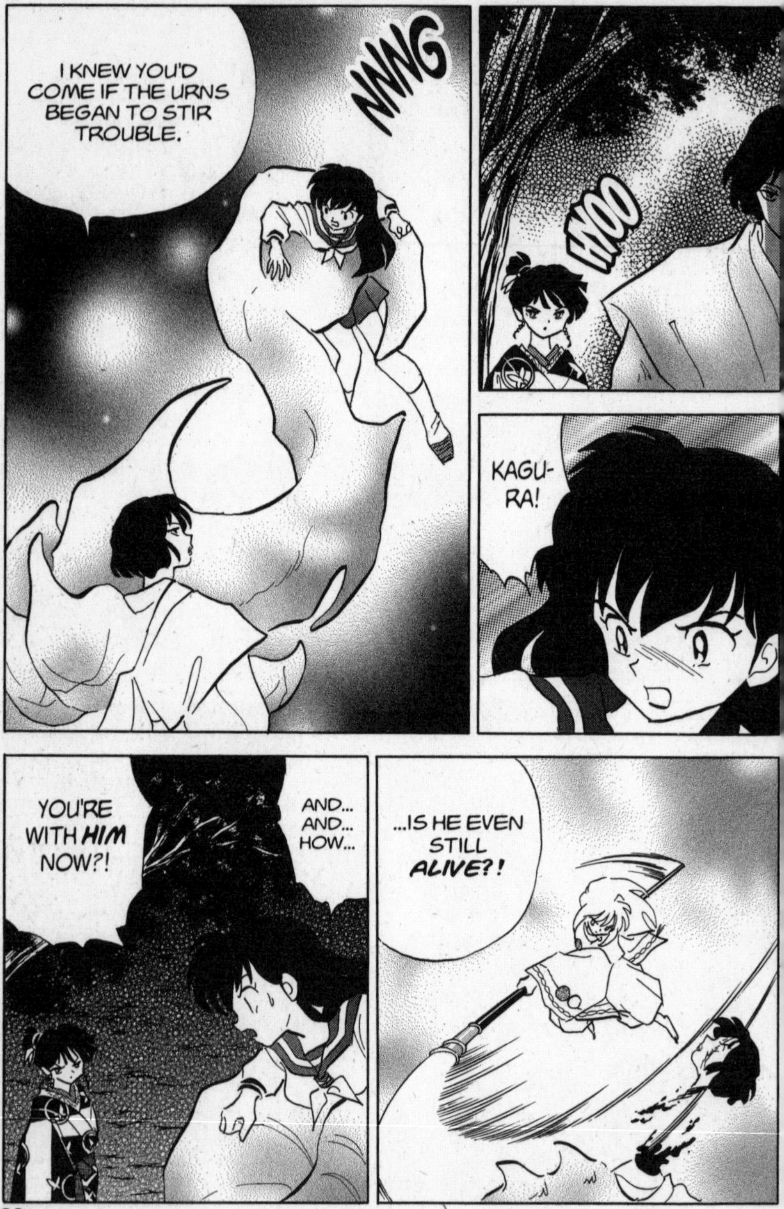
I KNEW YOU'D COME IF THE URNS BEGAN TO STIR TROUBLE.
NNNG
HOO
KAGU-RA!
YOU'RE WITH **HIM** NOW?!
AND... AND... HOW...
...IS HE EVEN STILL ***ALIVE?!***

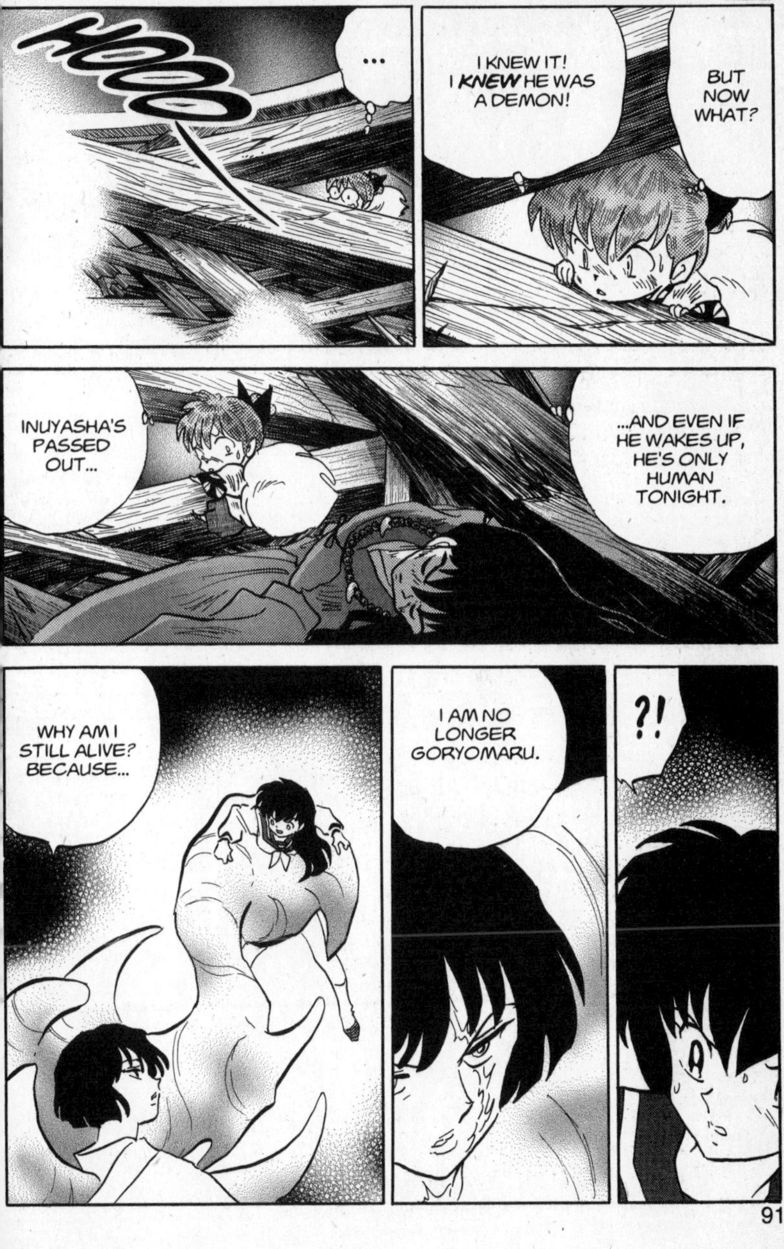
HOOO
...
I KNEW IT! I KNEW HE WAS A DEMON!
BUT NOW WHAT?
INUYASHA'S PASSED OUT...
...AND EVEN IF HE WAKES UP, HE'S ONLY HUMAN TONIGHT.
WHY AM I STILL ALIVE? BECAUSE...
I AM NO LONGER GORYOMARU.
?!

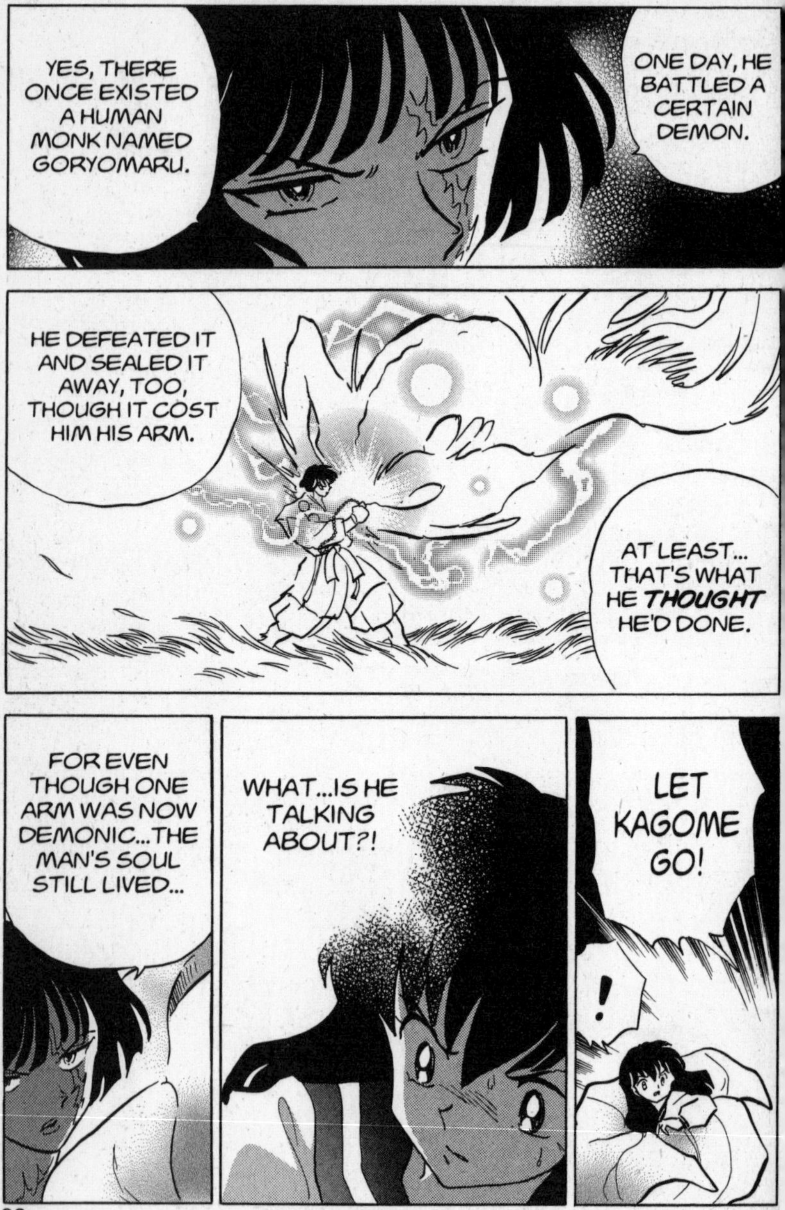
YES, THERE ONCE EXISTED A HUMAN MONK NAMED GORYOMARU.
ONE DAY, HE BATTLED A CERTAIN DEMON.
HE DEFEATED IT AND SEALED IT AWAY, TOO, THOUGH IT COST HIM HIS ARM.
AT LEAST... THAT'S WHAT HE *THOUGHT* HE'D DONE.
FOR EVEN THOUGH ONE ARM WAS NOW DEMONIC...THE MAN'S SOUL STILL LIVED...
WHAT...IS HE TALKING ABOUT?!
LET KAGOME GO!
!

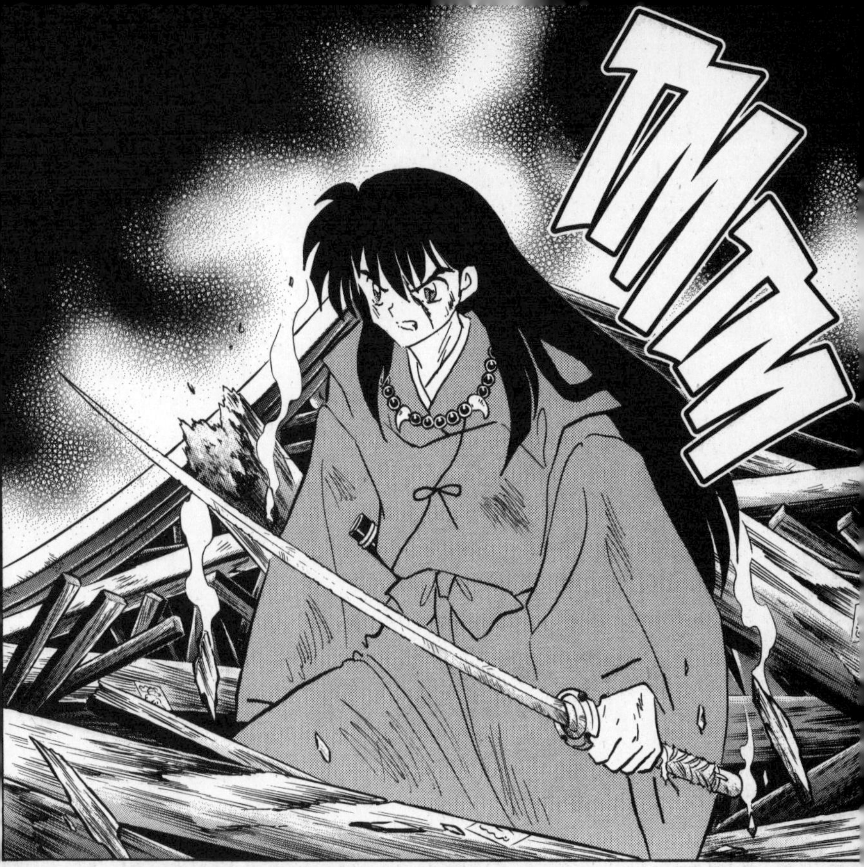
TWANG

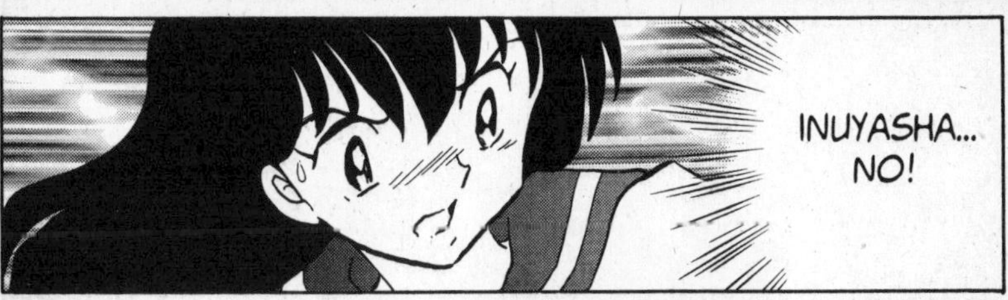
INUYASHA... NO!

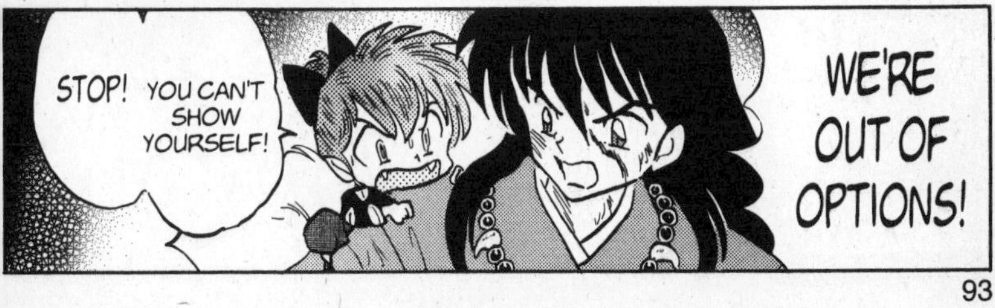
STOP! YOU CAN'T SHOW YOURSELF!
WE'RE OUT OF OPTIONS!

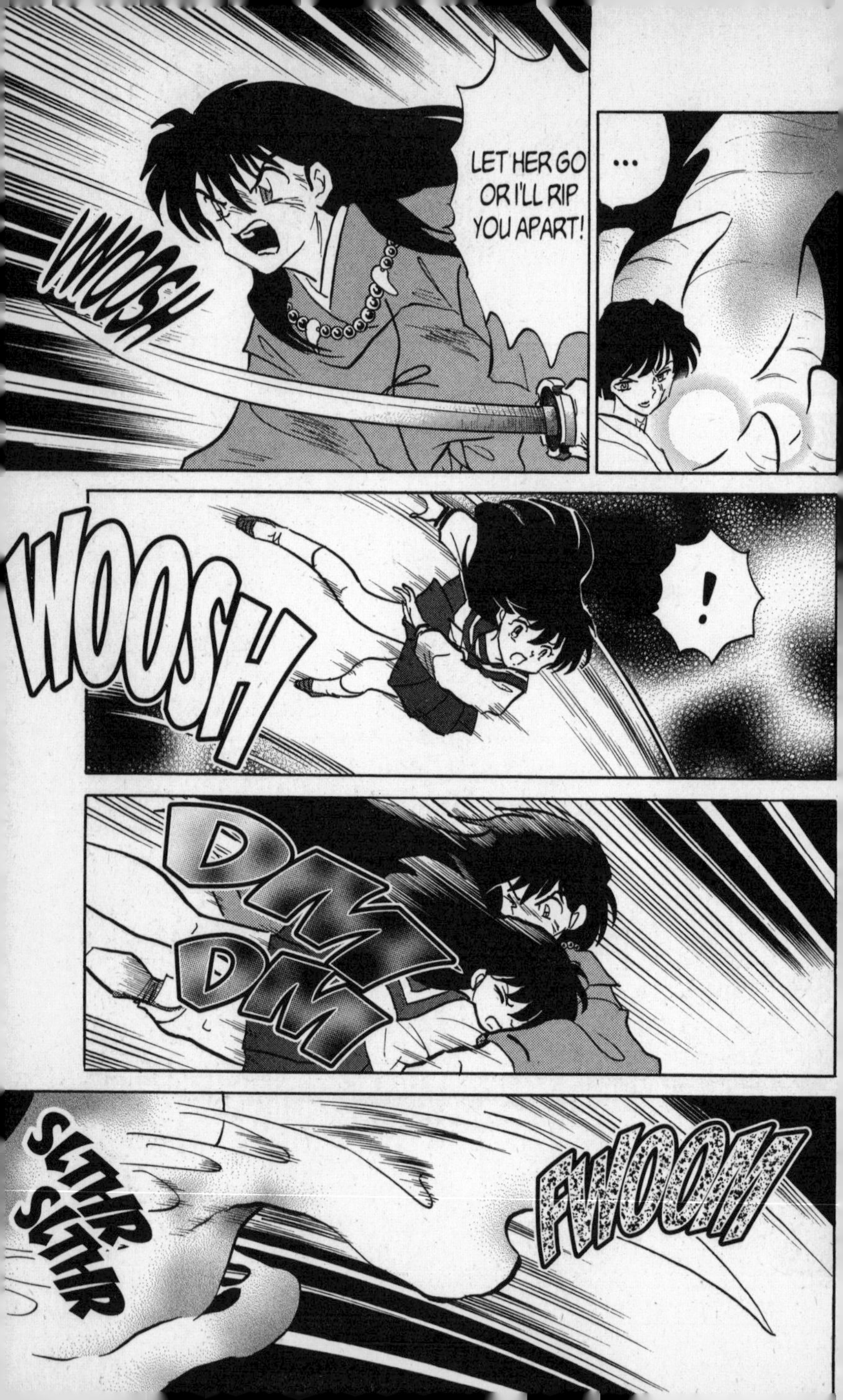
WOOSH
LET HER GO OR I'LL RIP YOU APART!
...
WOOSH
!
DM DM
SLTHR SLTHR
FWOOM

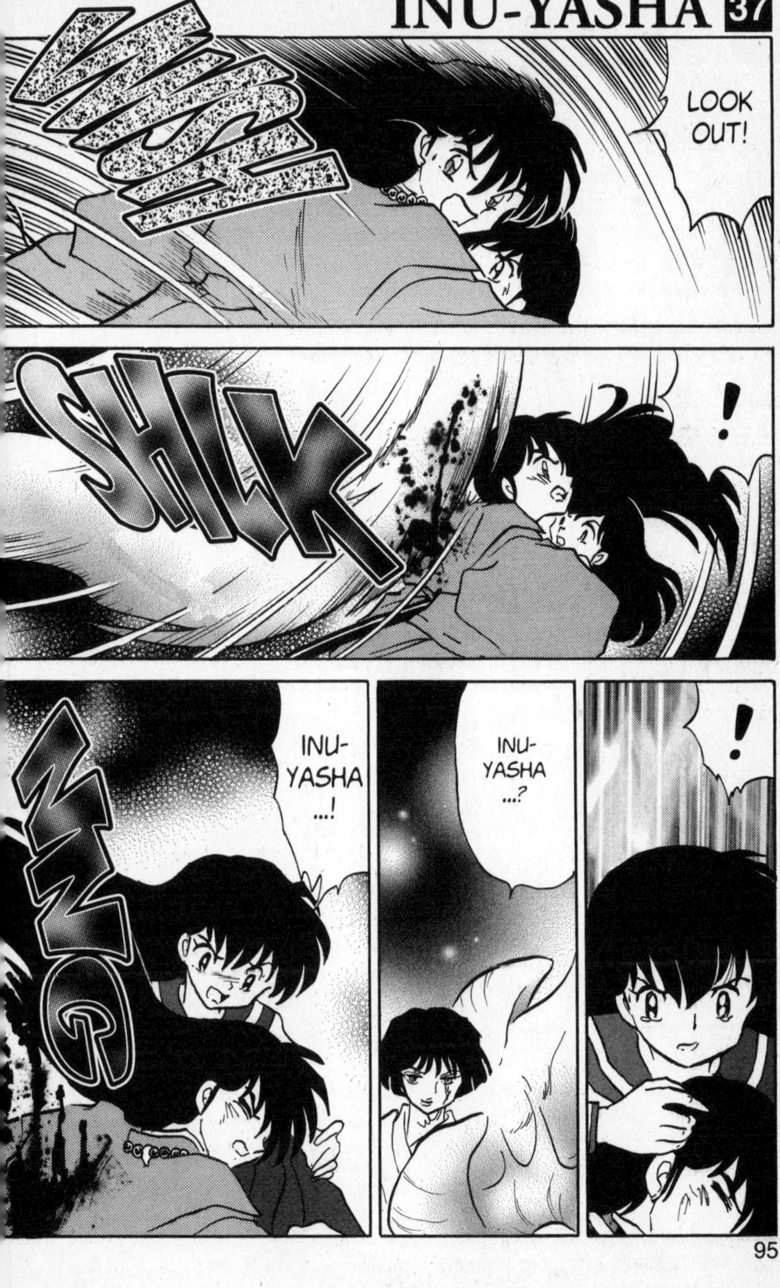
LOOK OUT!
!
INU-YASHA ...!
INU-YASHA ...?
!

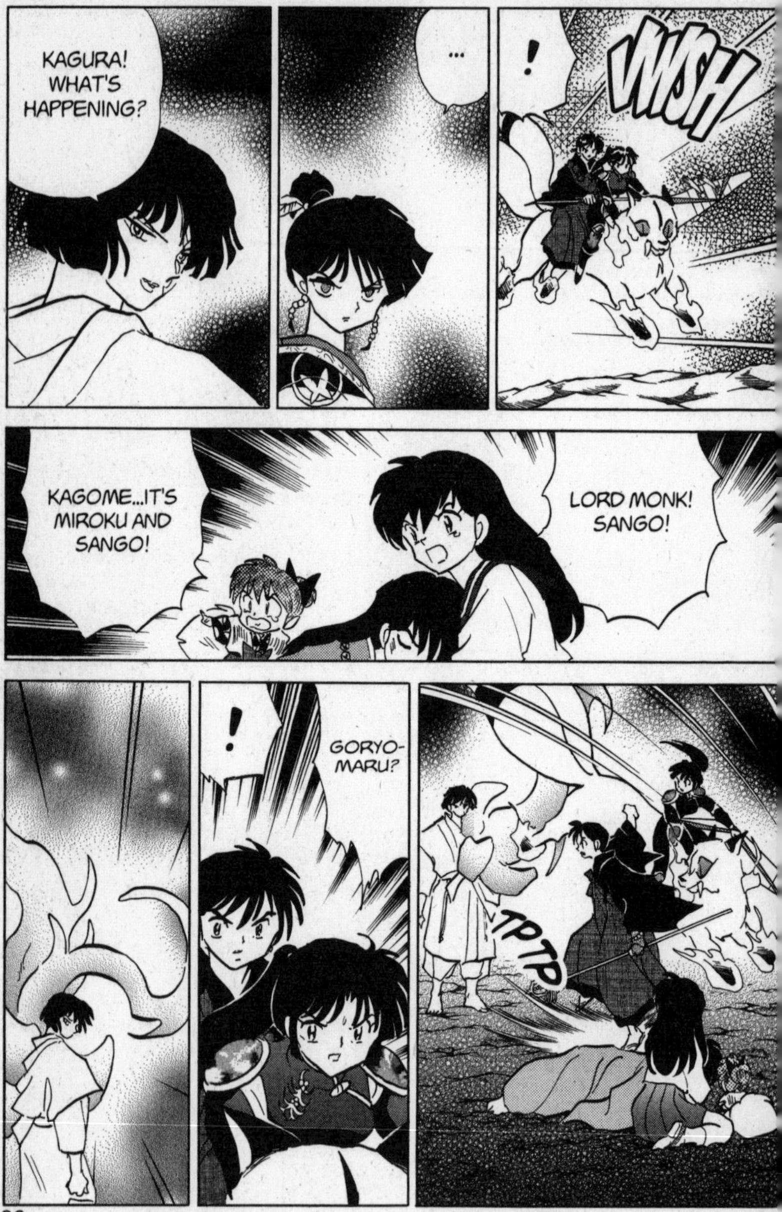

KAGURA! WHAT'S HAPPENING?
...
!
VWSH
KAGOME...IT'S MIROKU AND SANGO!
LORD MONK! SANGO!
!
GORYO-MARU?
TP TP

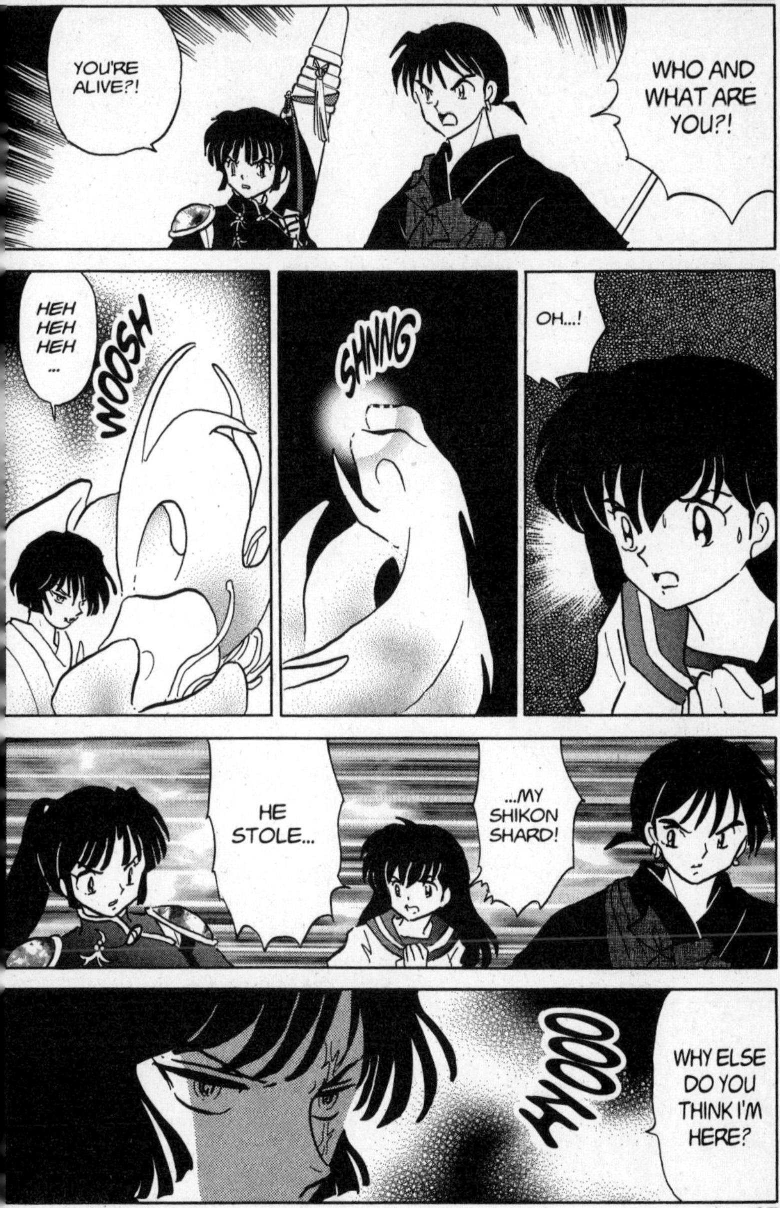
YOU'RE ALIVE?!
WHO AND WHAT ARE YOU?!
HEH HEH HEH ...
WOOSH
SHNNG
OH...!
HE STOLE...
...MY SHIKON SHARD!
HYOOO
WHY ELSE DO YOU THINK I'M HERE?

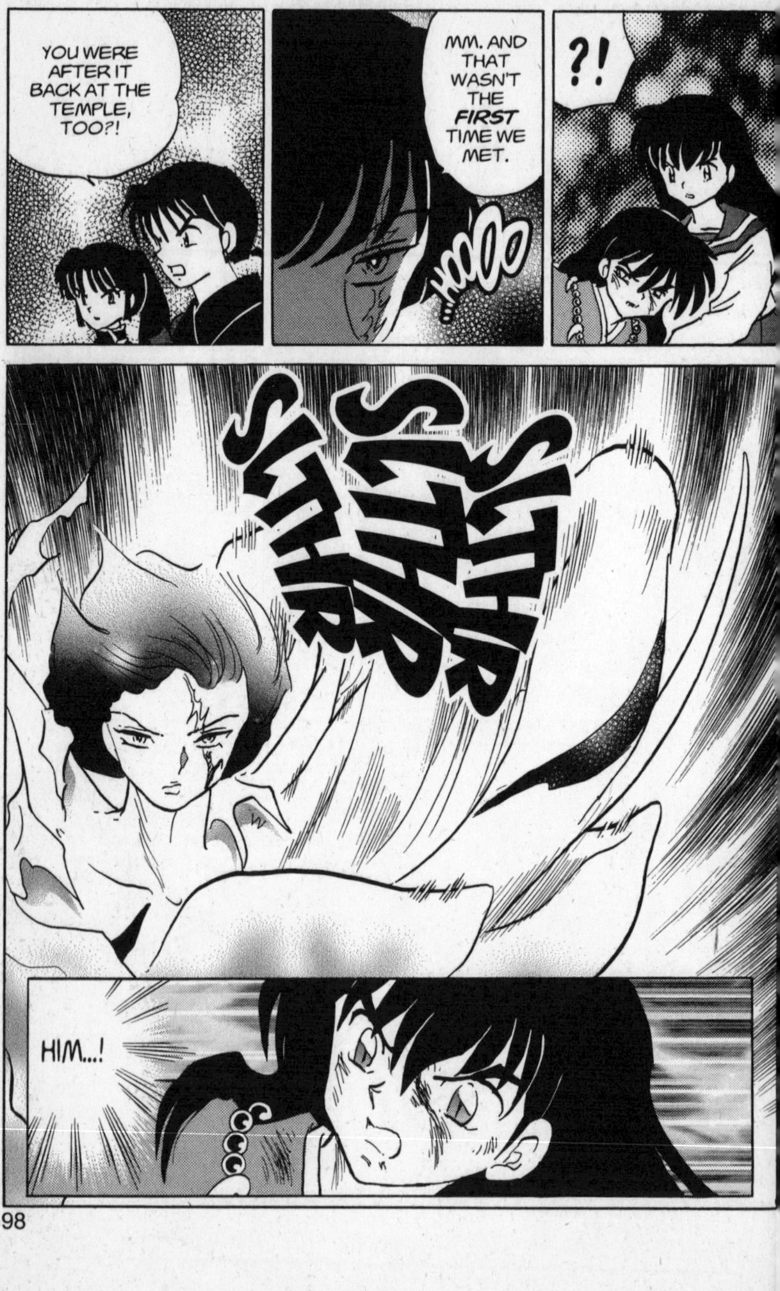
YOU WERE AFTER IT BACK AT THE TEMPLE, TOO?!
MM. AND THAT WASN'T THE *FIRST* TIME WE MET.
HOOOO
?!
HIM...!

SCROLL 6
METAMORPHOSIS

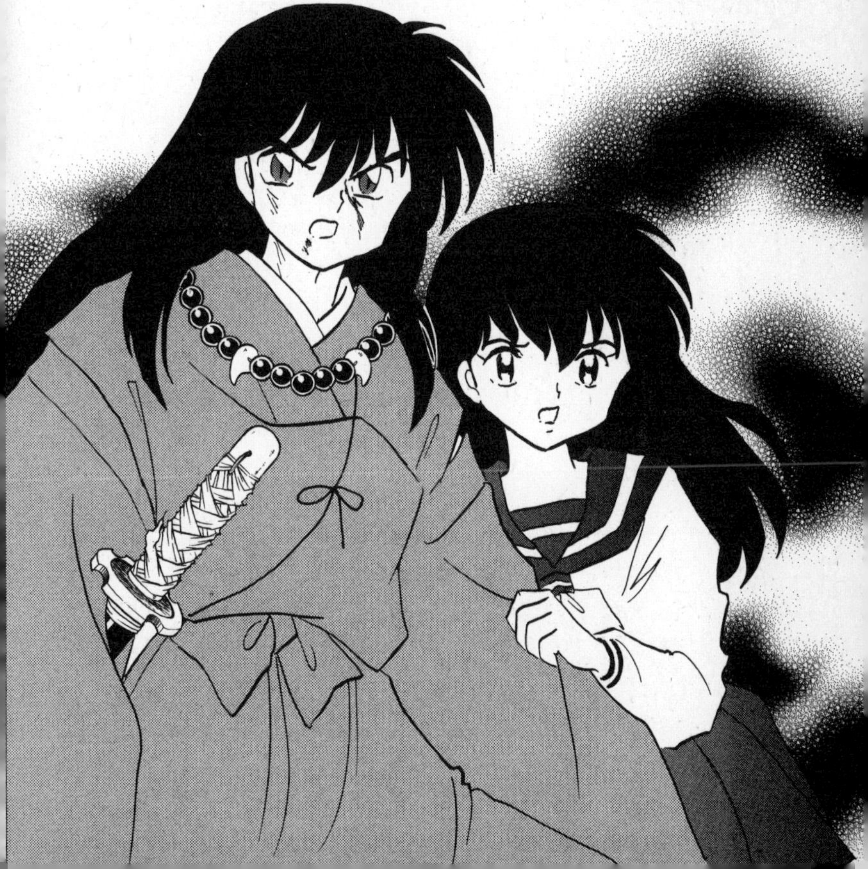

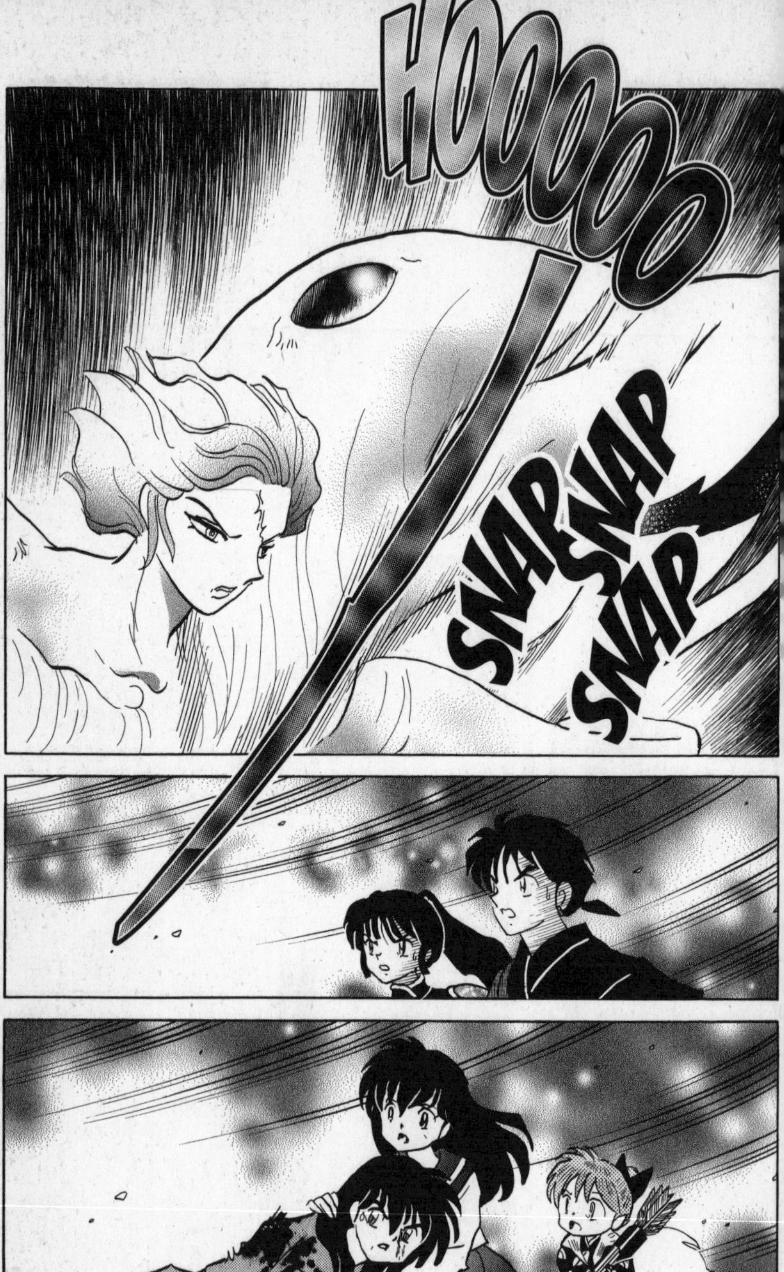
HOOOOO
SNAP
SNAP
SNAP

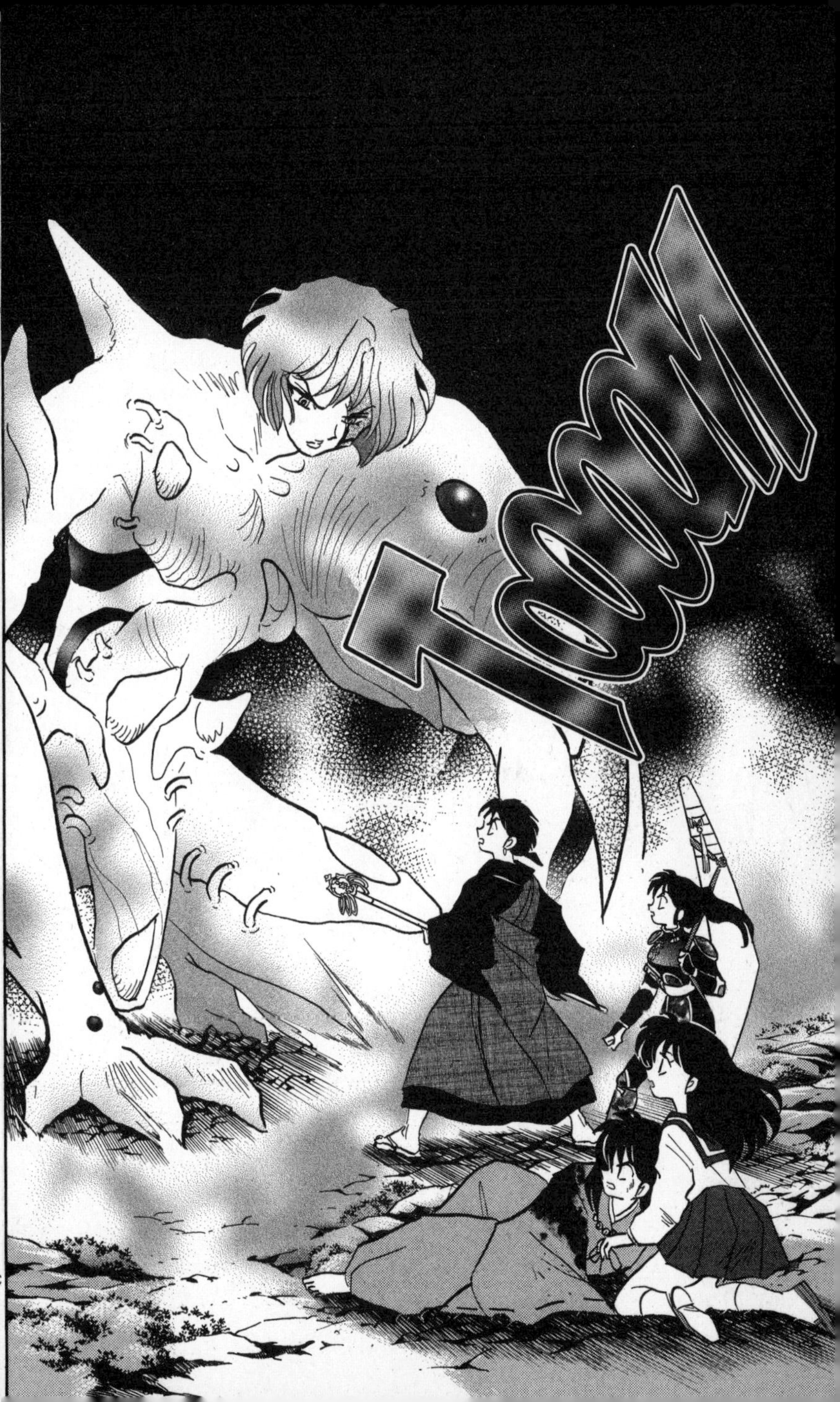
TOOOM

HEH HEH HEH...

REMEMBER ME...?

M-MONK...! IT'S...

MORYO-MARU!

THE DEMON HAKUDOSHI CREATED FROM THOSE DEMONS' CORPSES!

BUT...

102

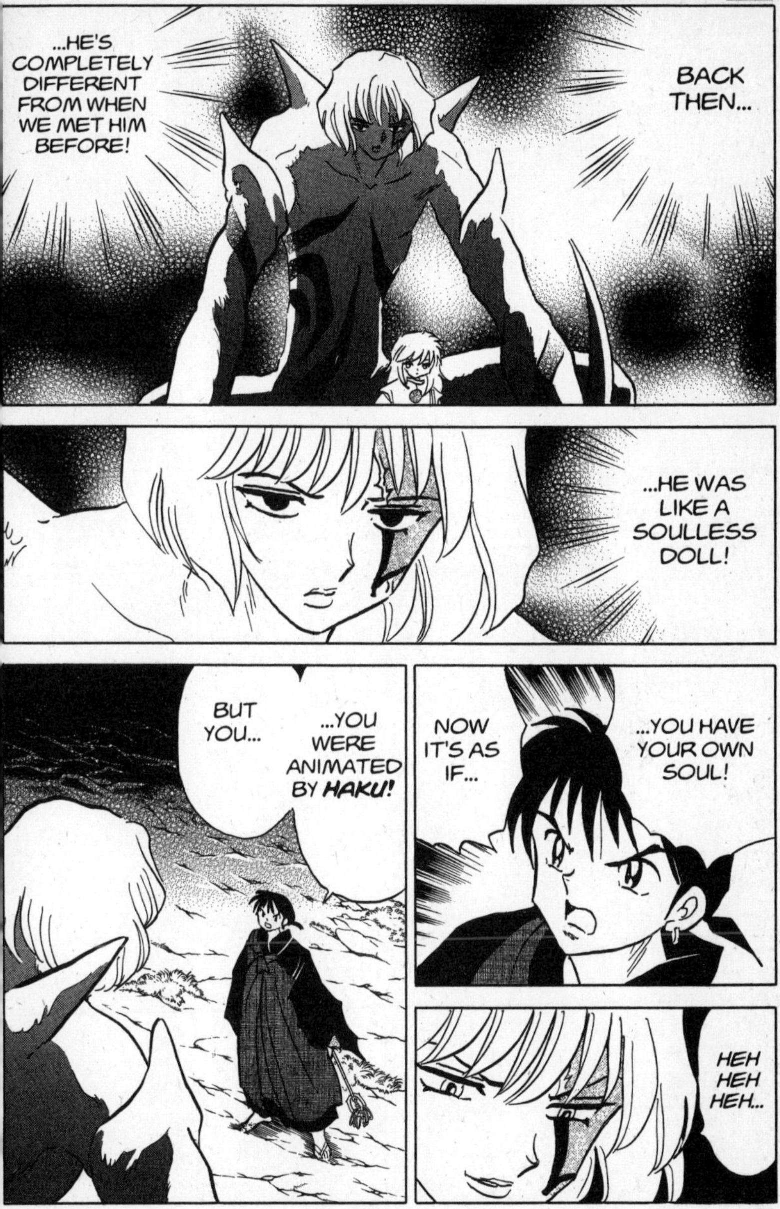
...HE'S COMPLETELY DIFFERENT FROM WHEN WE MET HIM BEFORE!
BACK THEN...
...HE WAS LIKE A SOULLESS DOLL!
BUT YOU...
...YOU WERE ANIMATED BY **HAKU!**
NOW IT'S AS IF...
...YOU HAVE YOUR OWN SOUL!
HEH HEH HEH...

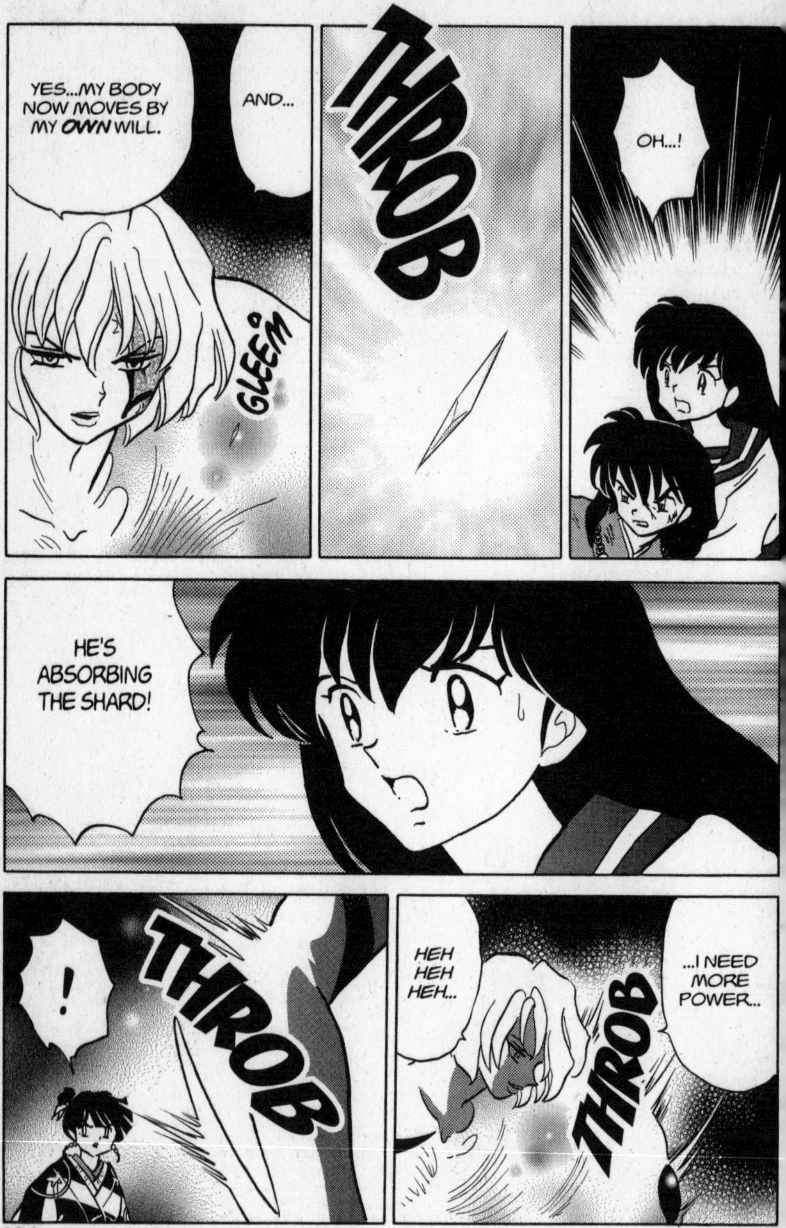
YES...MY BODY NOW MOVES BY MY OWN WILL.
AND...
GLEEM
THROB
OH...!
HE'S ABSORBING THE SHARD!
!
THROB
HEH HEH HEH...
THROB
...I NEED MORE POWER...

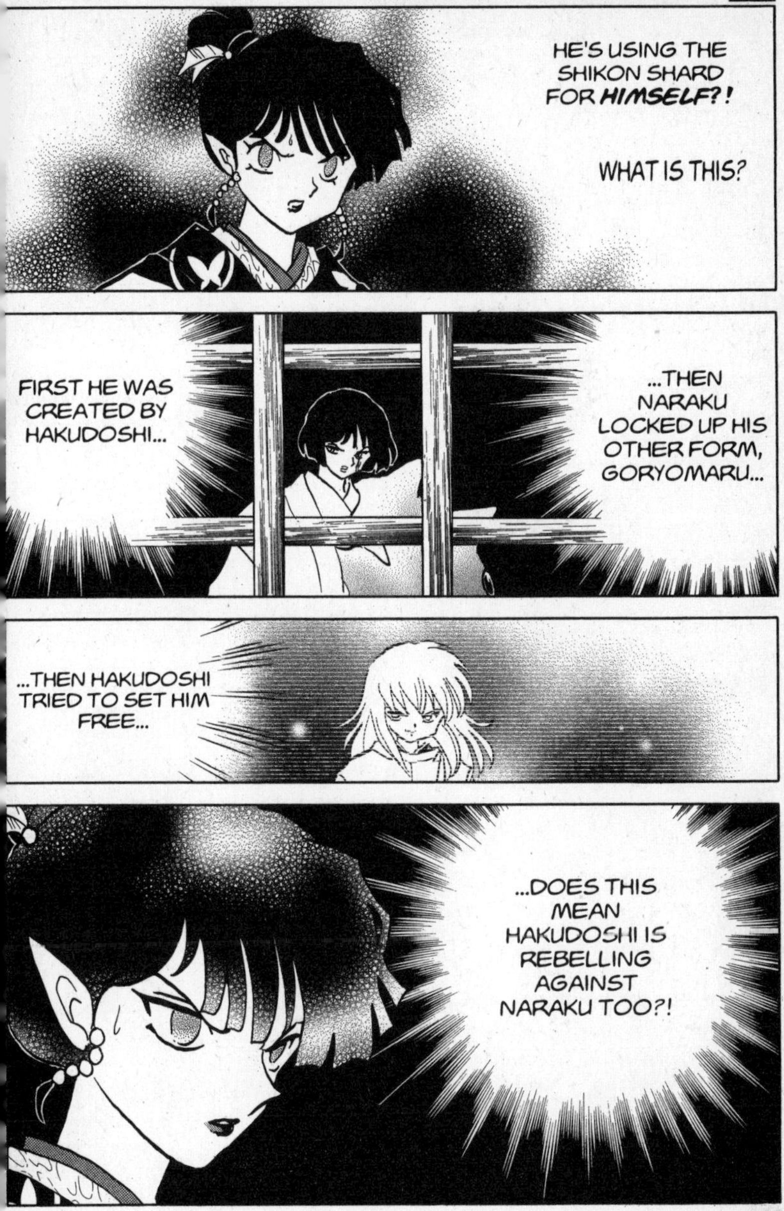
HE'S USING THE SHIKON SHARD FOR HIMSELF?!
WHAT IS THIS?
FIRST HE WAS CREATED BY HAKUDOSHI...
...THEN NARAKU LOCKED UP HIS OTHER FORM, GORYOMARU...
...THEN HAKUDOSHI TRIED TO SET HIM FREE...
...DOES THIS MEAN HAKUDOSHI IS REBELLING AGAINST NARAKU TOO?!

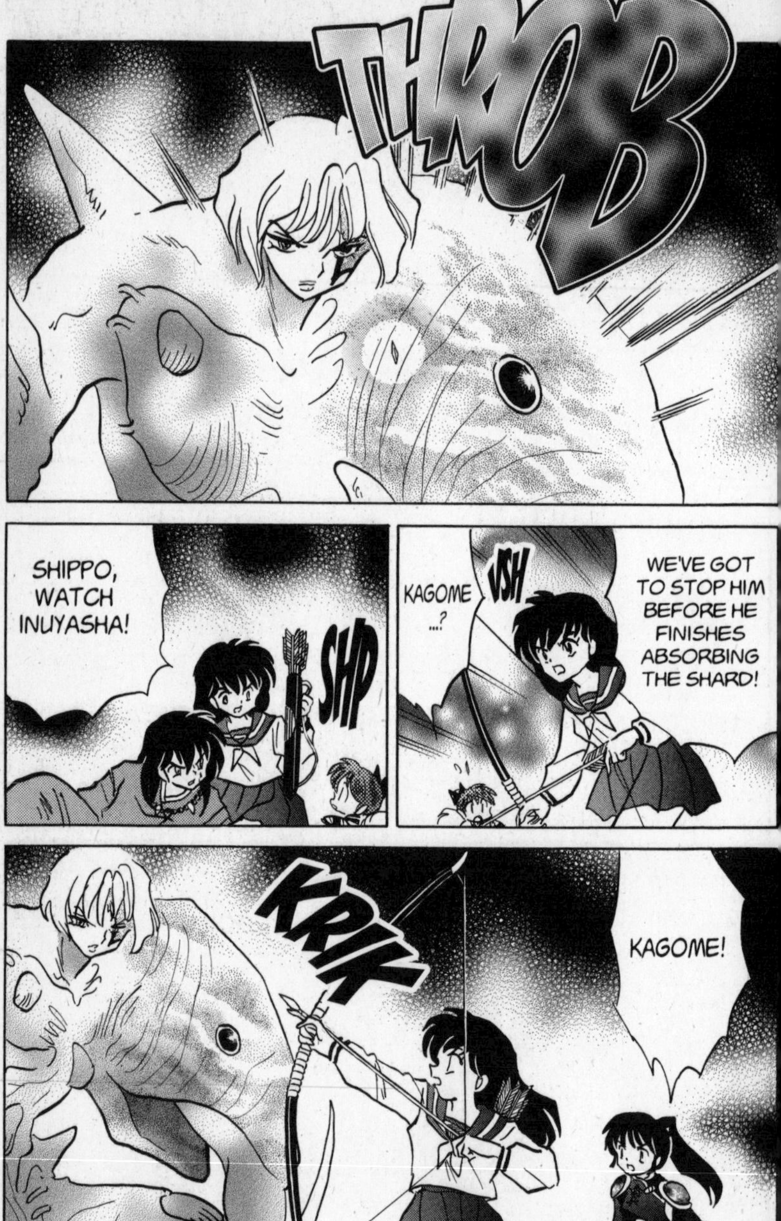
THROB
SHIPPO, WATCH INUYASHA!
SHP
KAGOME ...?
VSH
WE'VE GOT TO STOP HIM BEFORE HE FINISHES ABSORBING THE SHARD!
KRIK
KAGOME!

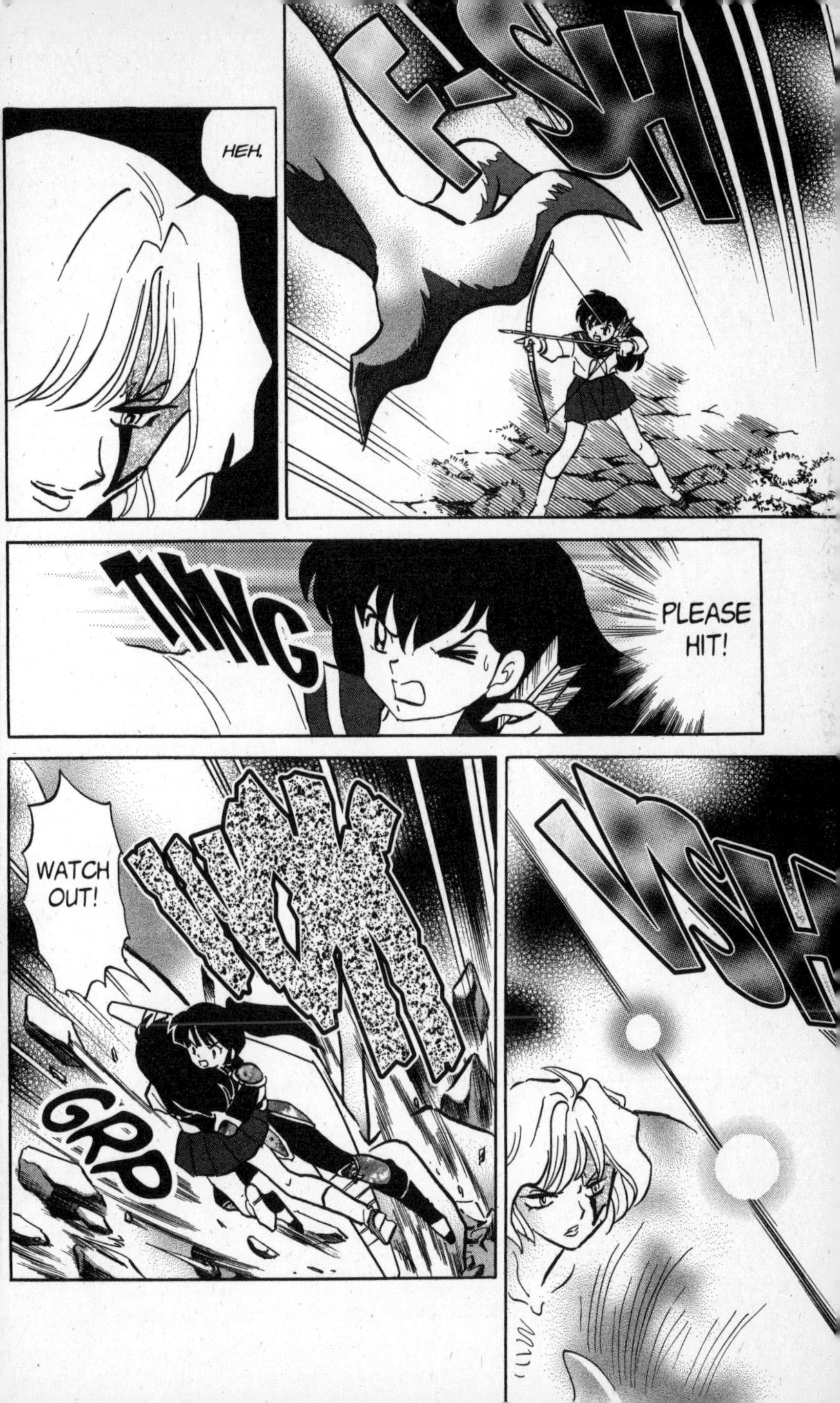
HEH.
TWNG
PLEASE HIT!
WATCH OUT!
GRP

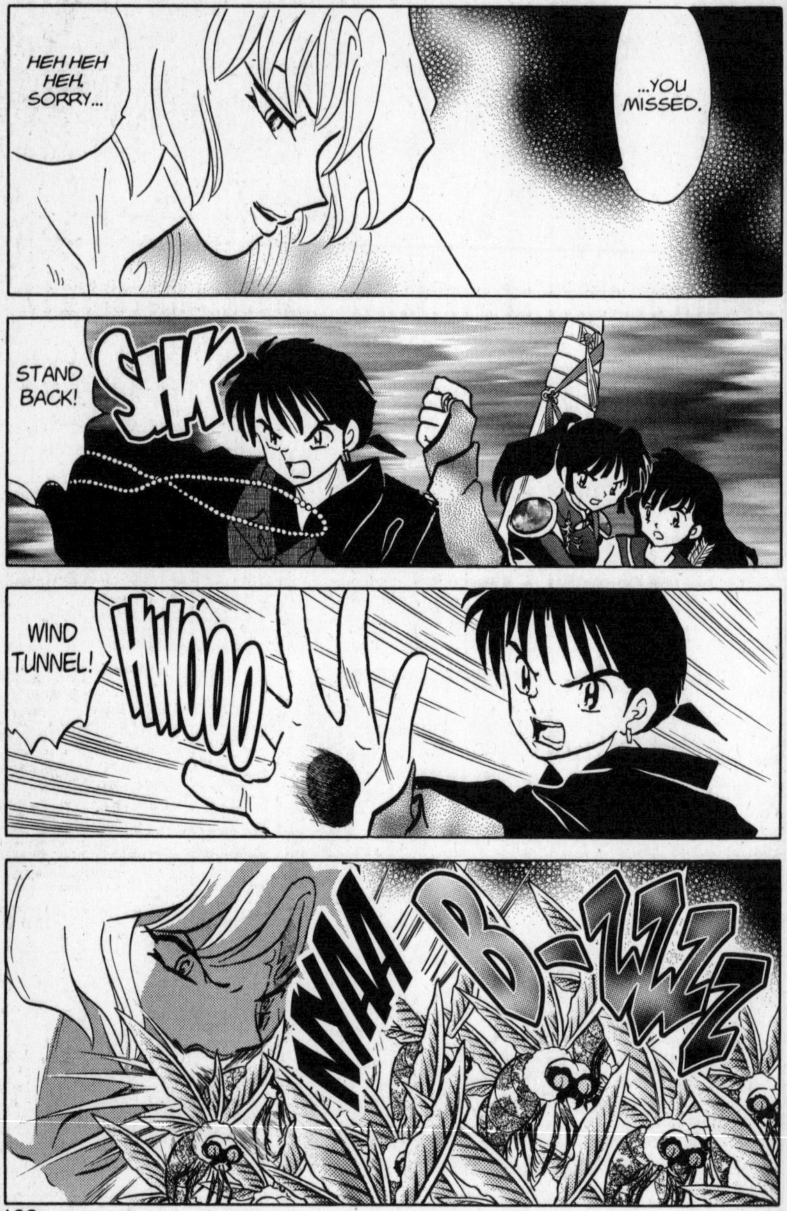
HEH HEH HEH. SORRY...
...YOU MISSED.
STAND BACK!
SHK
WIND TUNNEL!
HWOOO
NYAA
B-ZZZZ

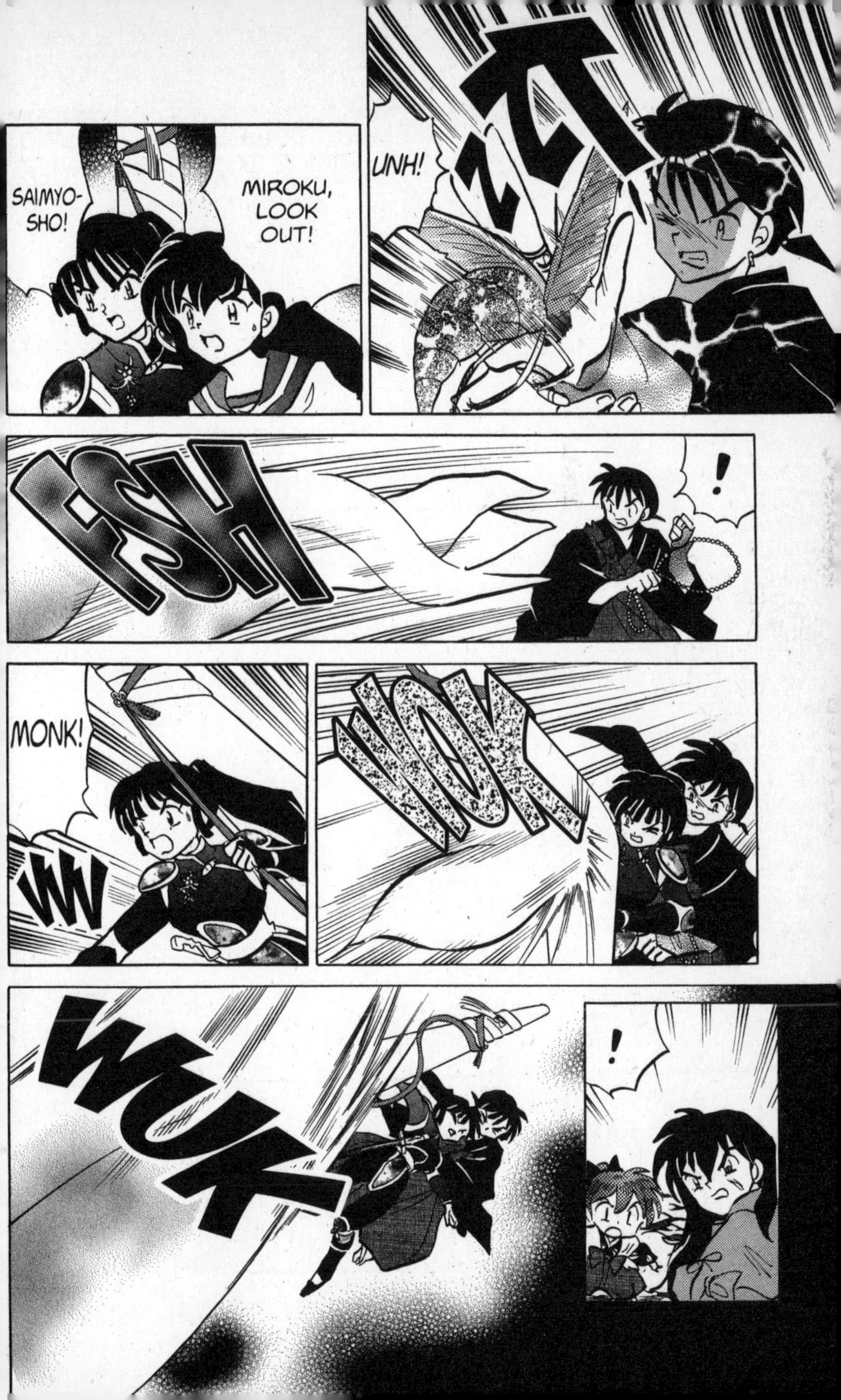
SAIMYO-SHO!
MIROKU, LOOK OUT!
UNH!
FSSH
!
MONK!
WUK
!

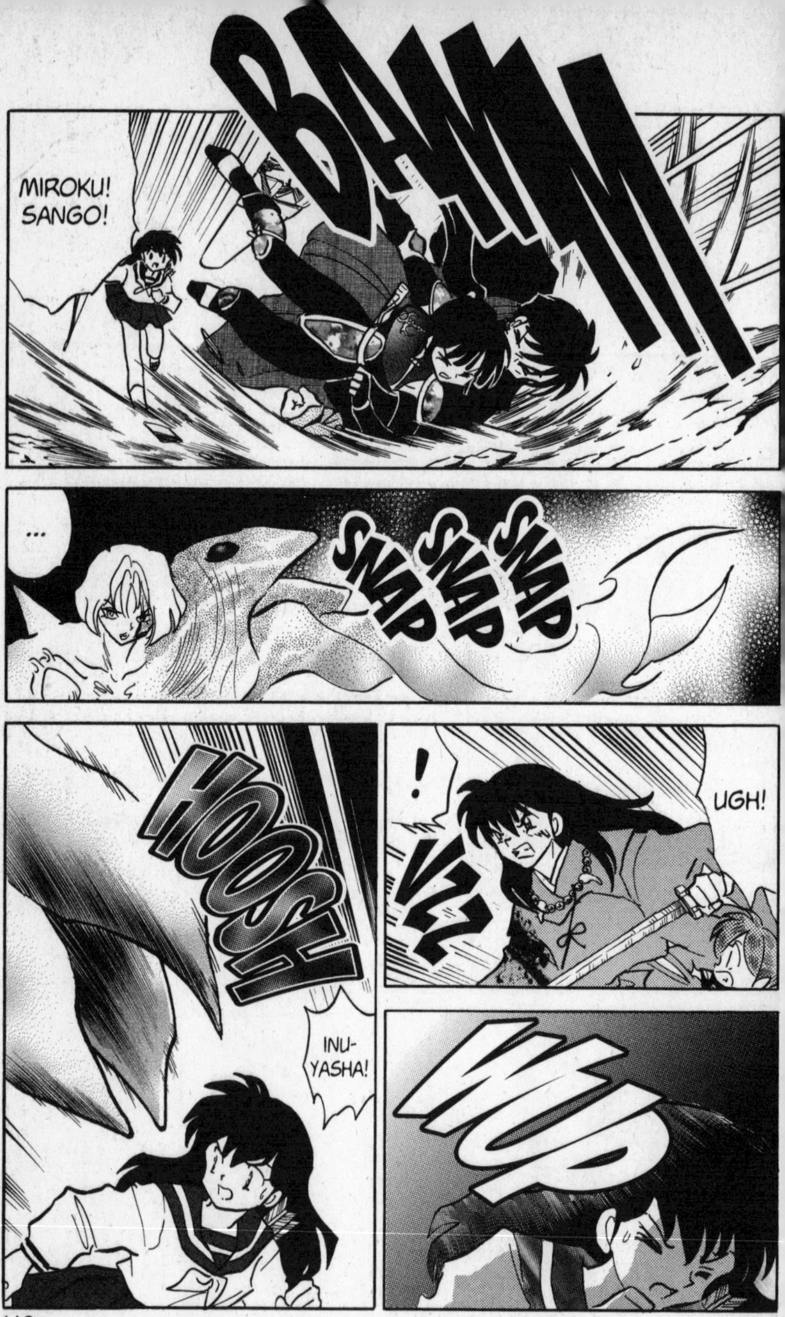
BAMM
MIROKU! SANGO!
...
SNAP SNAP SNAP
HOOSH
INU-YASHA!
!
VZZ
UGH!
WUP

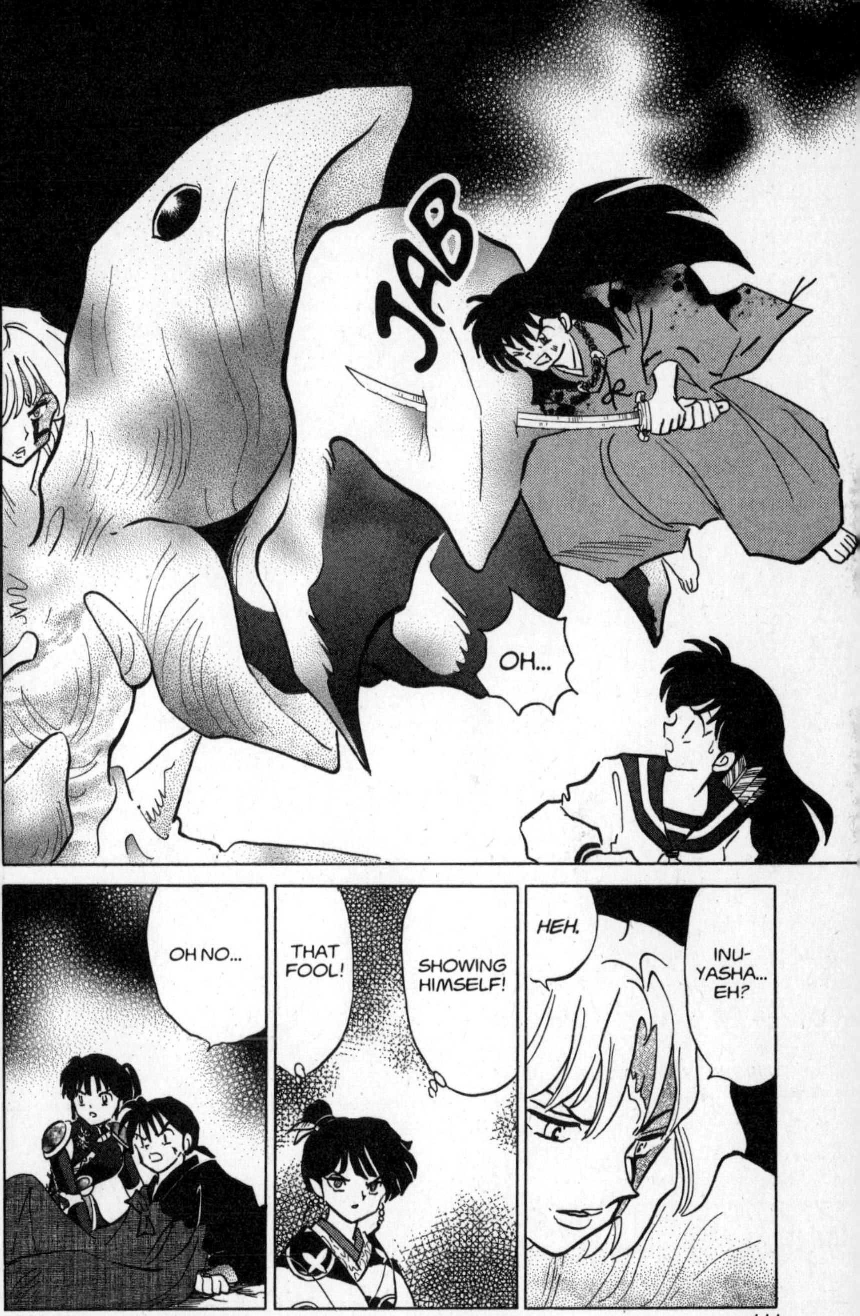
JAB
OH...
OH NO...
THAT FOOL!
SHOWING HIMSELF!
HEH.
INU-YASHA... EH?

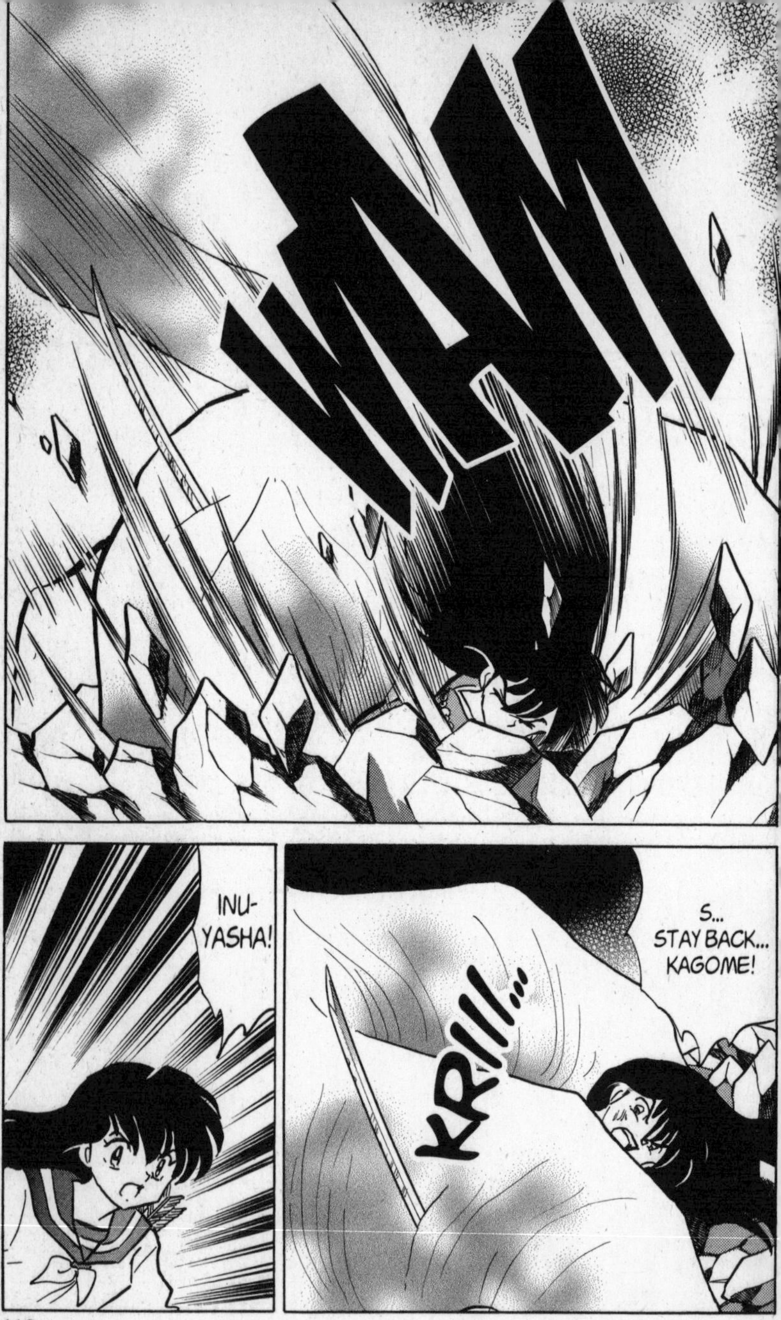
INU-
YASHA!
S...
STAY BACK...
KAGOME!
KRIII...

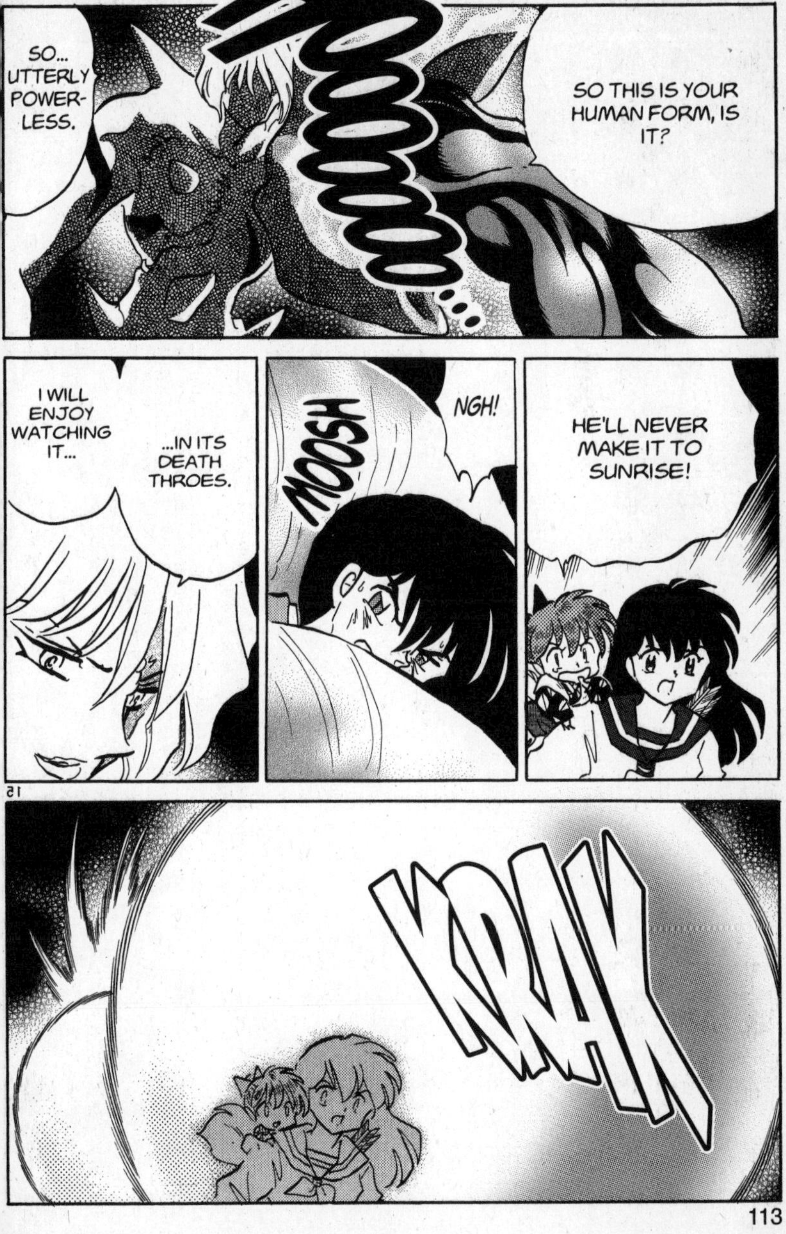
SO... UTTERLY POWER-LESS.
HOOOOOOO...
SO THIS IS YOUR HUMAN FORM, IS IT?
I WILL ENJOY WATCHING IT...
...IN ITS DEATH THROES.
MOOSH
NGH!
HE'LL NEVER MAKE IT TO SUNRISE!
KRAK

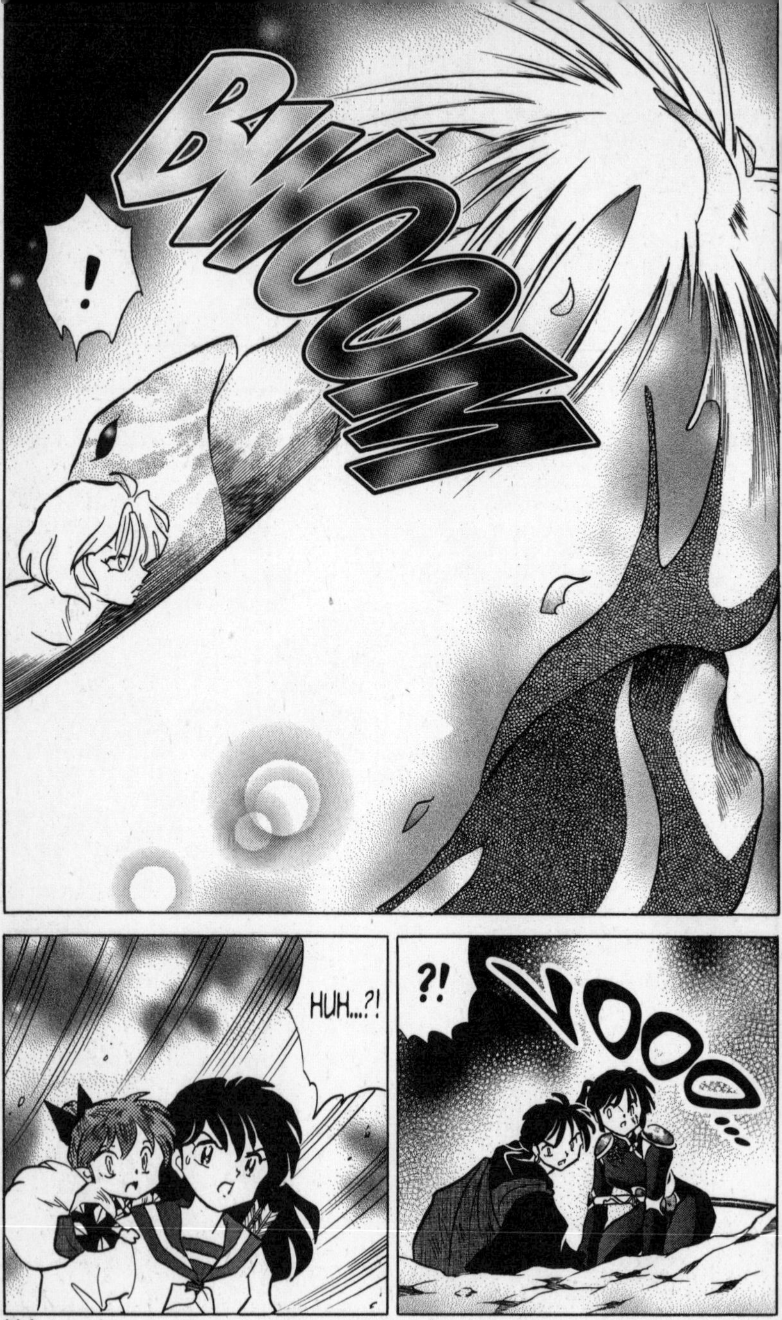

!
BWOOM
HUH...?!
?!
VOOO...

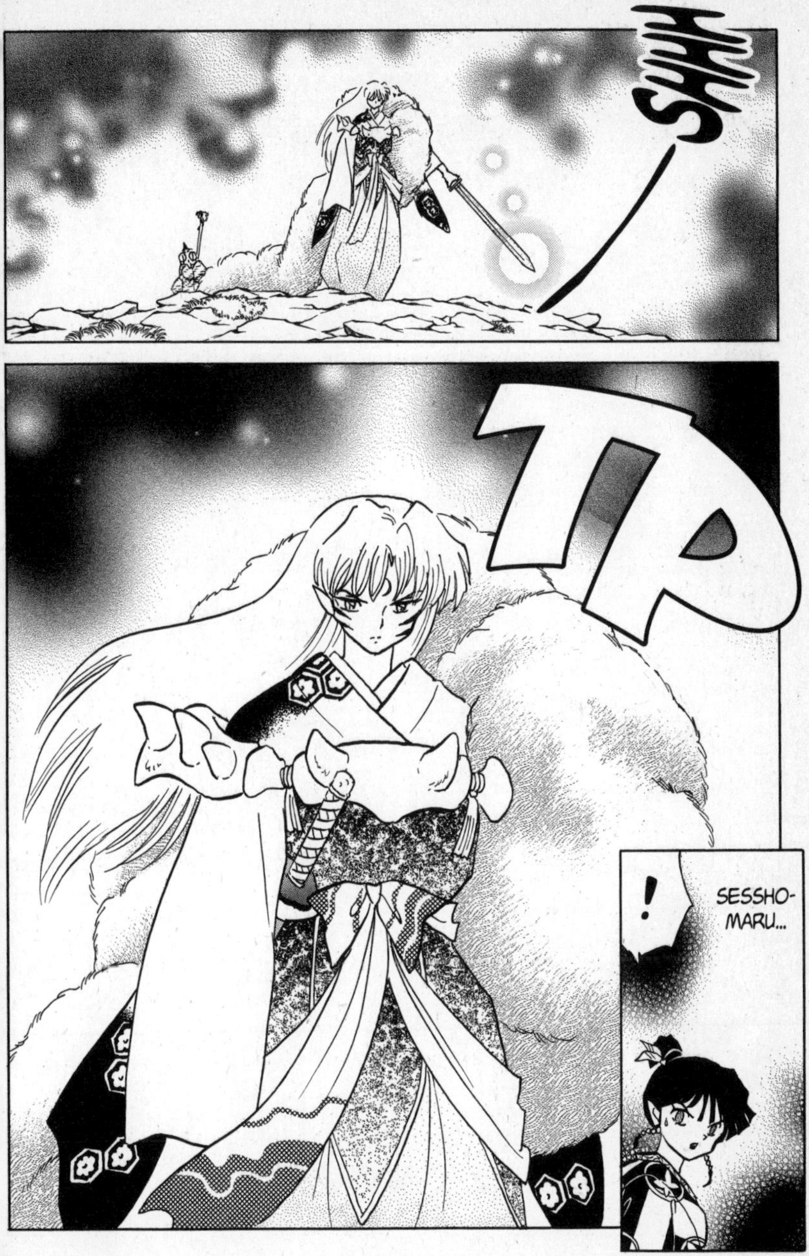
SHHHH
TIP
!
SESSHO-
MARU...

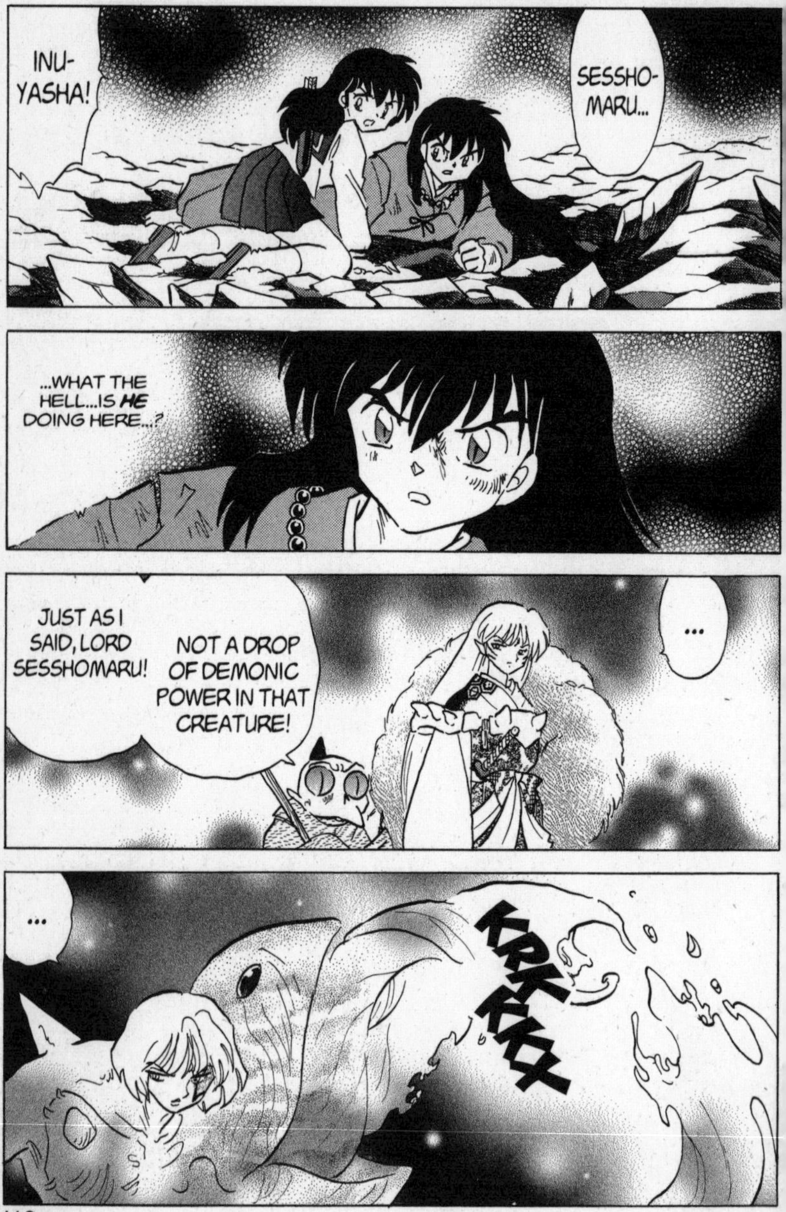
INU-YASHA!
SESSHO-MARU...
...WHAT THE HELL...IS HE DOING HERE...?
JUST AS I SAID, LORD SESSHOMARU!
NOT A DROP OF DEMONIC POWER IN THAT CREATURE!
...
...
KRKKKK

SCROLL 7

THE VANISHED POWER

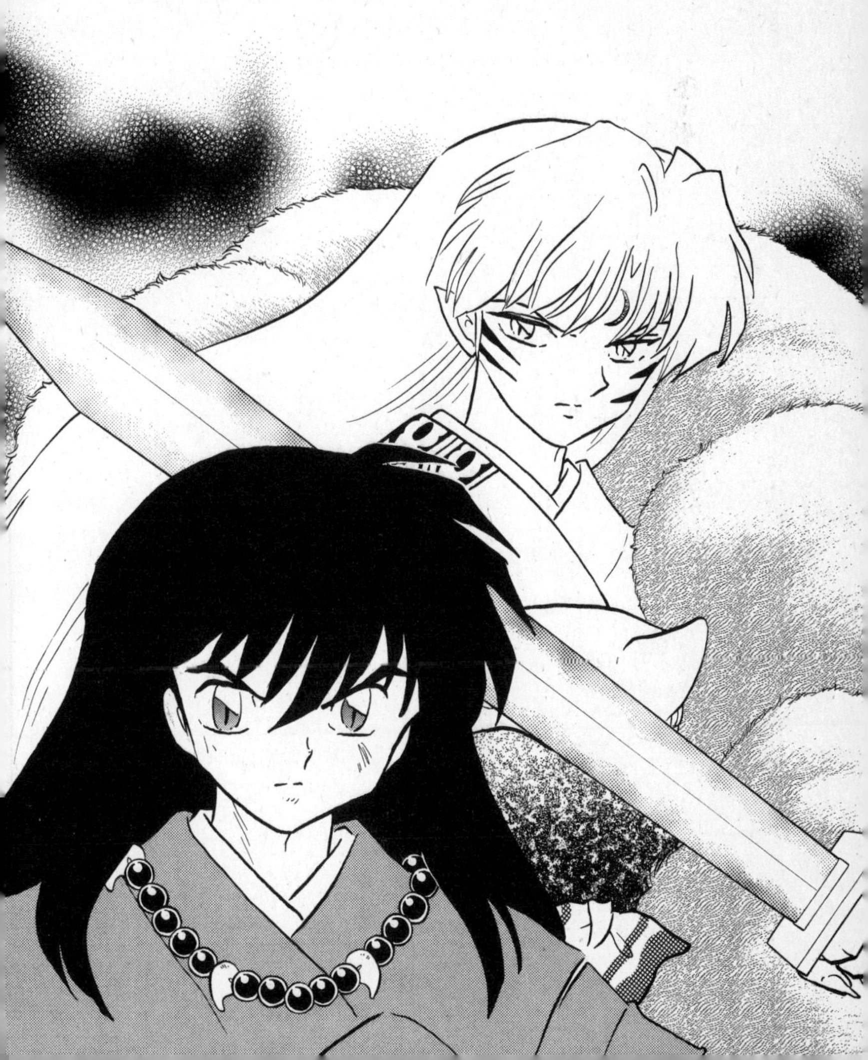

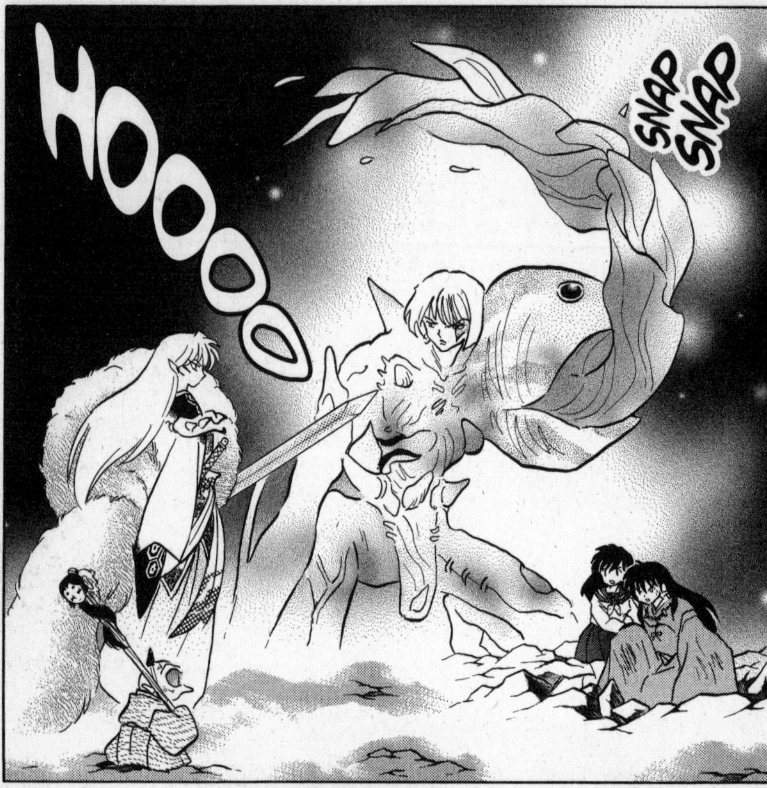
HOOOO
SNAP SNAP
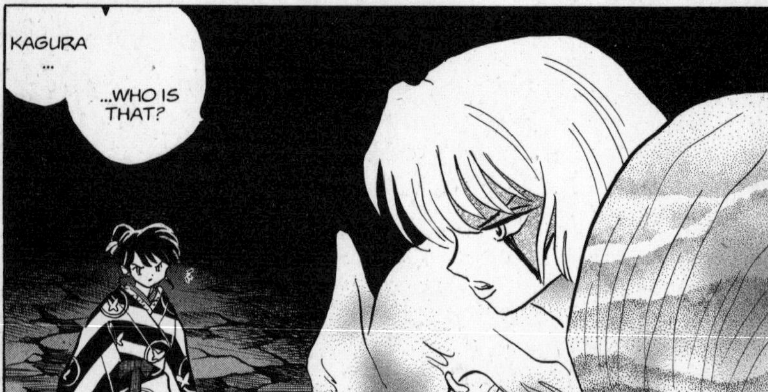
KAGURA ... ...WHO IS THAT?

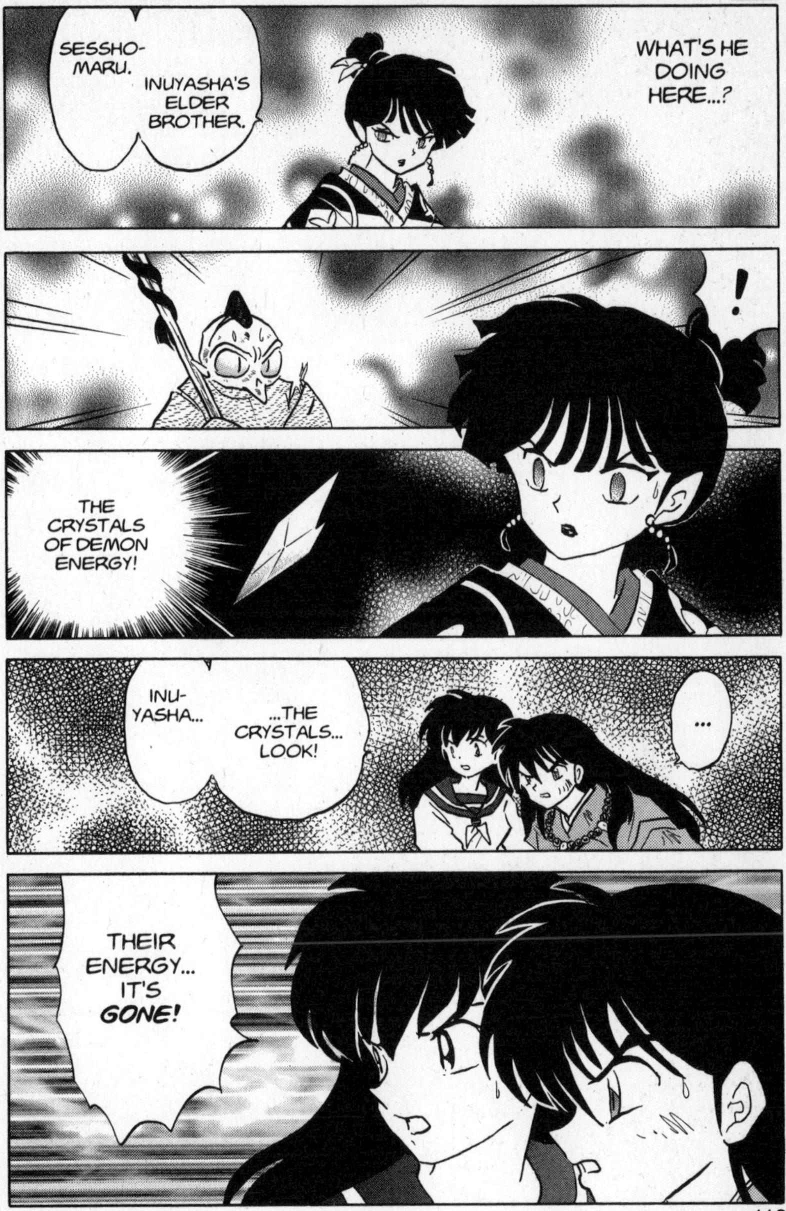
SESSHO-MARU.
INUYASHA'S ELDER BROTHER.
WHAT'S HE DOING HERE...?
!
THE CRYSTALS OF DEMON ENERGY!
INU-YASHA...
...THE CRYSTALS... LOOK!
...
THEIR ENERGY... IT'S *GONE!*

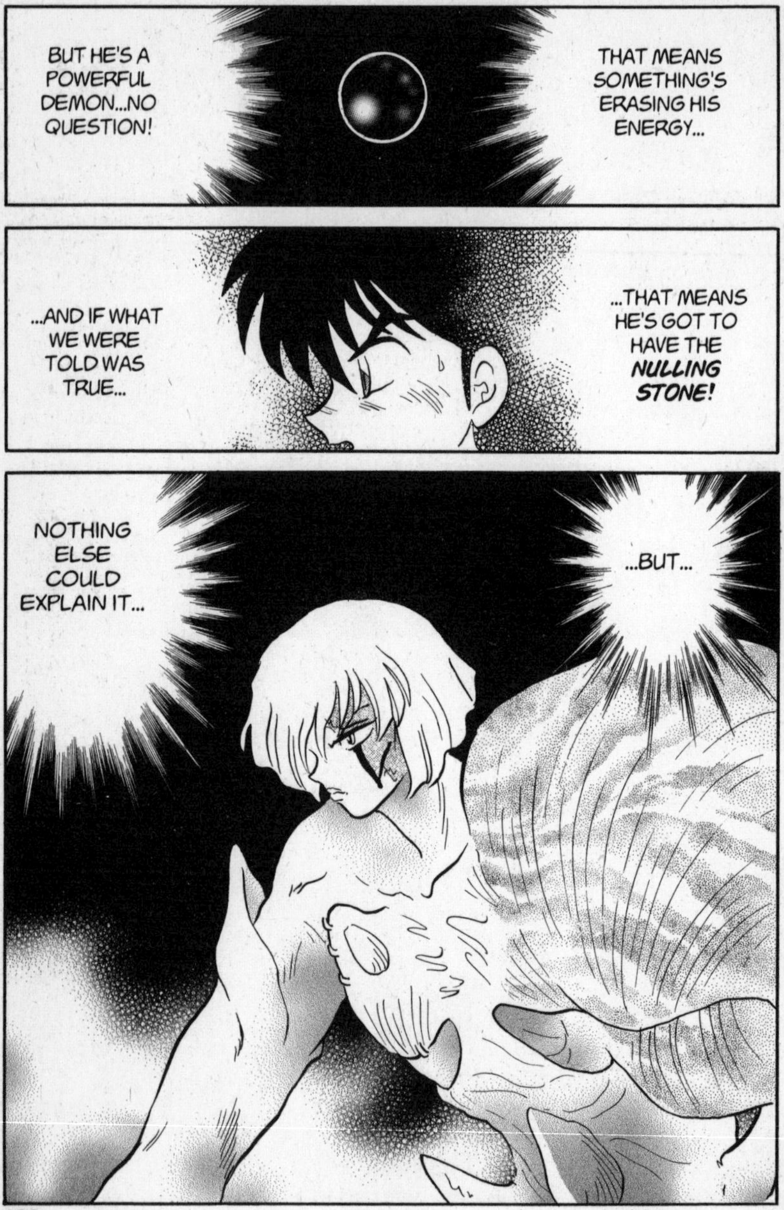
BUT HE'S A POWERFUL DEMON...NO QUESTION!
THAT MEANS SOMETHING'S ERASING HIS ENERGY...
...AND IF WHAT WE WERE TOLD WAS TRUE...
...THAT MEANS HE'S GOT TO HAVE THE NULLING STONE!
NOTHING ELSE COULD EXPLAIN IT...
...BUT...

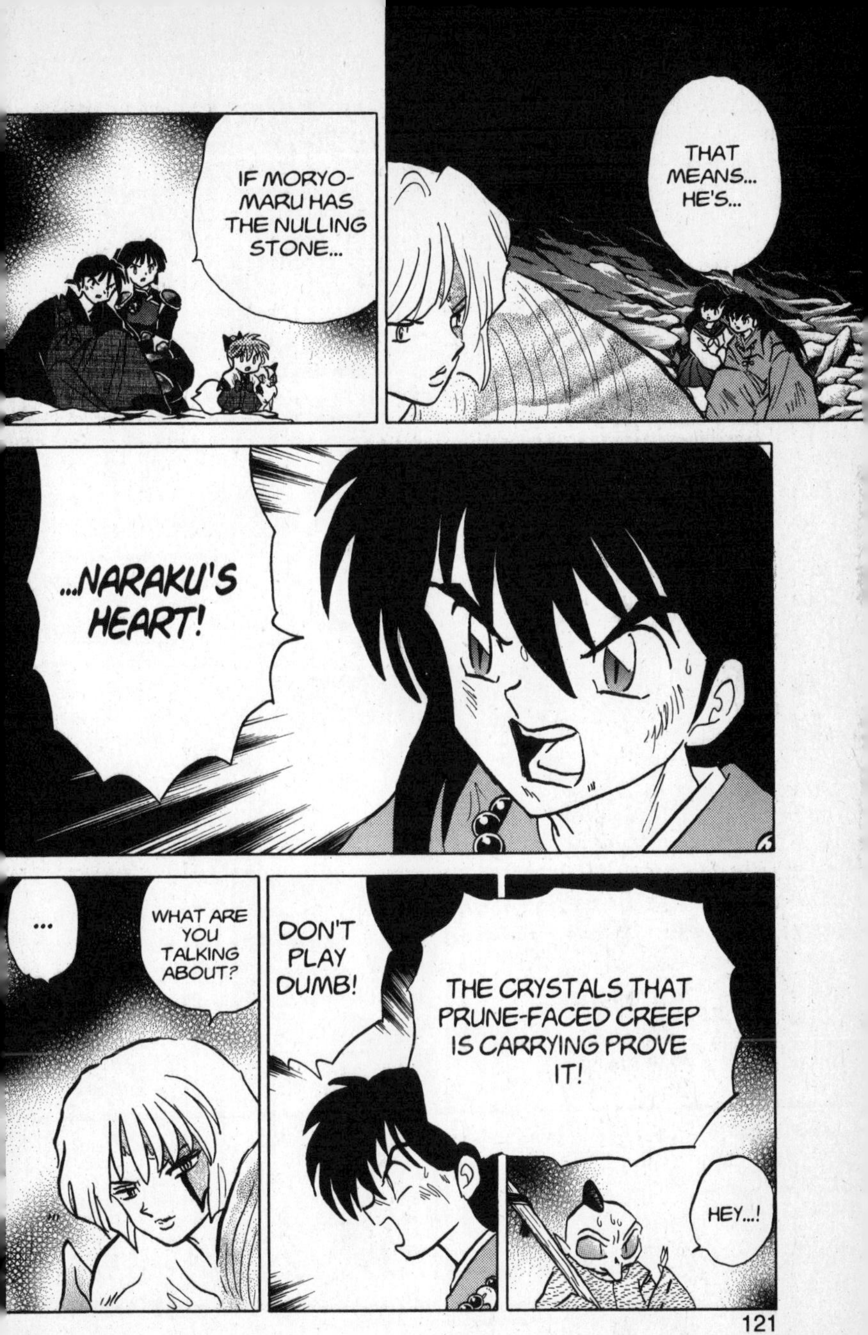
IF MORYO-MARU HAS THE NULLING STONE...
THAT MEANS... HE'S...
...NARAKU'S HEART!
...
WHAT ARE YOU TALKING ABOUT?
DON'T PLAY DUMB!
THE CRYSTALS THAT PRUNE-FACED CREEP IS CARRYING PROVE IT!
HEY...!

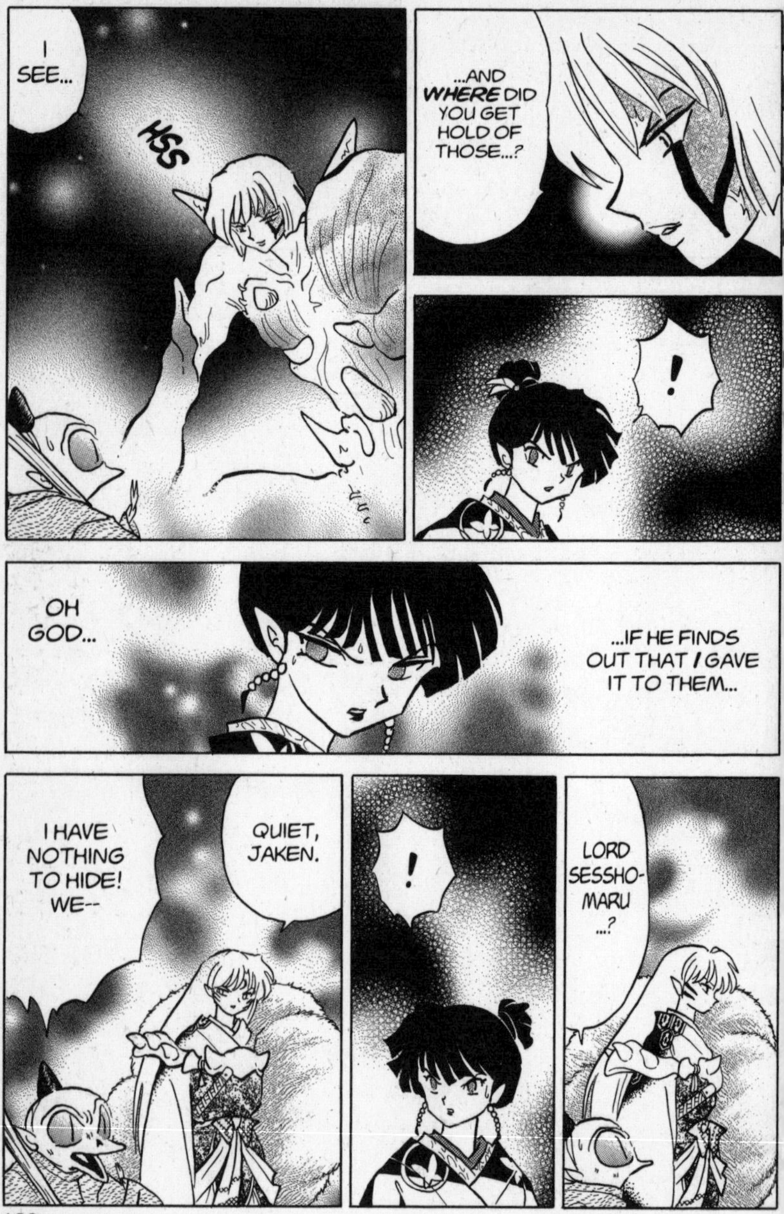
I SEE...
HSS
...AND WHERE DID YOU GET HOLD OF THOSE...?
!
OH GOD...
...IF HE FINDS OUT THAT I GAVE IT TO THEM...
I HAVE NOTHING TO HIDE! WE--
QUIET, JAKEN.
!
LORD SESSHO-MARU ...?

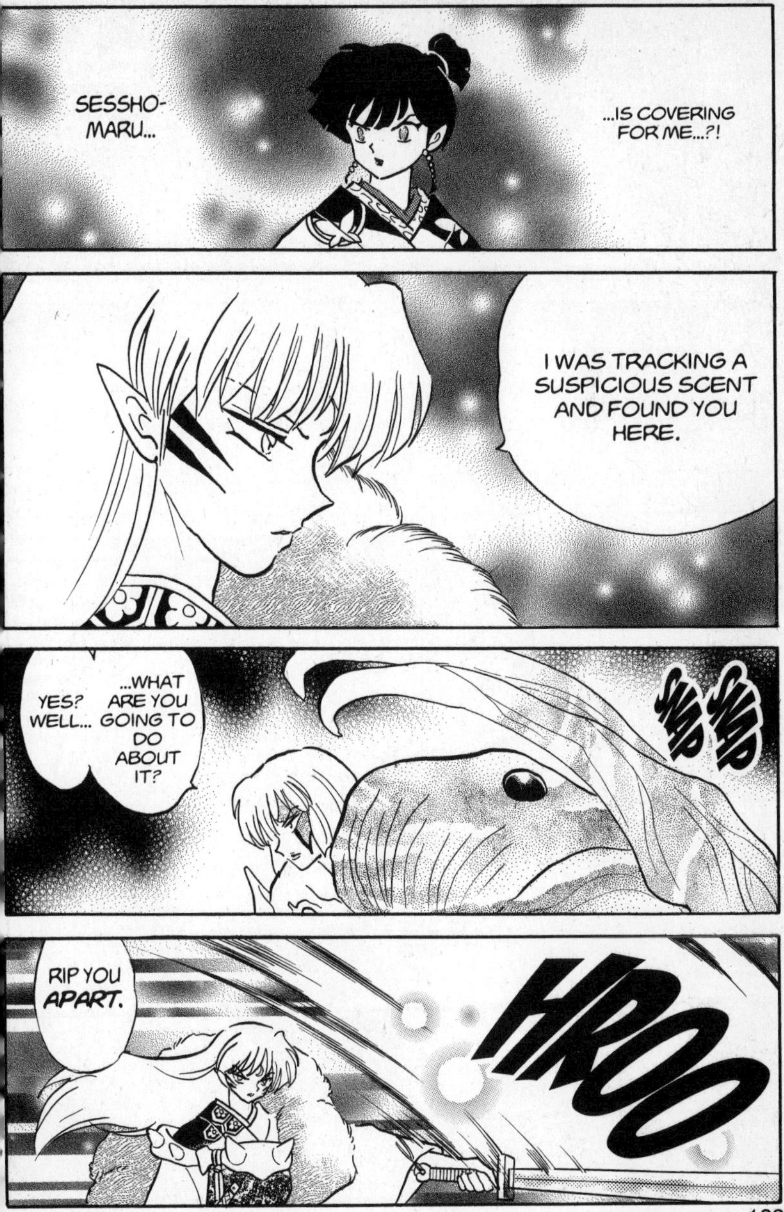
SESSHO-MARU...
...IS COVERING FOR ME...?!
I WAS TRACKING A SUSPICIOUS SCENT AND FOUND YOU HERE.
YES? WELL...
...WHAT ARE YOU GOING TO DO ABOUT IT?
SNAP SNAP
RIP YOU APART.
HROO

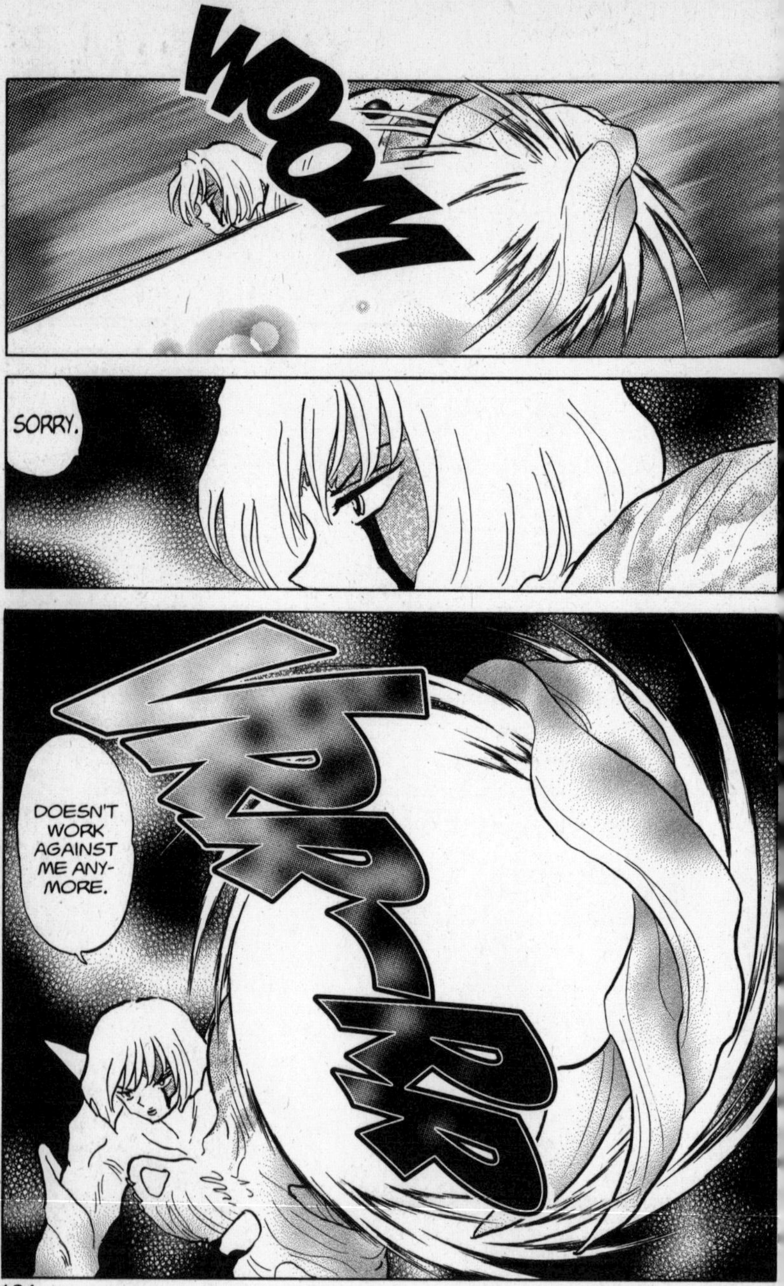
WOOM
SORRY.
WOOM
DOESN'T WORK AGAINST ME ANY-MORE.

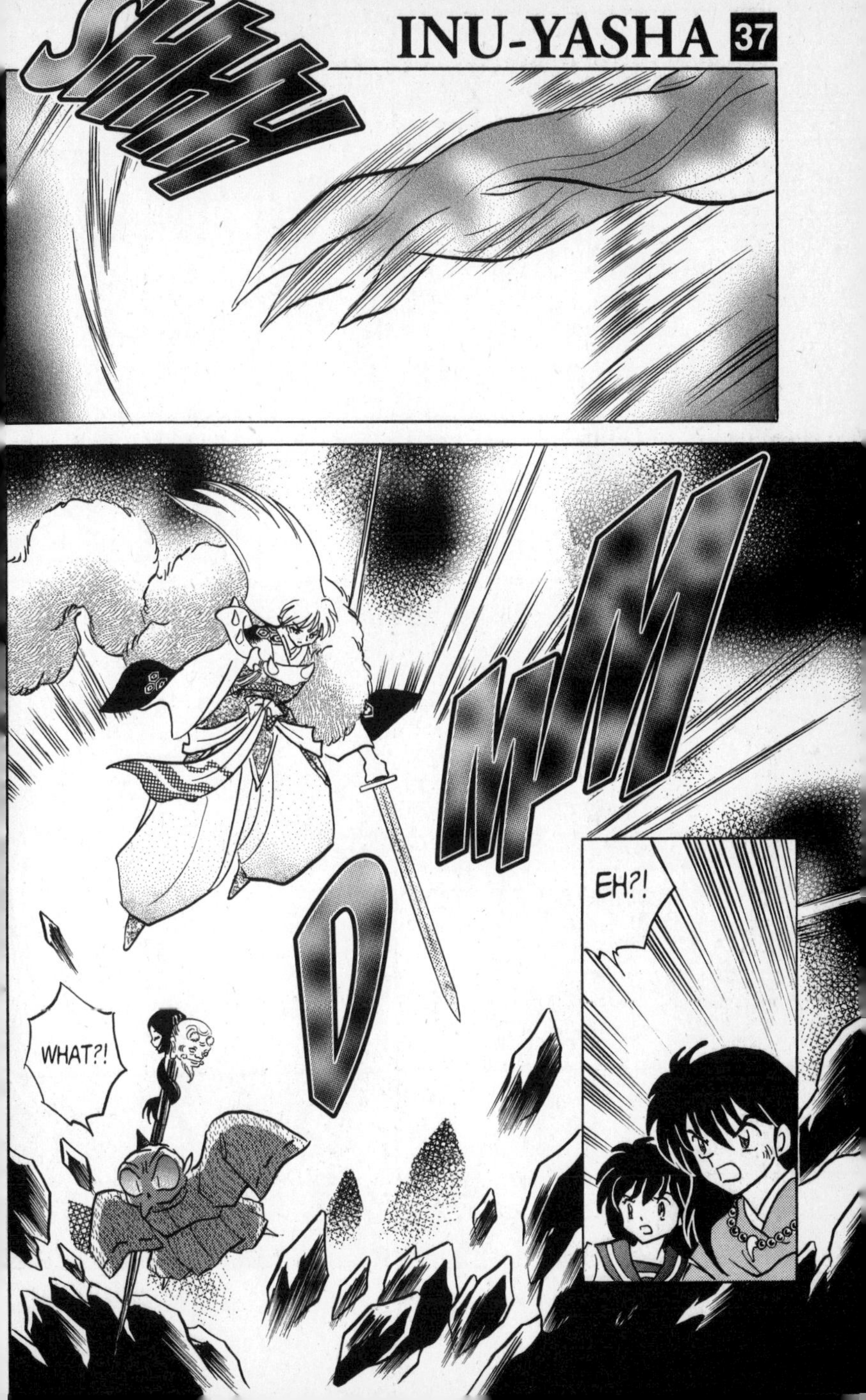
SHEEE
DOMM
EH?!
WHAT?!

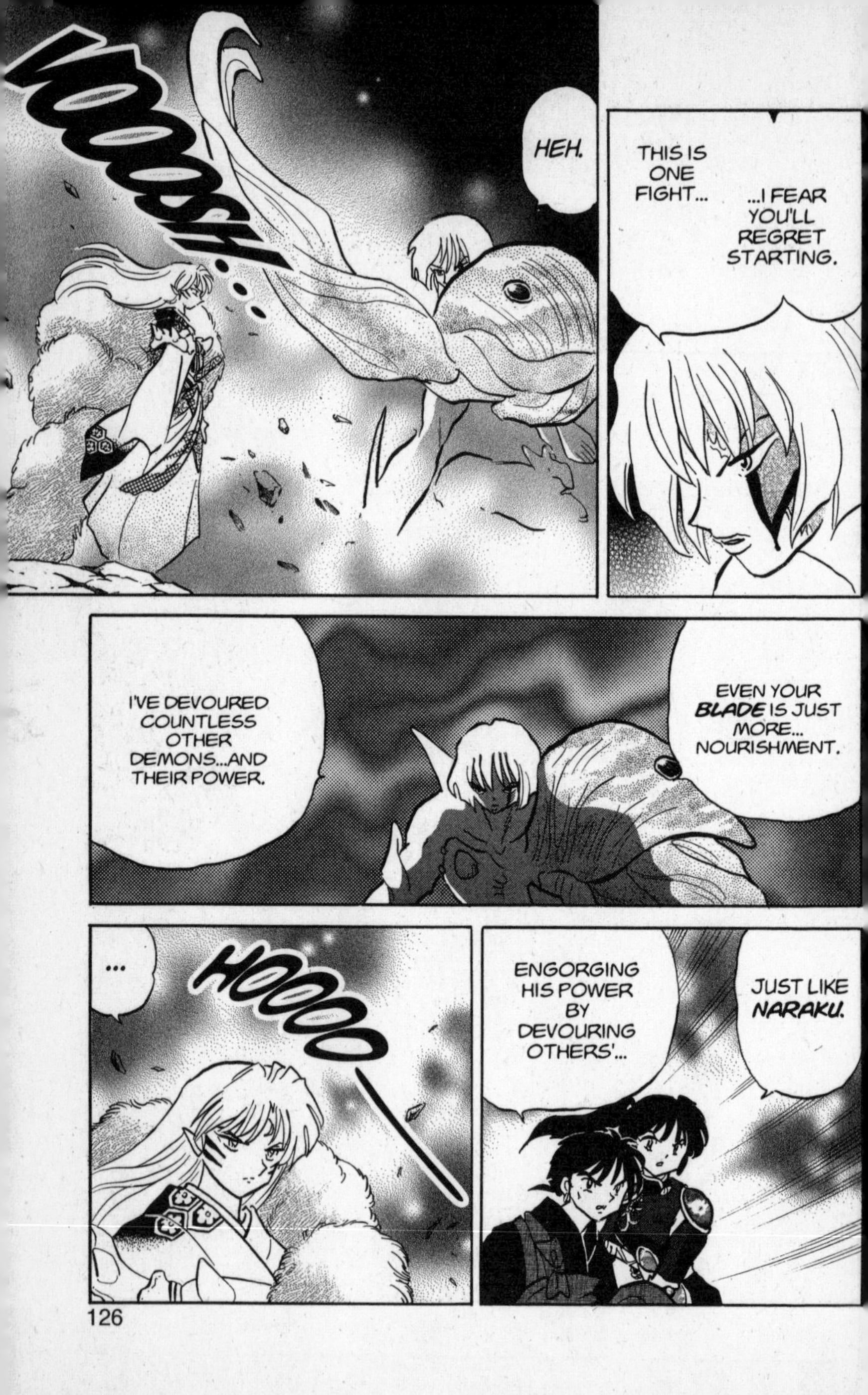
VOOOSH...
HEH.
THIS IS ONE FIGHT...
...I FEAR YOU'LL REGRET STARTING.
I'VE DEVOURED COUNTLESS OTHER DEMONS...AND THEIR POWER.
EVEN YOUR BLADE IS JUST MORE... NOURISHMENT.
...
HOOOO
ENGORGING HIS POWER BY DEVOURING OTHERS'...
JUST LIKE NARAKU.

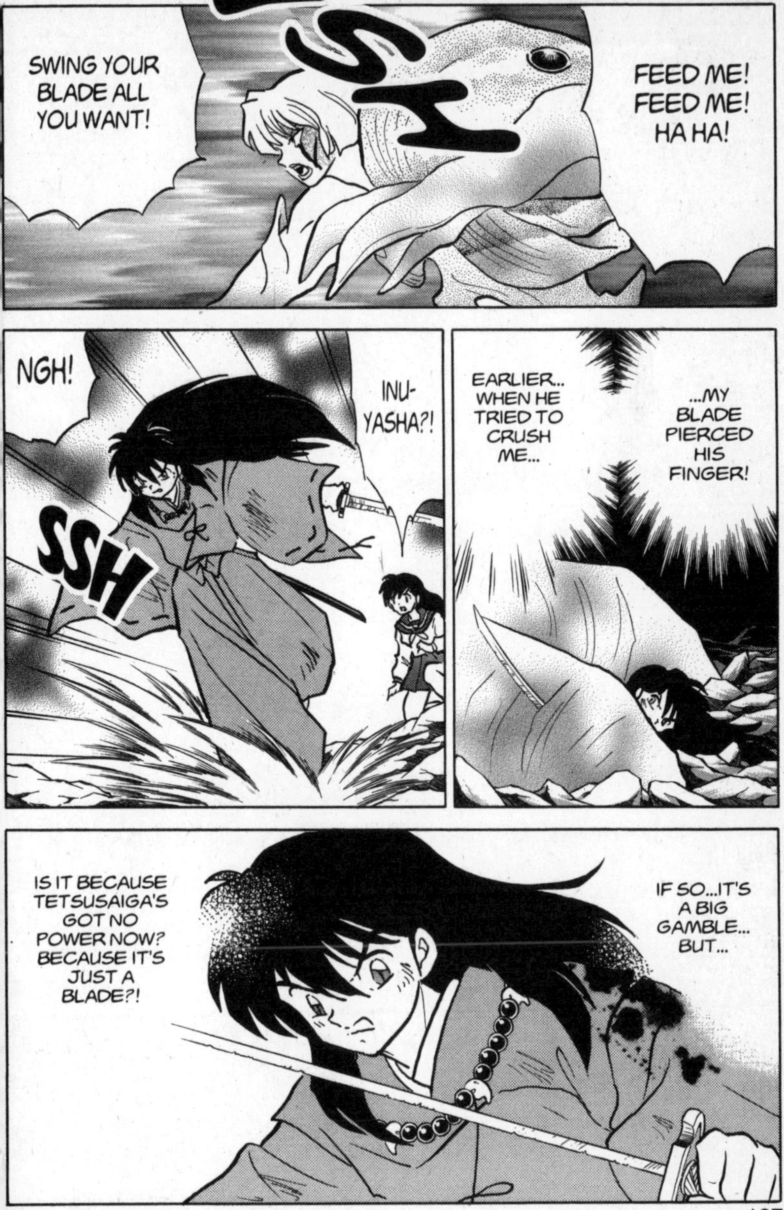
SWING YOUR BLADE ALL YOU WANT!
VSSH
FEED ME! FEED ME! HA HA!
NGH!
SSH
INU-YASHA?!
EARLIER... WHEN HE TRIED TO CRUSH ME...
...MY BLADE PIERCED HIS FINGER!
IS IT BECAUSE TETSUSAIGA'S GOT NO POWER NOW? BECAUSE IT'S JUST A BLADE?!
IF SO...IT'S A BIG GAMBLE... BUT...

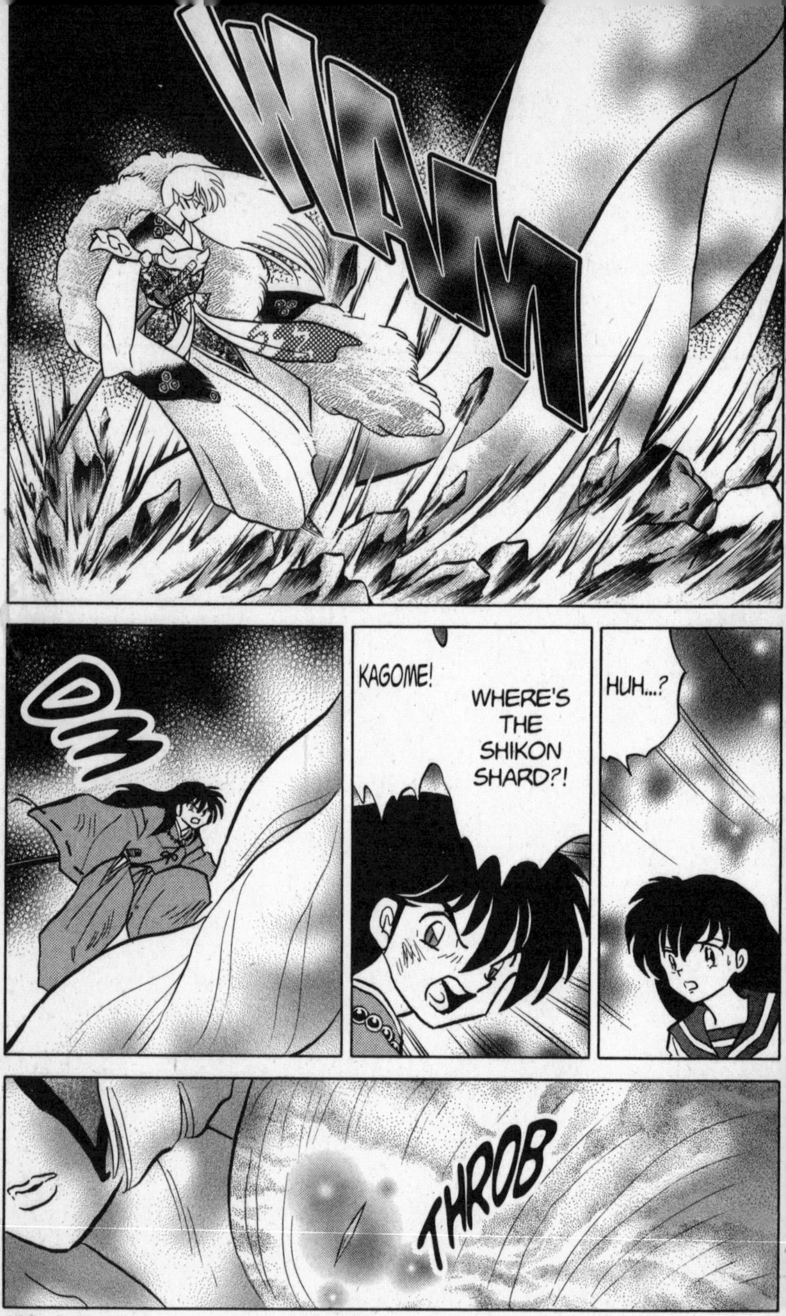
WHAM
DOM
KAGOME!
WHERE'S THE SHIKON SHARD?!
HUH...?
THROB

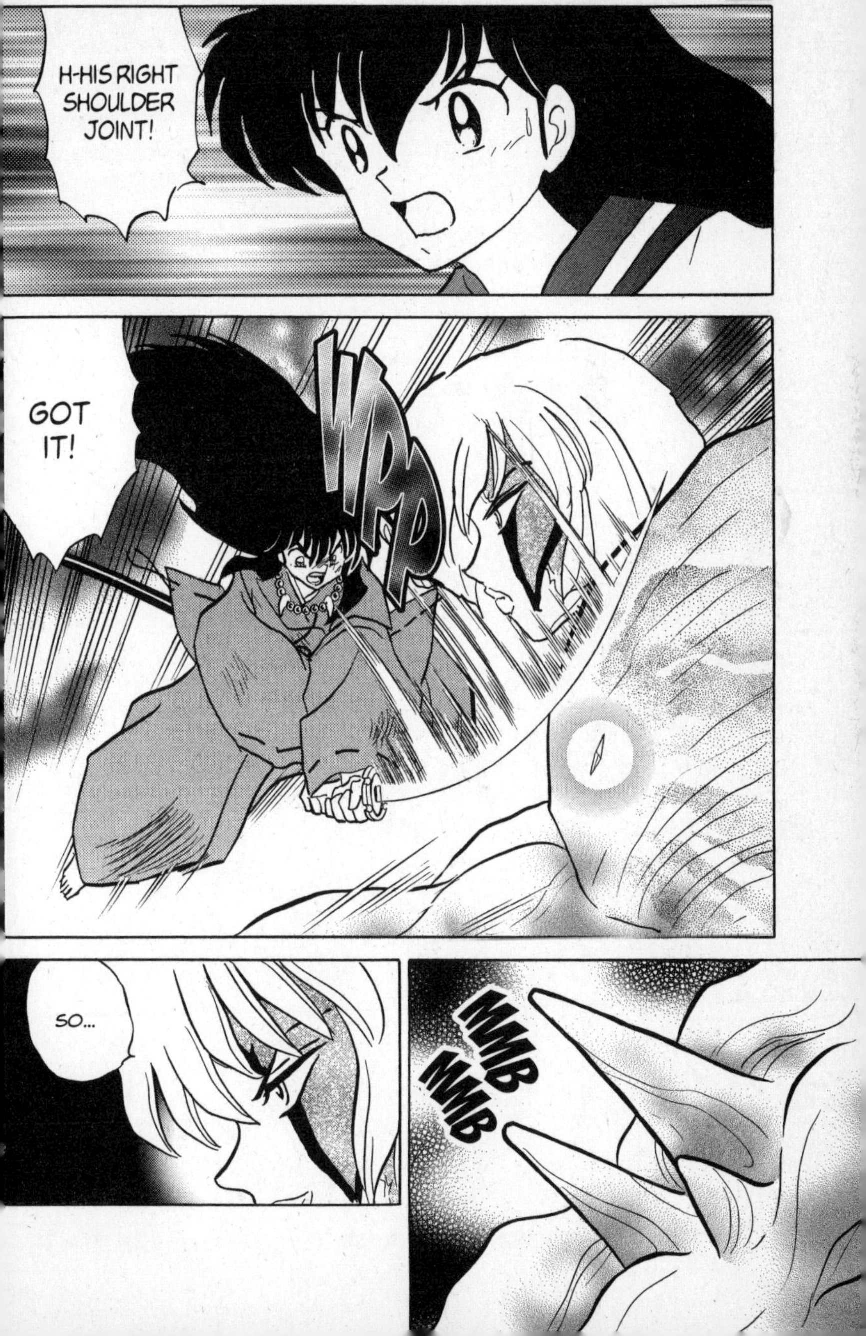
H-HIS RIGHT SHOULDER JOINT!
GOT IT!
WPP
SO...
MMMB MMMB

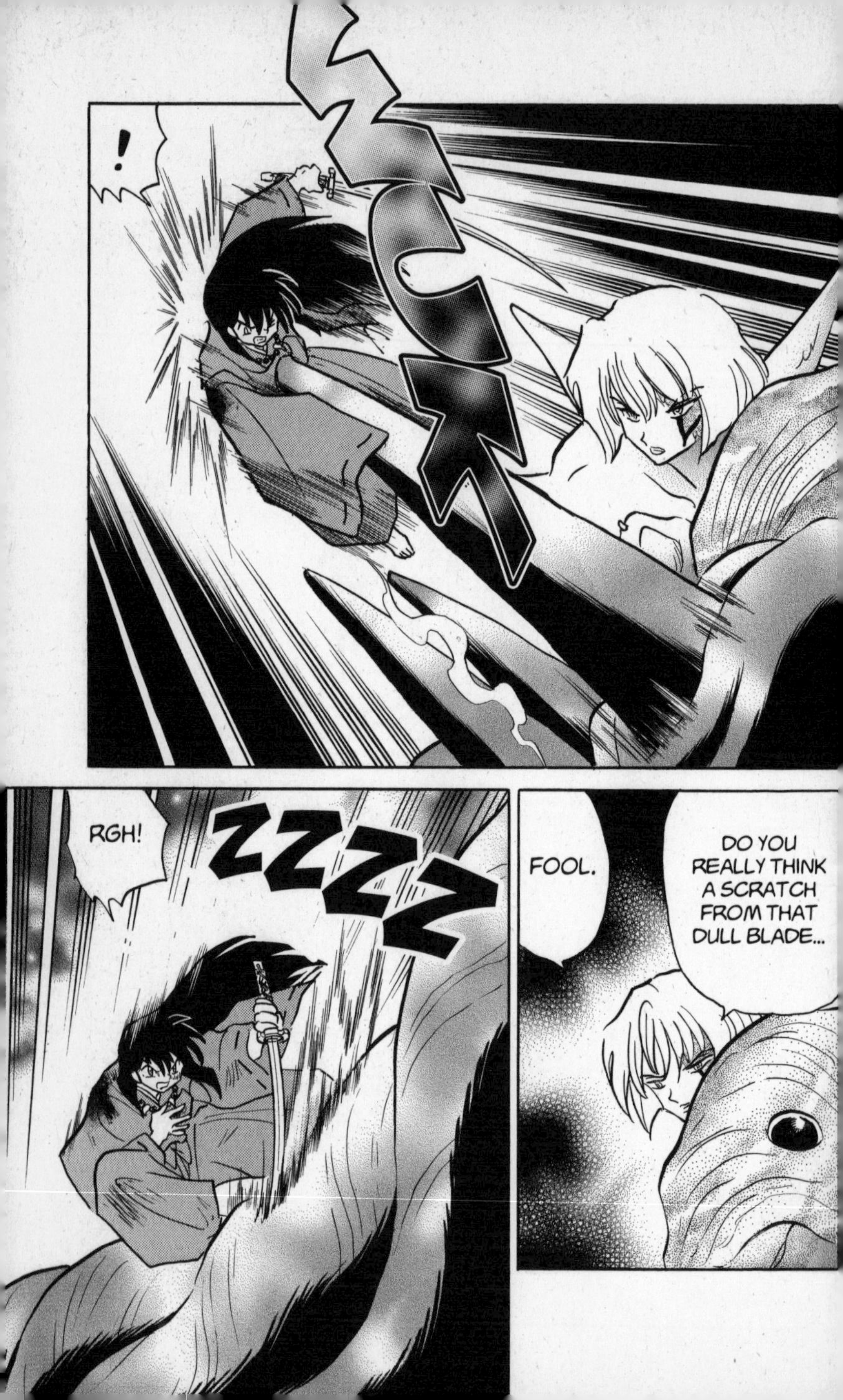
!
RGH!
FOOL.
DO YOU REALLY THINK A SCRATCH FROM THAT DULL BLADE...

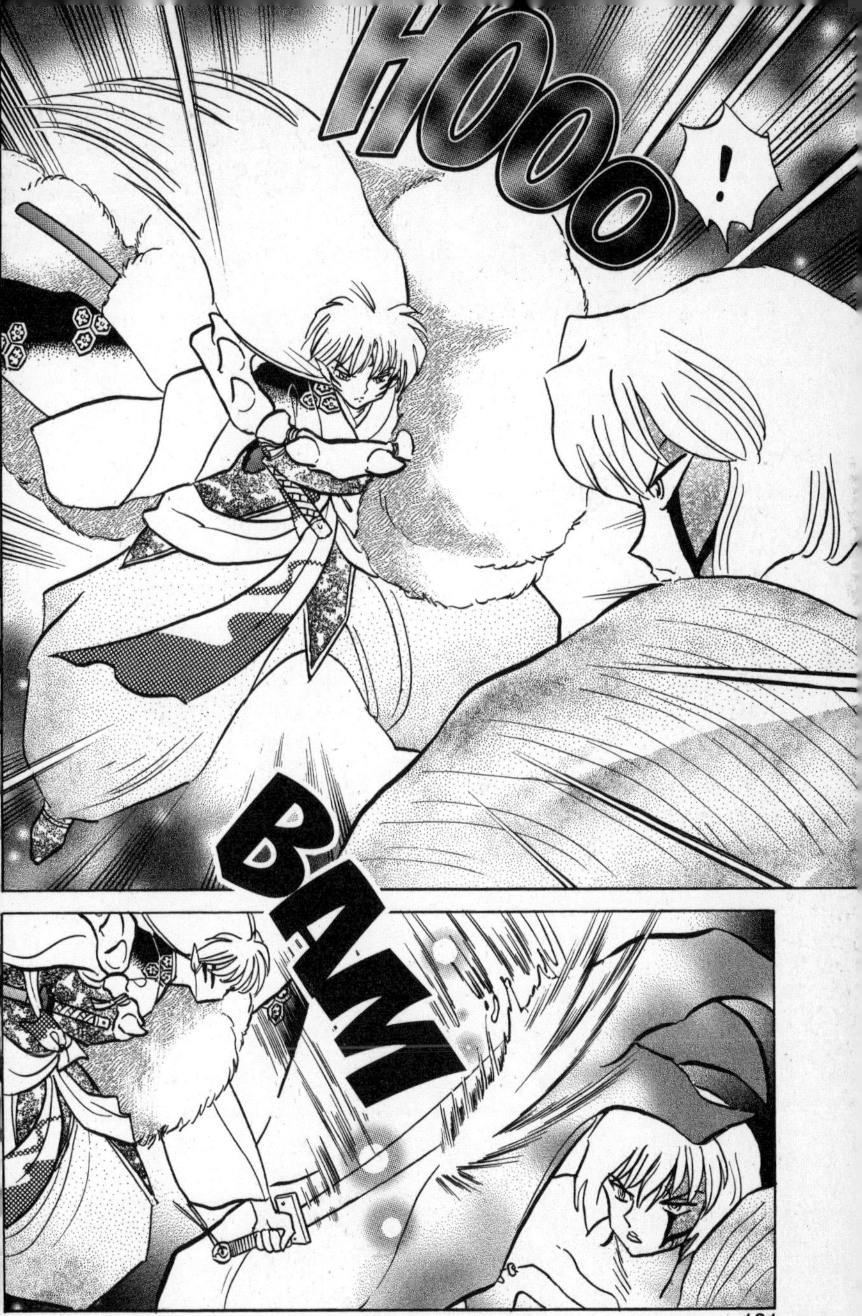
HOOOO
!
BAM

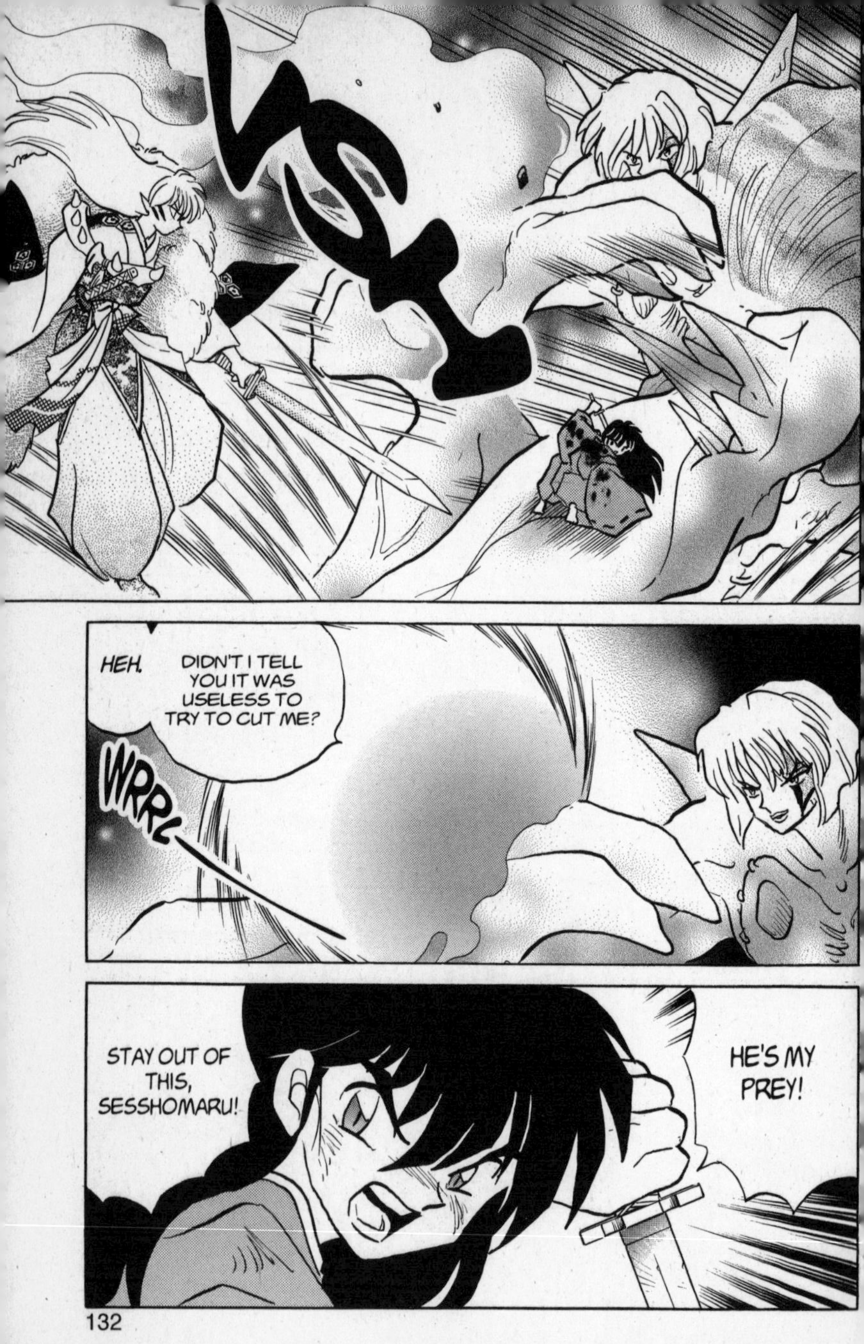
HEH.
DIDN'T I TELL YOU IT WAS USELESS TO TRY TO CUT ME?
WRRL
STAY OUT OF THIS, SESSHOMARU!
HE'S MY PREY!

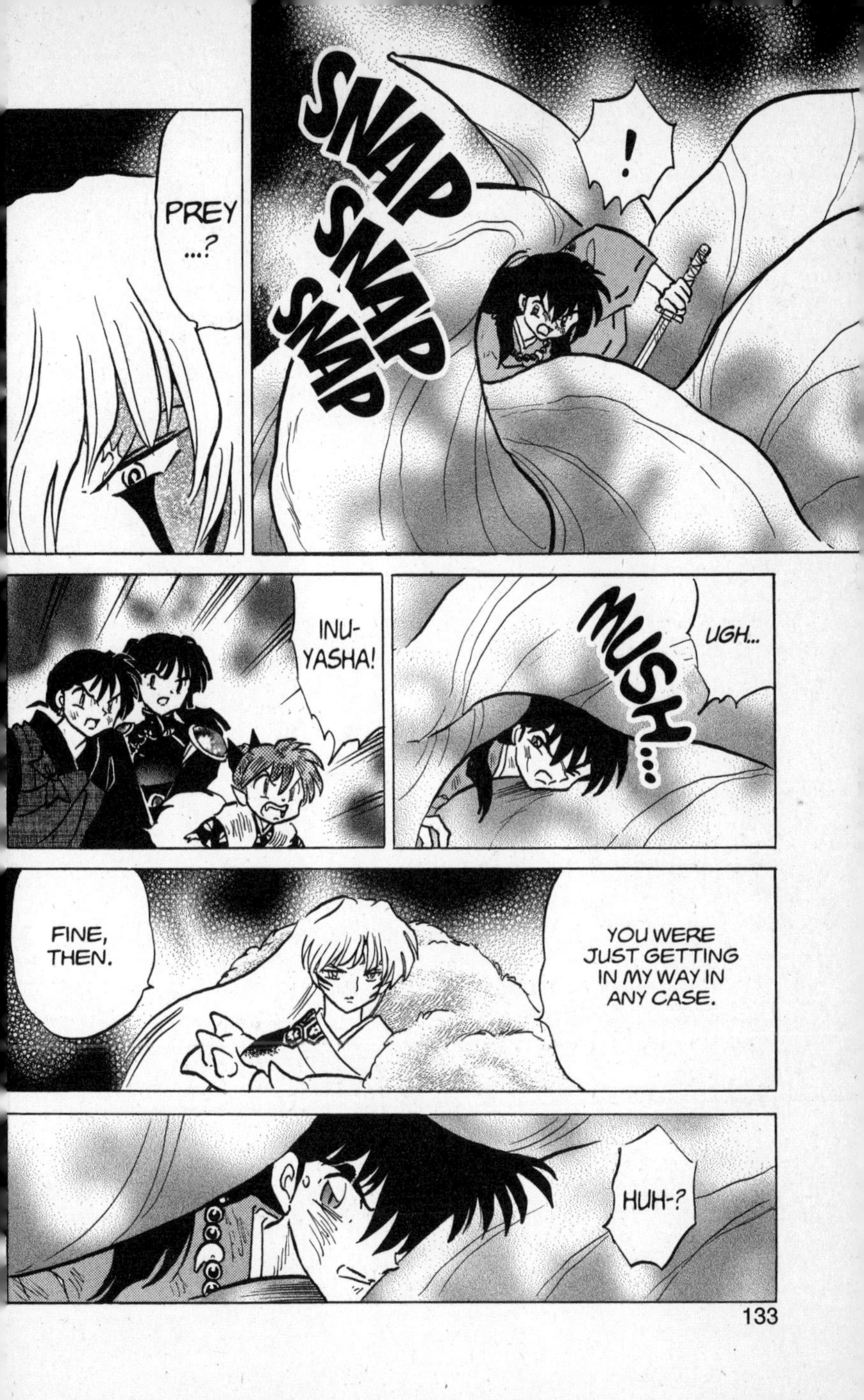
PREY ...?
SNAP SNAP SNAP
!
INU-YASHA!
MUSH...
UGH...
FINE, THEN.
YOU WERE JUST GETTING IN MY WAY IN ANY CASE.
HUH-?

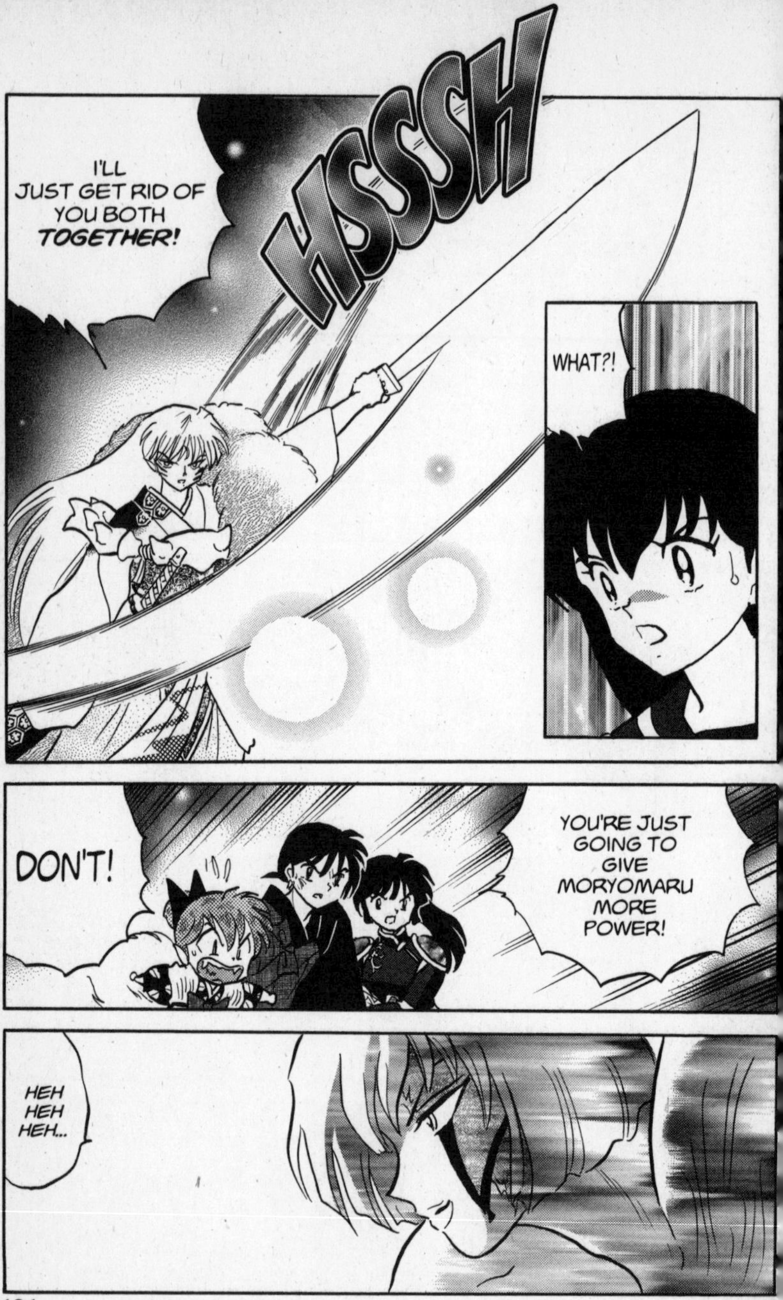
I'LL JUST GET RID OF YOU BOTH TOGETHER!
HSSSH
WHAT?!
DON'T!
YOU'RE JUST GOING TO GIVE MORYOMARU MORE POWER!
HEH HEH HEH...

SCROLL 8
THE VESSEL

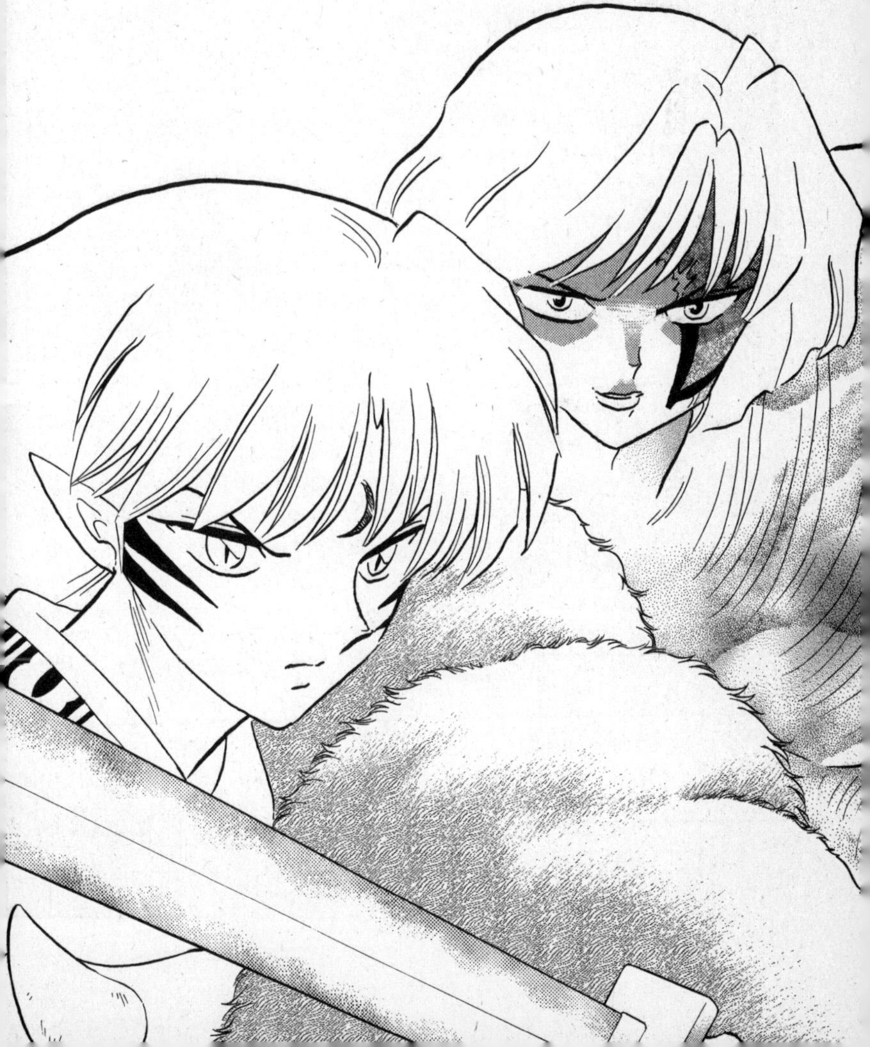

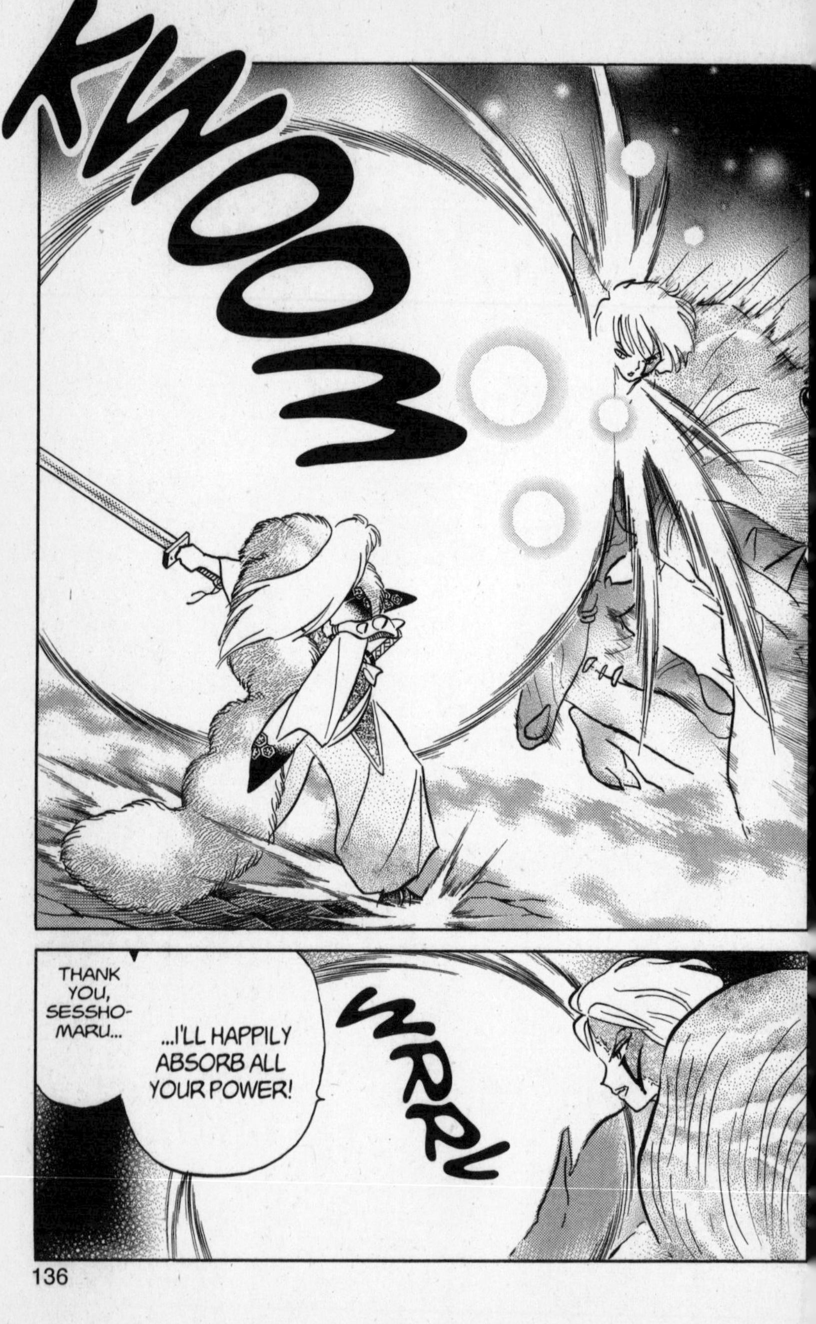
KWOOM
THANK YOU, SESSHO-MARU...
...I'LL HAPPILY ABSORB ALL YOUR POWER!
WRRU

WILL YOU NOW?!

HWOOO

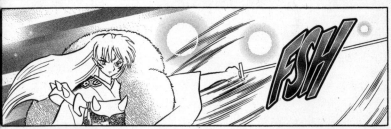

FSH

DMM

WRL...

HEH...

SESSHO-MARU, YOU IDIOT!!

YOU'RE JUST MAKING HIM STRONGER!

WHO ARE YOU TO CALL LORD SESSHO-MARU AN IDIOT?!

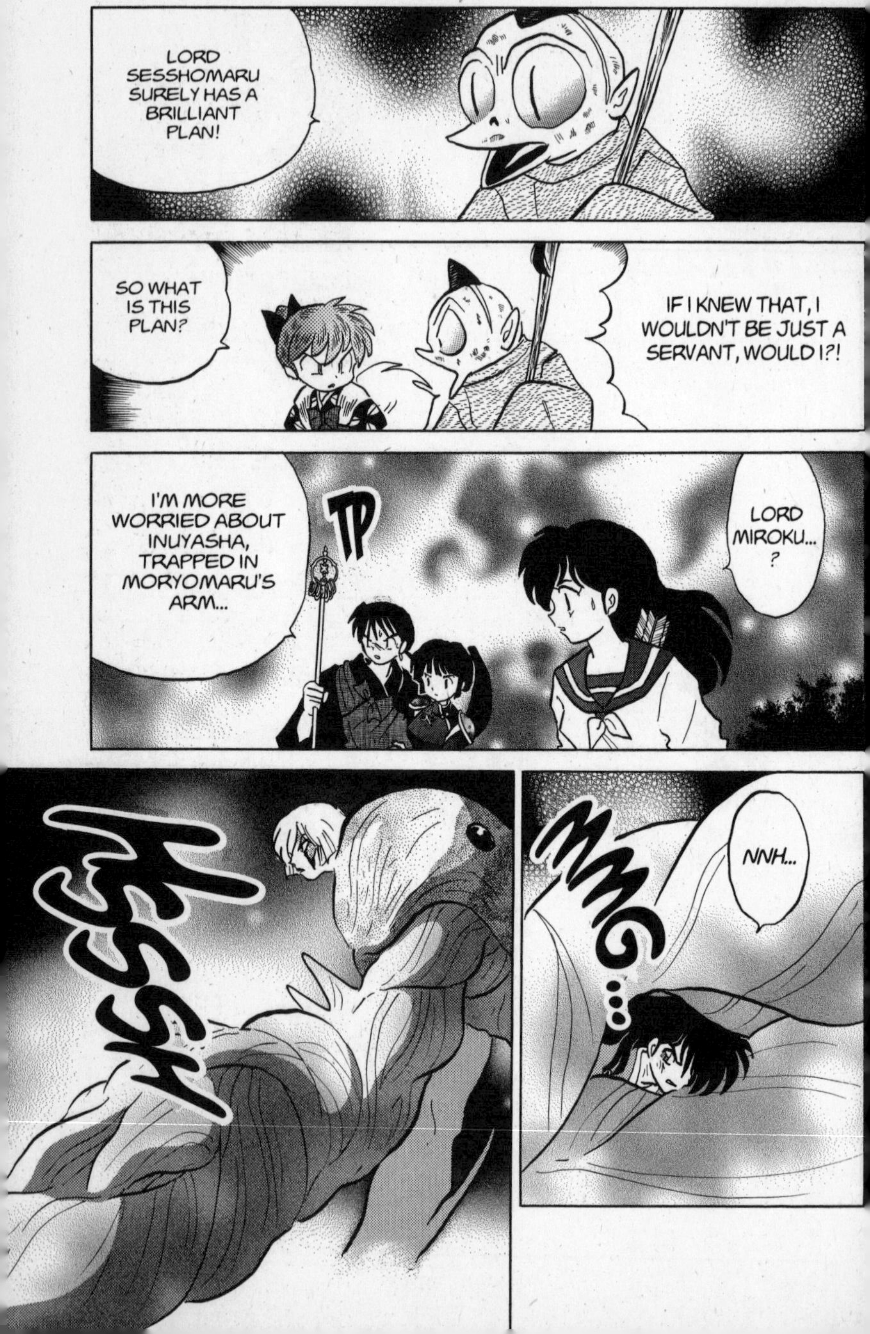
LORD SESSHOMARU SURELY HAS A BRILLIANT PLAN!
SO WHAT IS THIS PLAN?
IF I KNEW THAT, I WOULDN'T BE JUST A SERVANT, WOULD I?!
I'M MORE WORRIED ABOUT INUYASHA, TRAPPED IN MORYOMARU'S ARM...
TP
LORD MIROKU...?
HSSSH
MMG...
NNH...

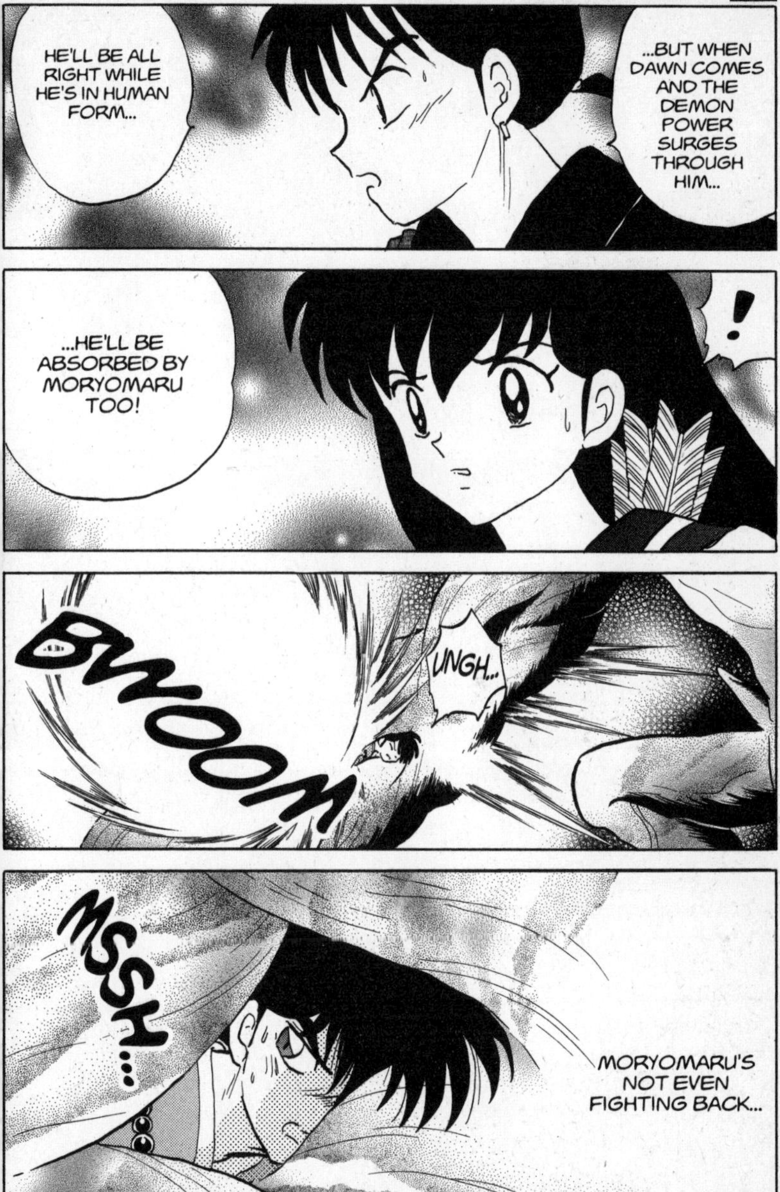
HE'LL BE ALL RIGHT WHILE HE'S IN HUMAN FORM...
...BUT WHEN DAWN COMES AND THE DEMON POWER SURGES THROUGH HIM...
...HE'LL BE ABSORBED BY MORYOMARU TOO!
!
BWOOM
UNGH...
MSSH...
MORYOMARU'S NOT EVEN FIGHTING BACK...

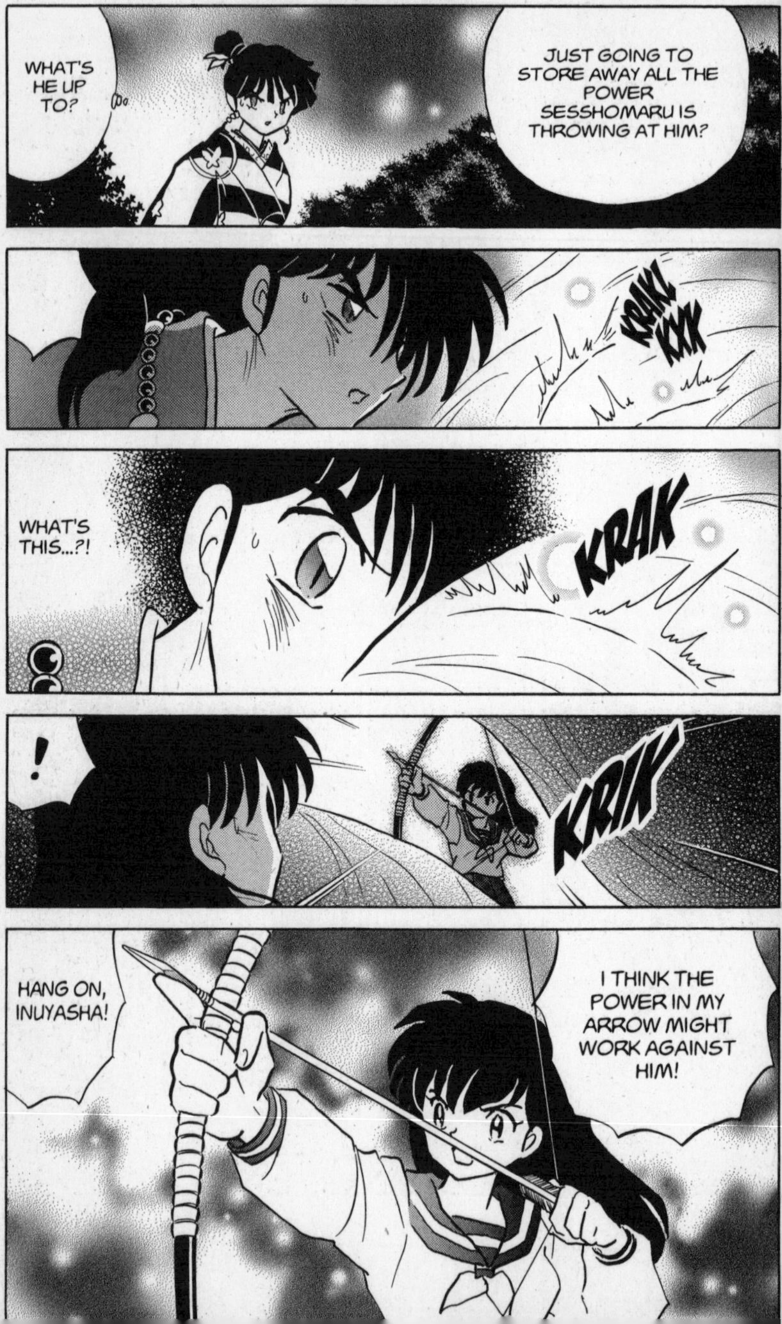
WHAT'S HE UP TO?
JUST GOING TO STORE AWAY ALL THE POWER SESSHOMARU IS THROWING AT HIM?
KRAK! KKK
WHAT'S THIS...?!
KRAK
!
KRIK
HANG ON, INUYASHA!
I THINK THE POWER IN MY ARROW MIGHT WORK AGAINST HIM!

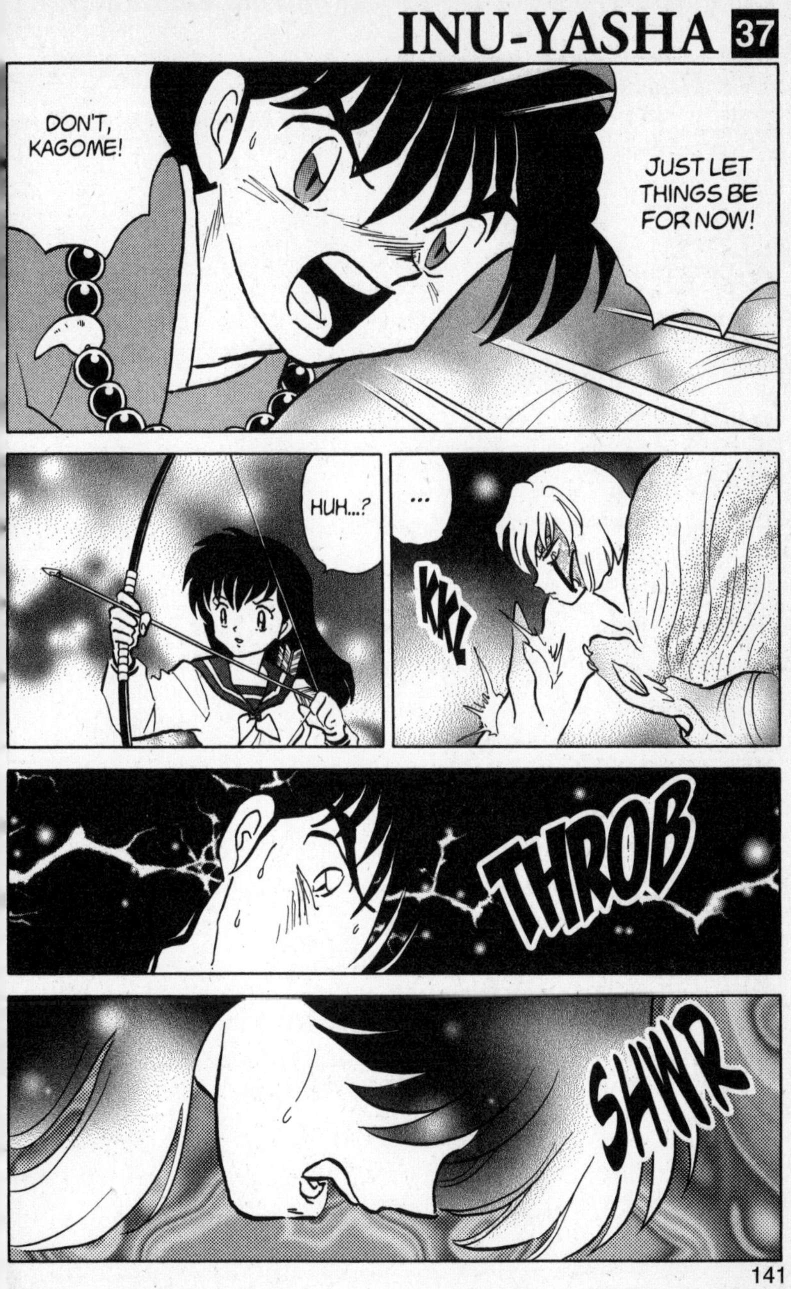
DON'T, KAGOME!
JUST LET THINGS BE FOR NOW!
HUH...?
...
KKL
THROB
SHWR

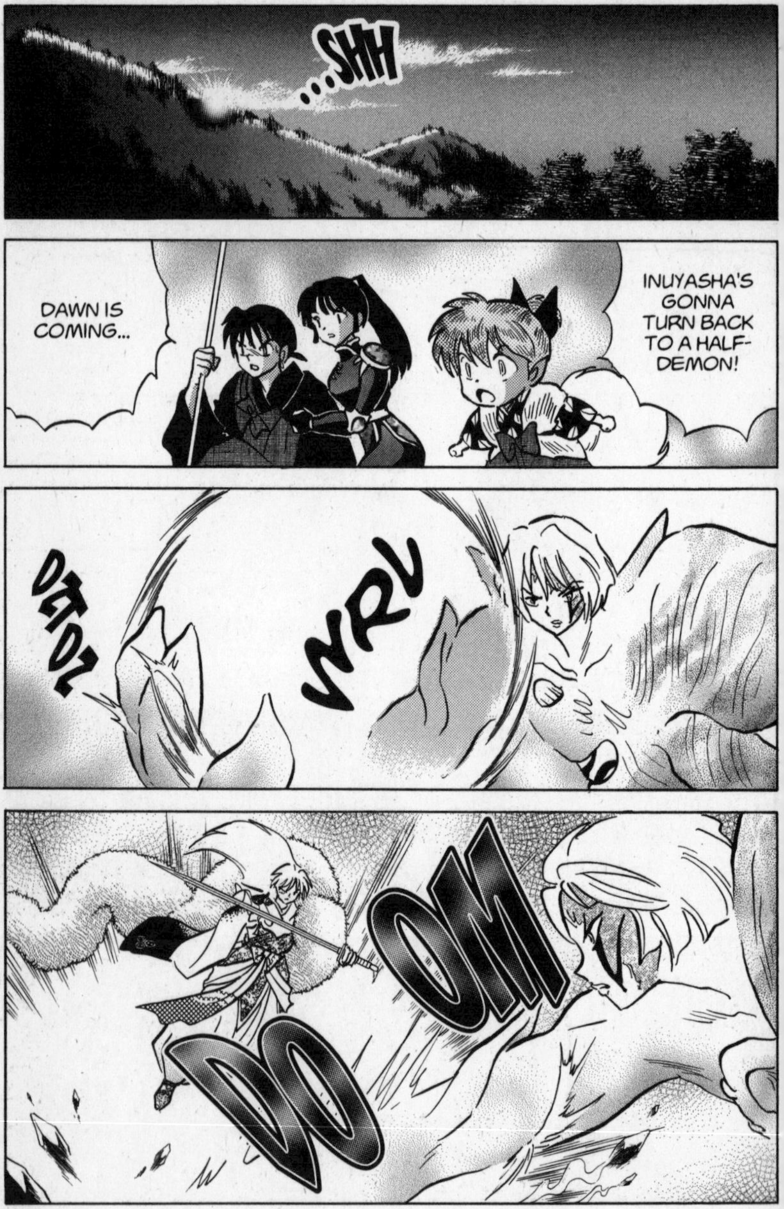
...SHH
DAWN IS COMING...
INUYASHA'S GONNA TURN BACK TO A HALF-DEMON!
WRL
DOOM

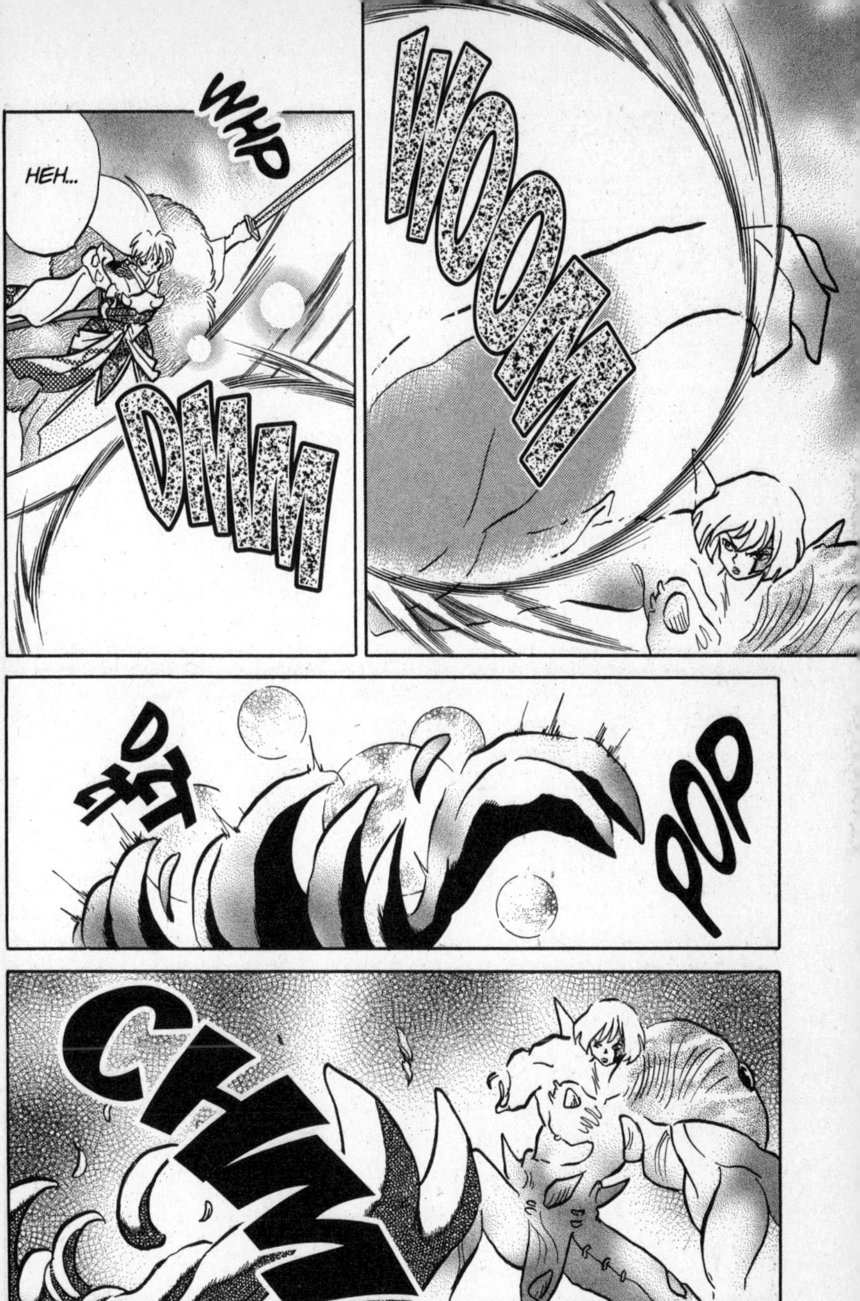
HEH...
WHP
DMM
WOOM
DIT
POP
CHM

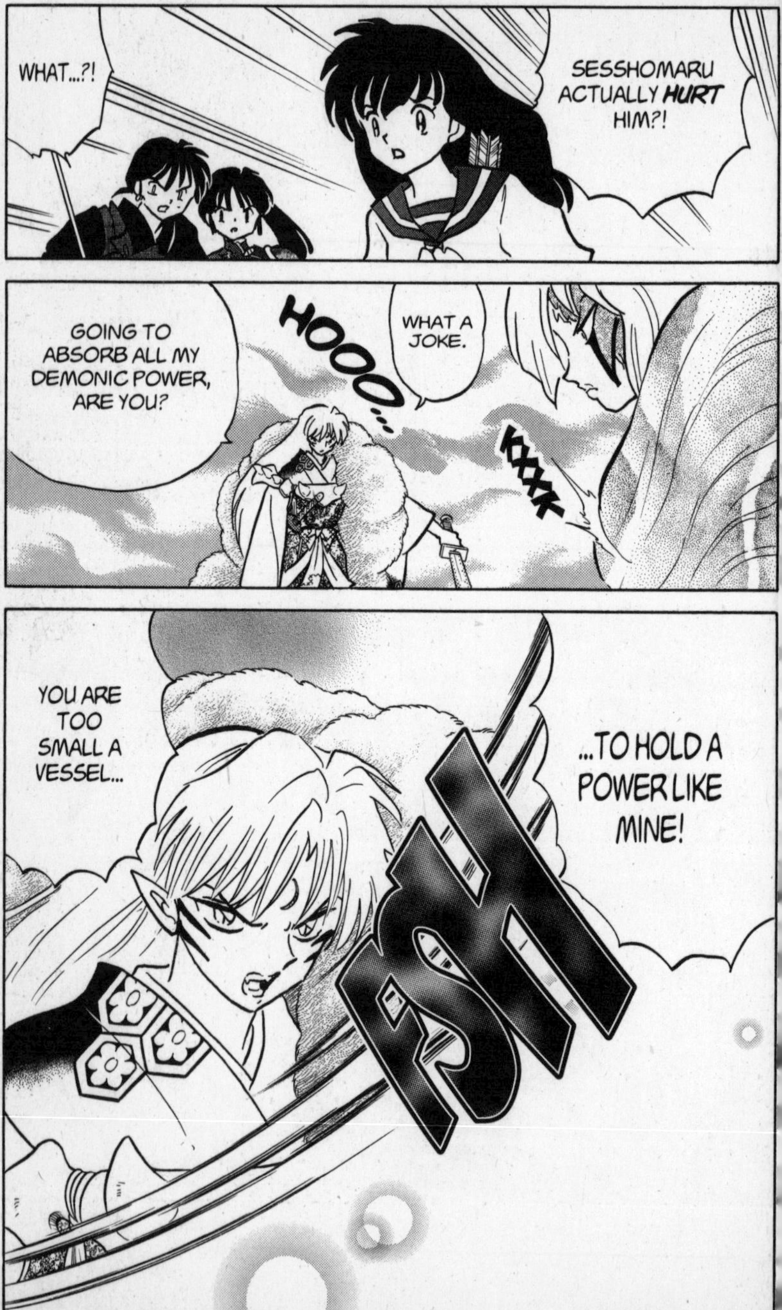
WHAT...?!
SESSHOMARU ACTUALLY HURT HIM?!
GOING TO ABSORB ALL MY DEMONIC POWER, ARE YOU?
HOOOO...
WHAT A JOKE.
KKKK
YOU ARE TOO SMALL A VESSEL...
FSH
...TO HOLD A POWER LIKE MINE!

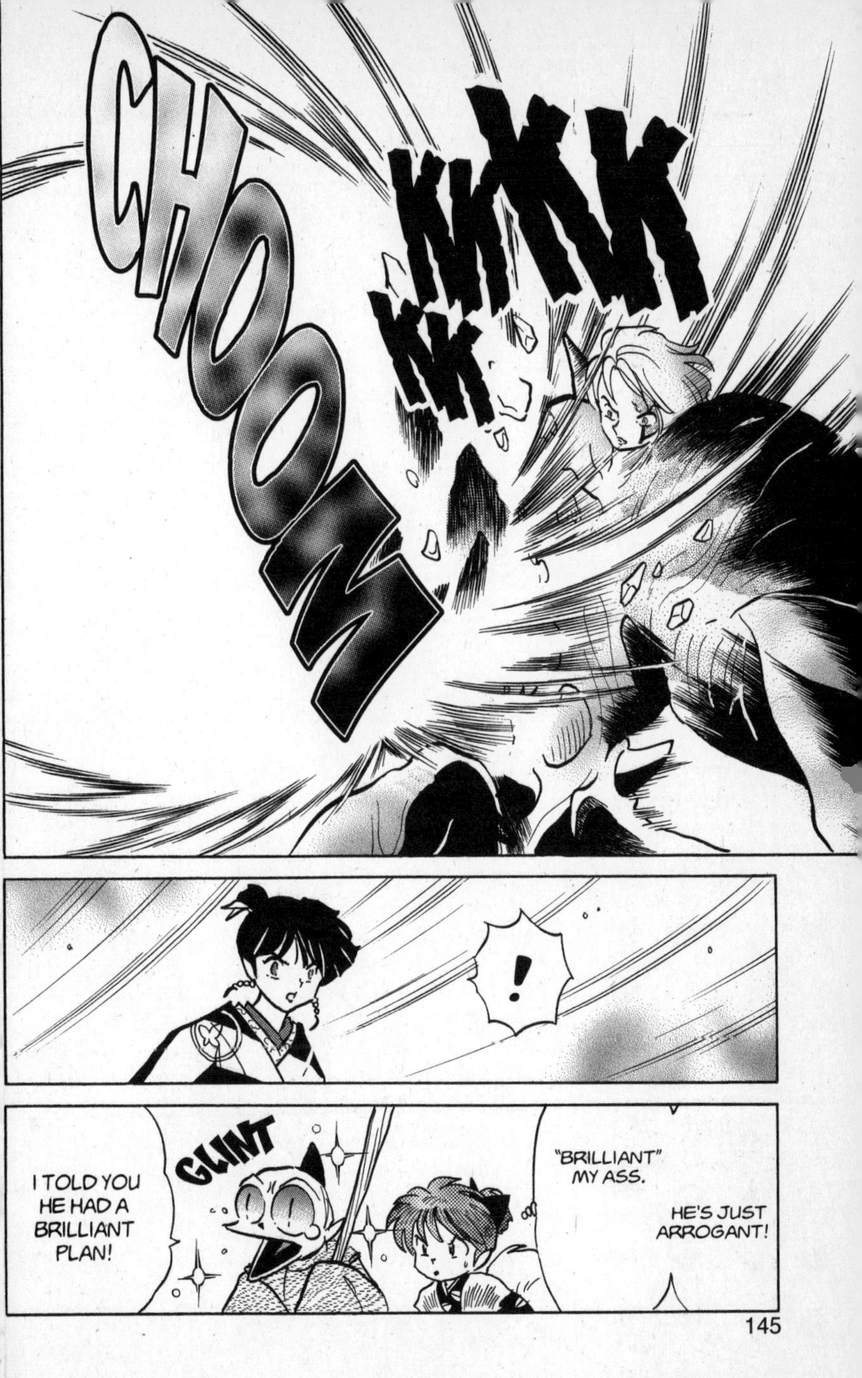
CHOOOM
KKKK
KK
!
I TOLD YOU HE HAD A BRILLIANT PLAN!
GLINT
"BRILLIANT" MY ASS.
HE'S JUST ARROGANT!

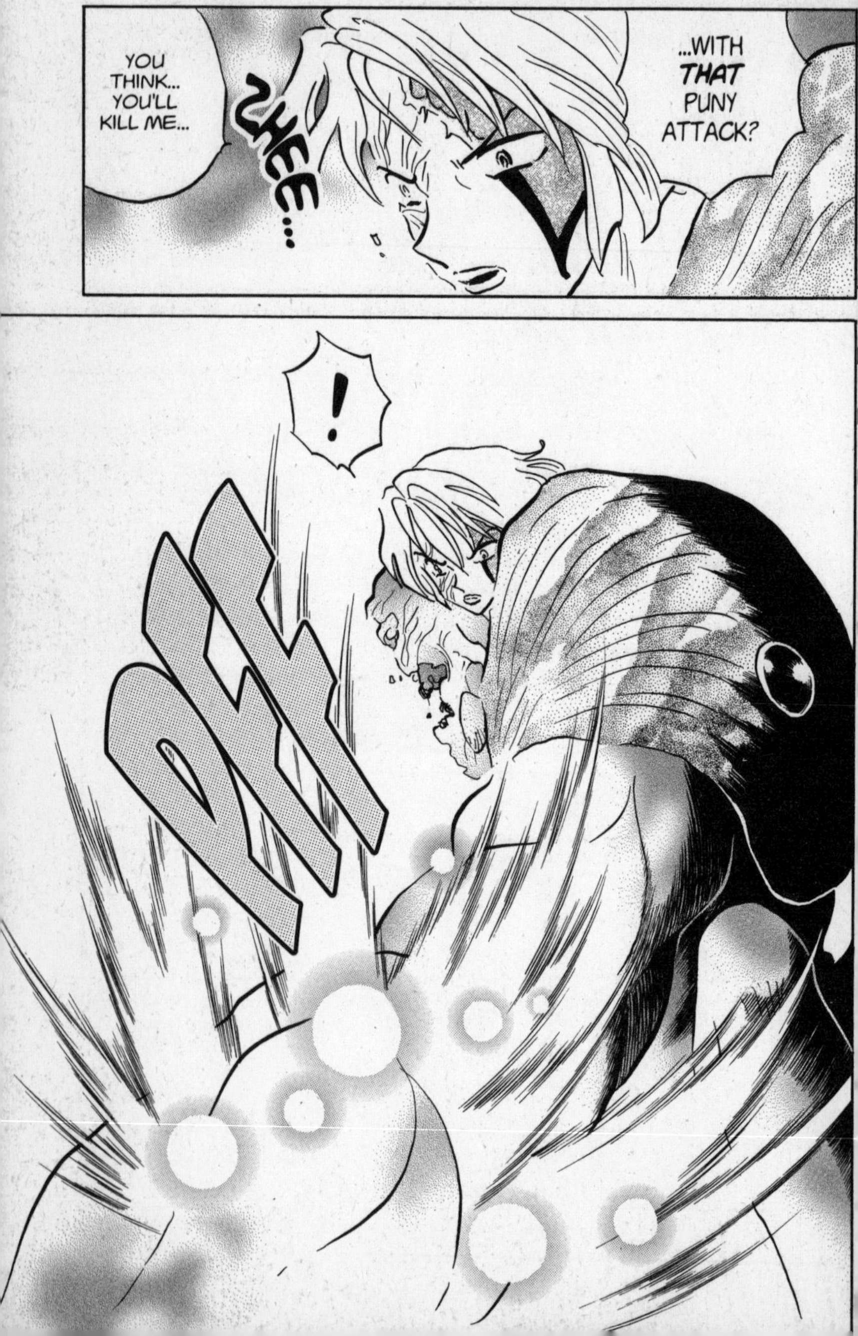
YOU THINK... YOU'LL KILL ME...
SHEE...
...WITH **THAT** PUNY ATTACK?
!

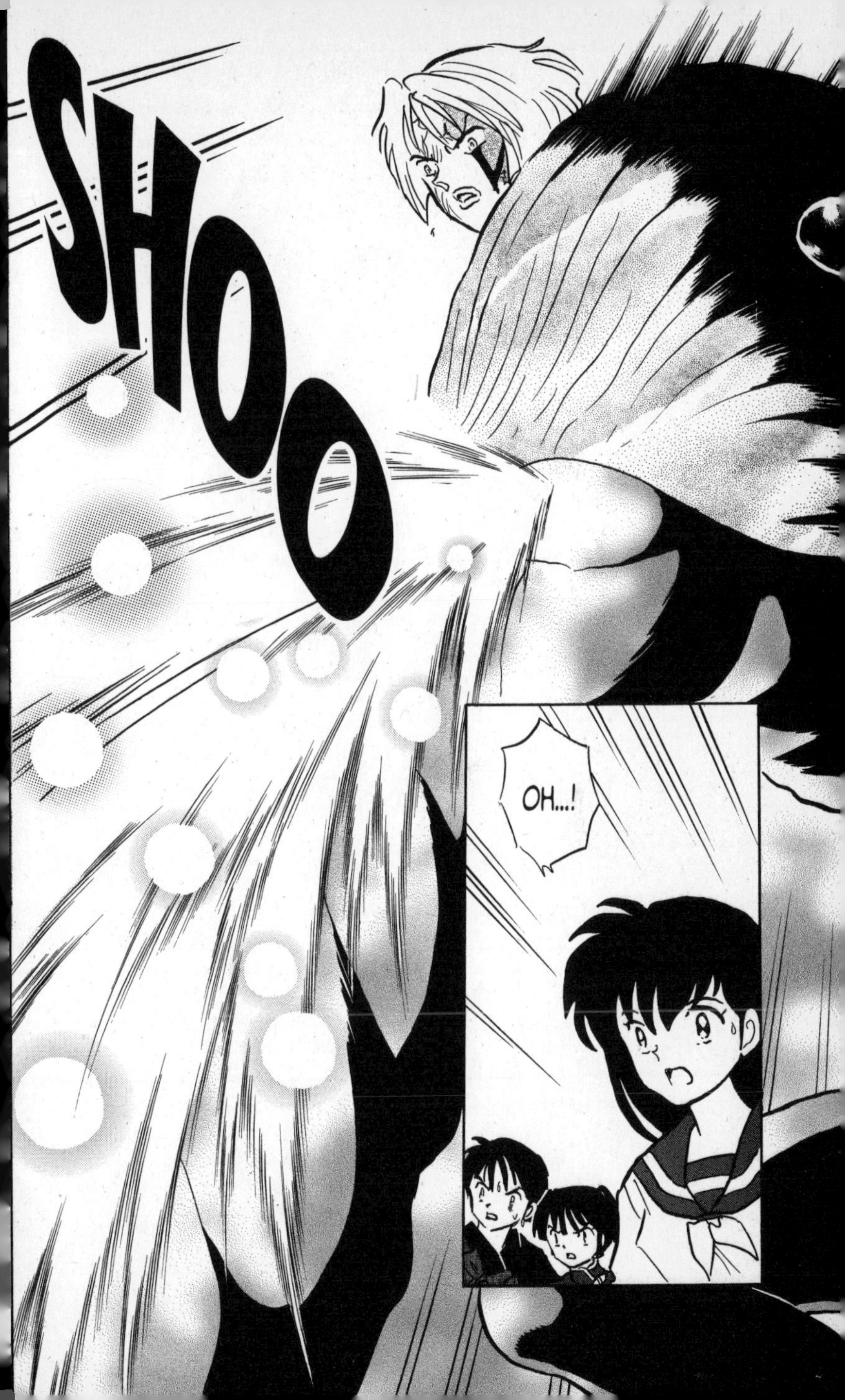
SHOO
OH...!

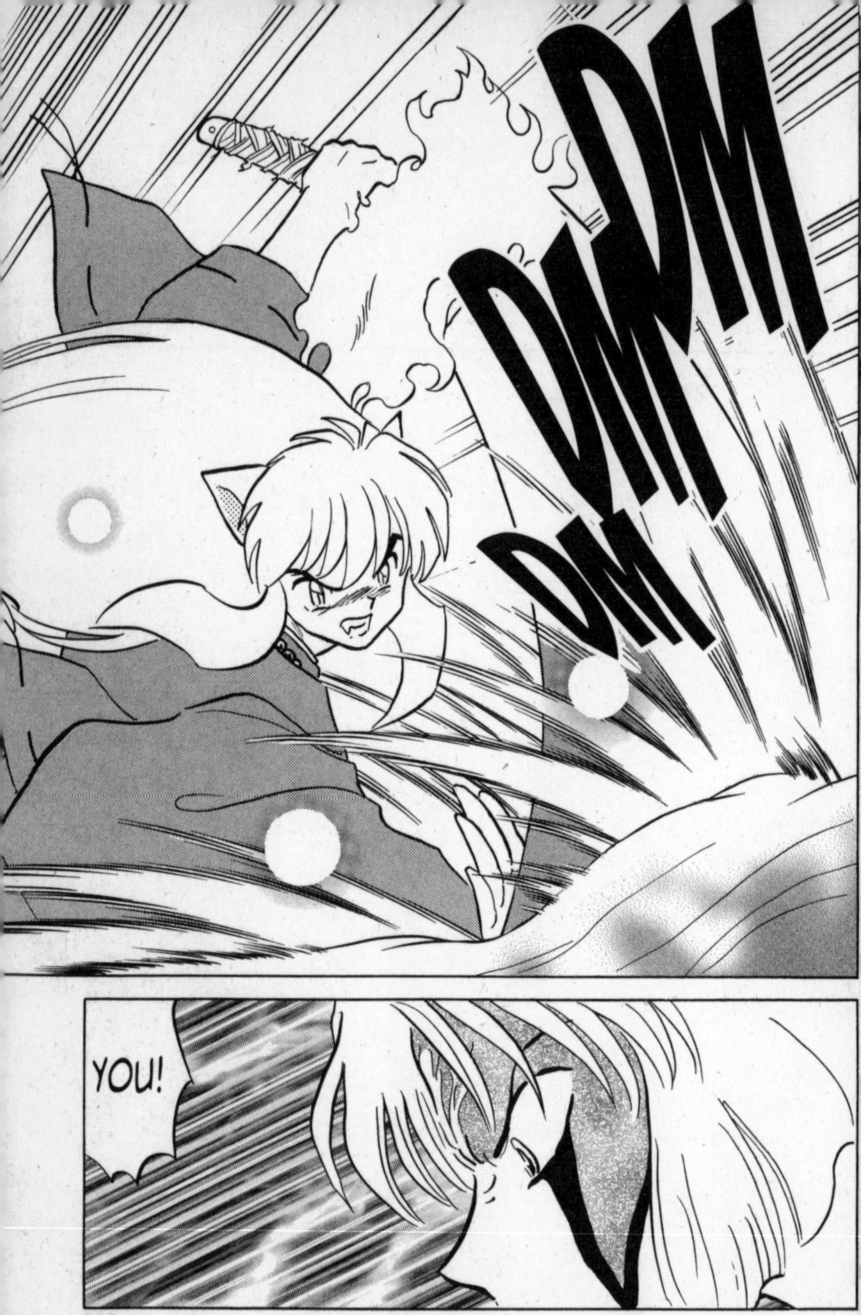
DM DM DM
YOU!

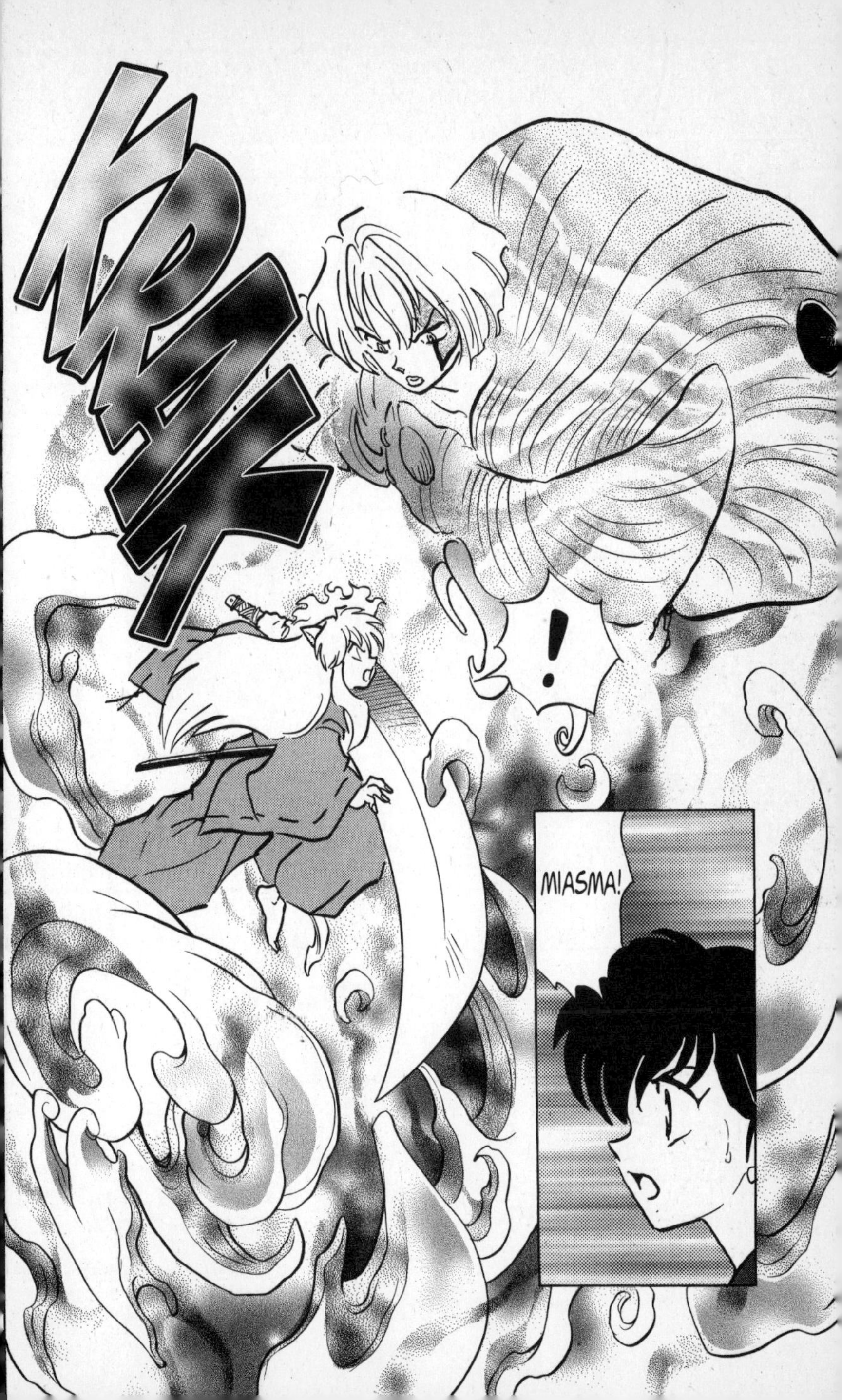
KRAK
!
MIASMA!

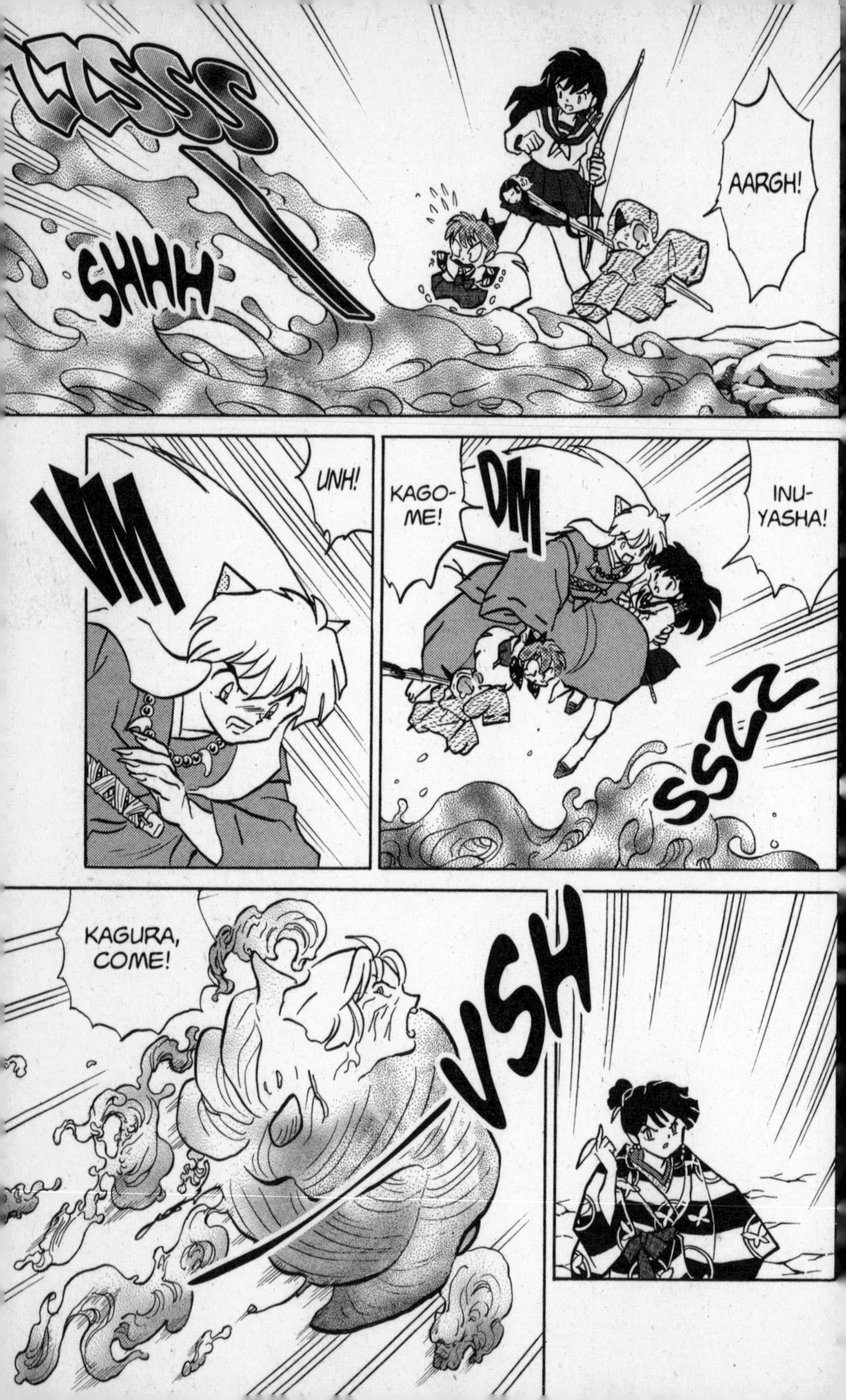

TZSSS
SHHH
AARGH!
VM
UNH!
KAGO-
ME!
DM
INU-
YASHA!
SSZZ
KAGURA,
COME!
VSH

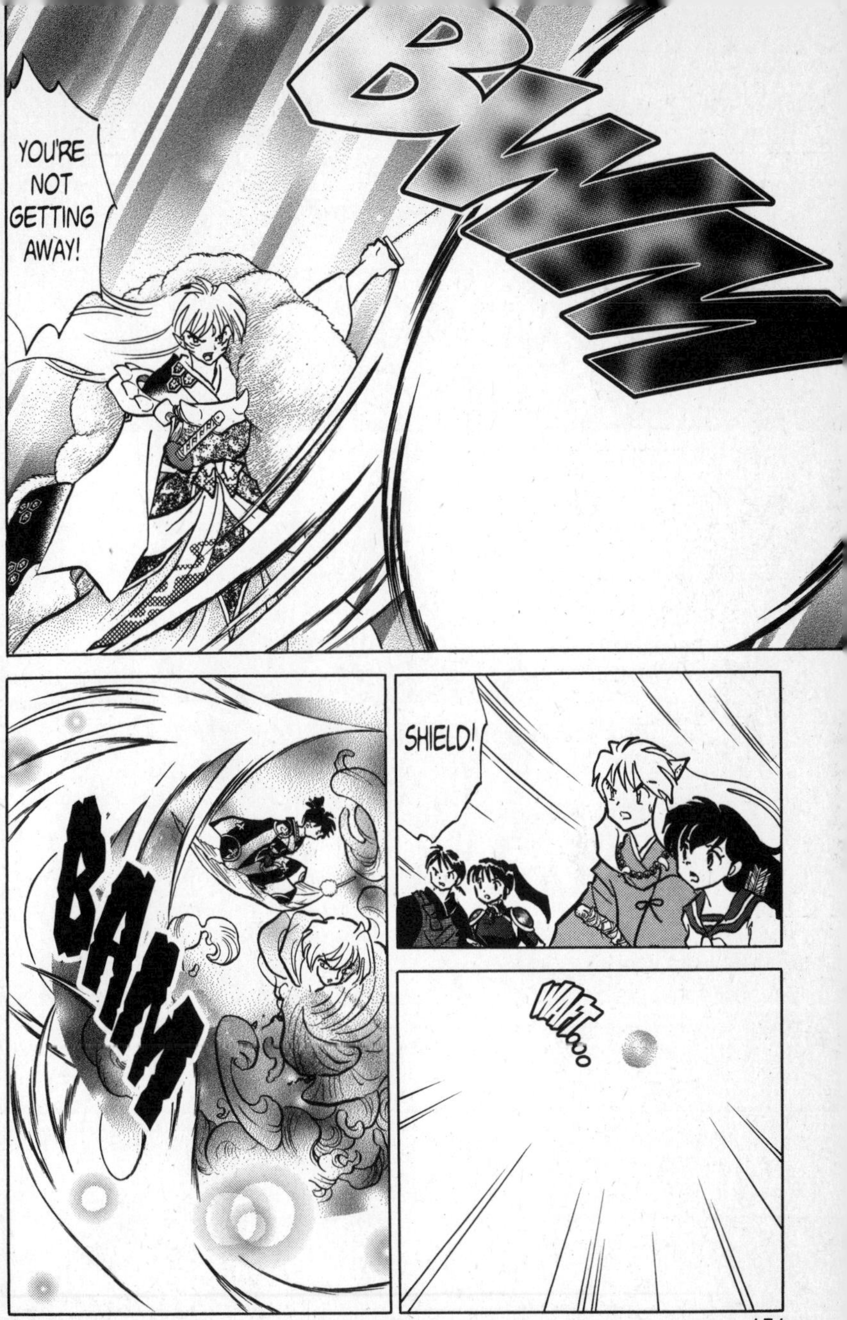
YOU'RE NOT GETTING AWAY!
BAM
SHIELD!
WAFT...

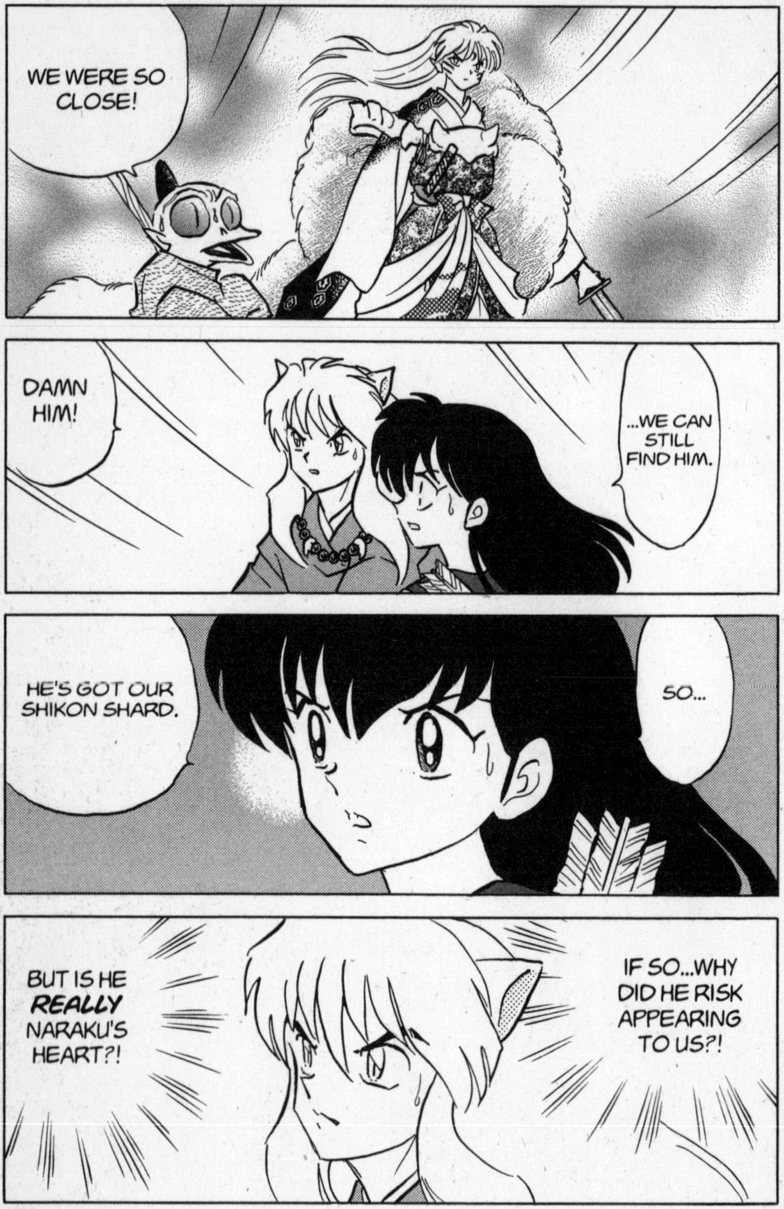
WE WERE SO CLOSE!
DAMN HIM!
...WE CAN STILL FIND HIM.
HE'S GOT OUR SHIKON SHARD.
SO...
BUT IS HE ***REALLY*** NARAKU'S HEART?!
IF SO...WHY DID HE RISK APPEARING TO US?!

SCROLL 9

WHERE IS THE CHILD?

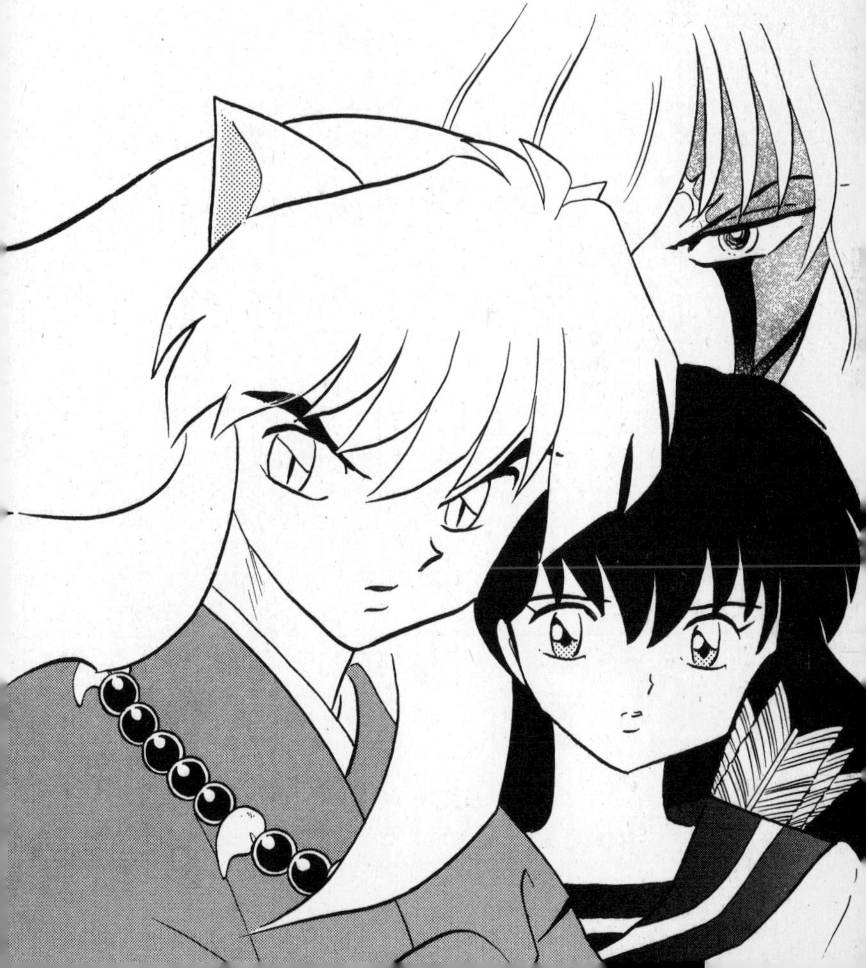

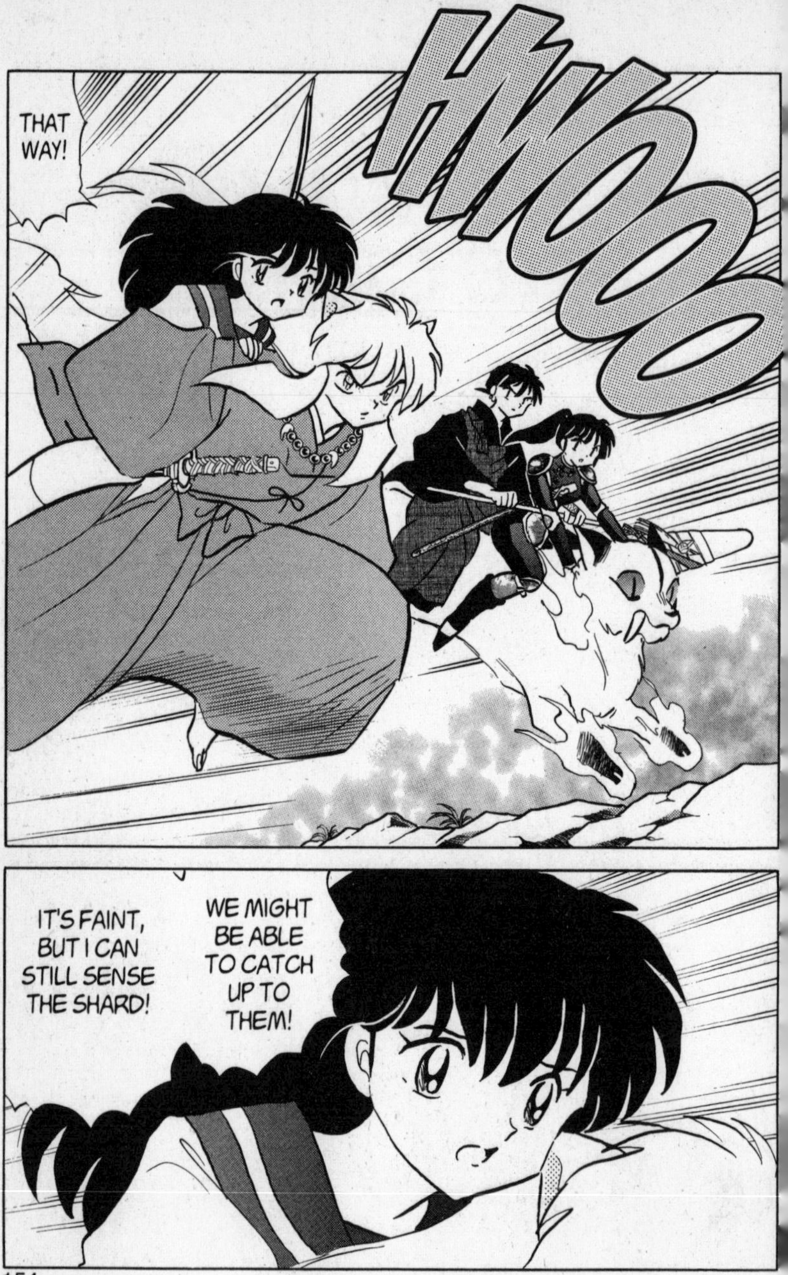
THAT WAY!
HWOOOO
IT'S FAINT, BUT I CAN STILL SENSE THE SHARD!
WE MIGHT BE ABLE TO CATCH UP TO THEM!

BUT... THERE ARE STILL...

...SO MANY QUES- TIONS.

NARAKU OBTAINED THE NULL STONE...

...IN ORDER TO CONCEAL WHERE HE'D HIDDEN HIS HEART.

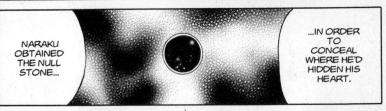

SO WE THINK MORYOMARU IS THAT HEART.

BUT THEN...

YEAH.

HE CAME TO STEAL OUR SHIKON SHARD.

IF NARAKU'S HIDING HIS HEART, WHY WOULD HE SEND IT OUT INTO THE OPEN TO FIGHT?!

HE'S RIGHT...

...THIS COULDN'T HAVE BEEN ON NARAKU'S ORDERS!

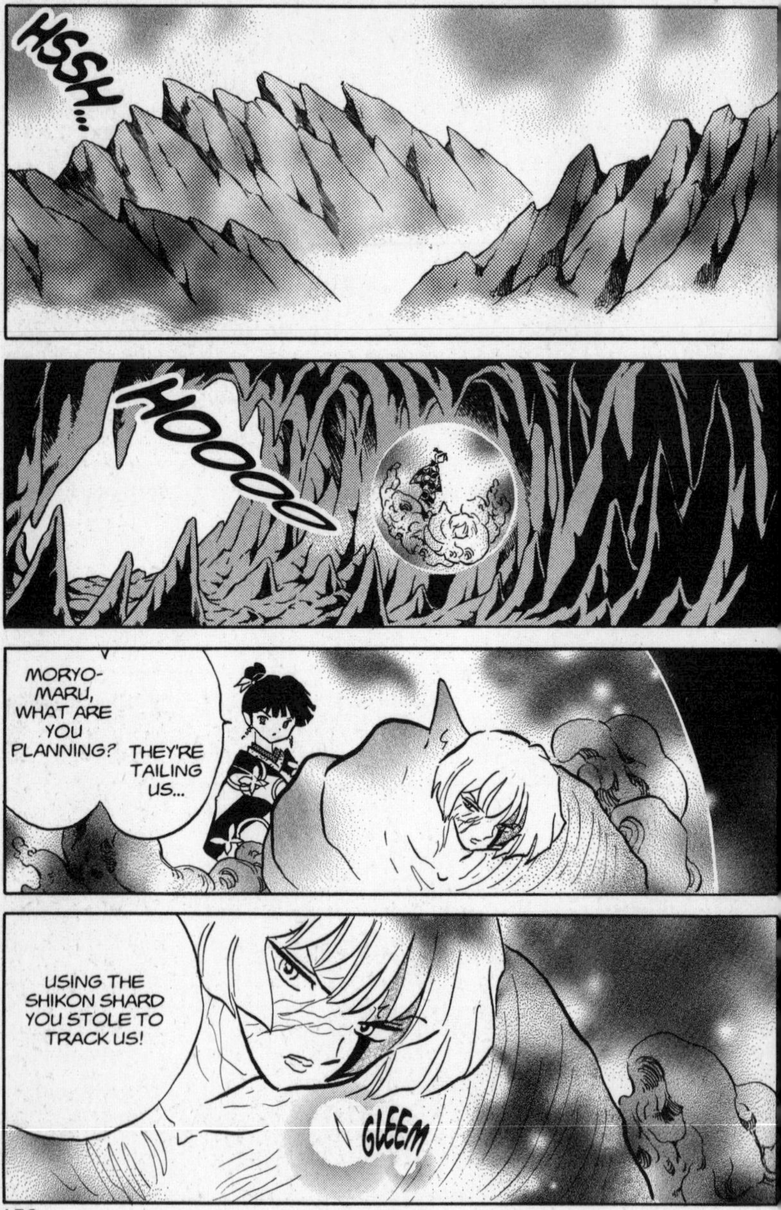
HSSH...
HOOOO
MORYO-MARU, WHAT ARE YOU PLANNING?
THEY'RE TAILING US...
USING THE SHIKON SHARD YOU STOLE TO TRACK US!
GLEEM

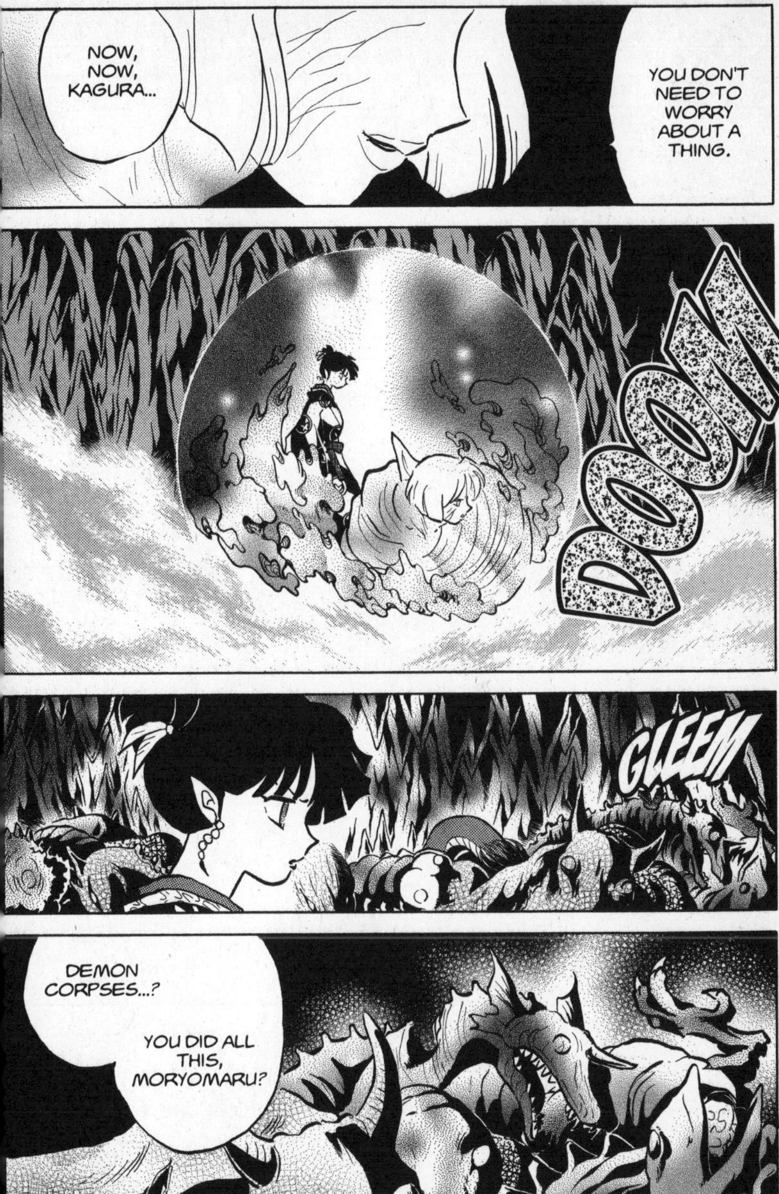
NOW, NOW, KAGURA...
YOU DON'T NEED TO WORRY ABOUT A THING.
DOOOM
GLEEM
DEMON CORPSES...?
YOU DID ALL THIS, MORYOMARU?

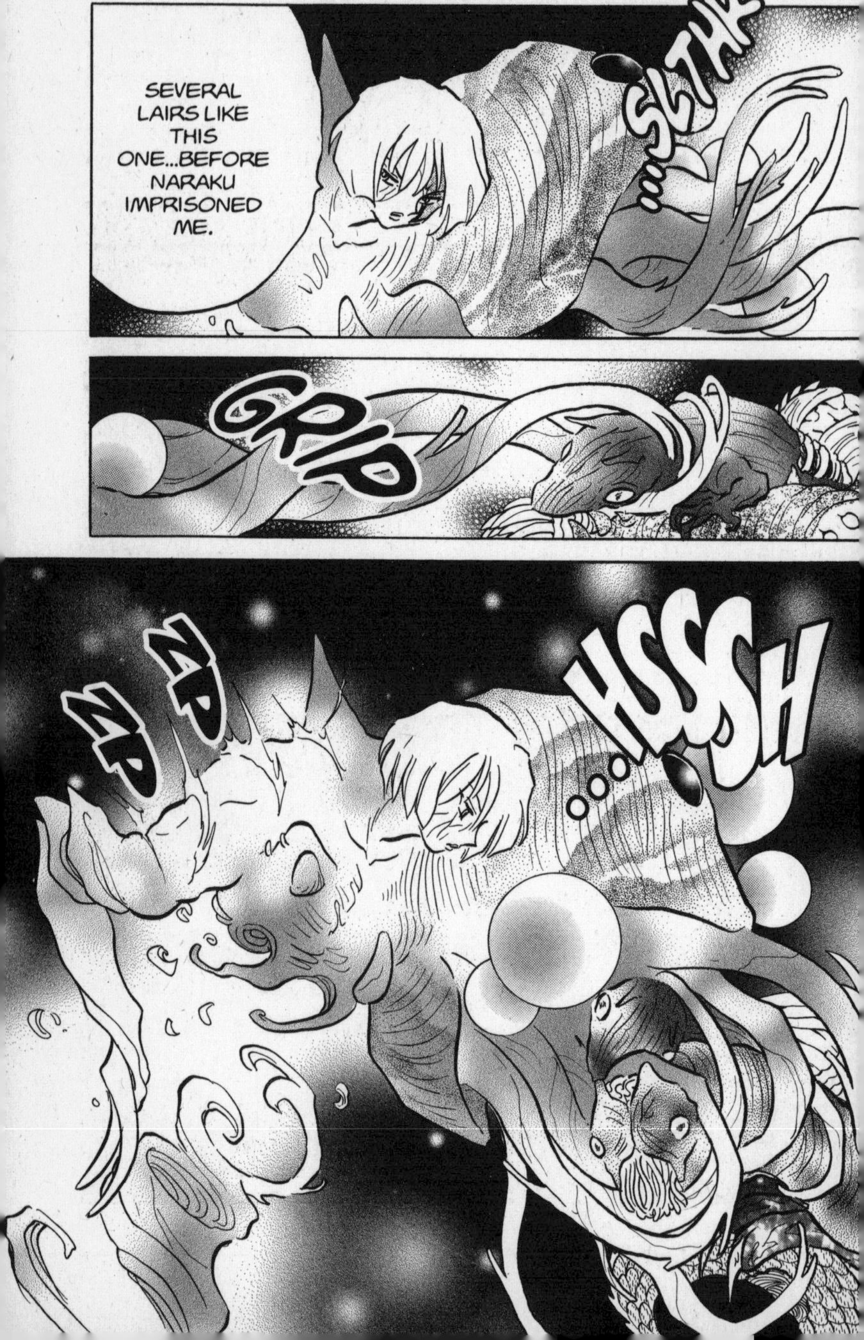

SEVERAL LAIRS LIKE THIS ONE...BEFORE NARAKU IMPRISONED ME.
...SLTHR
GRIP
ZAP ZAP
...HSSSH

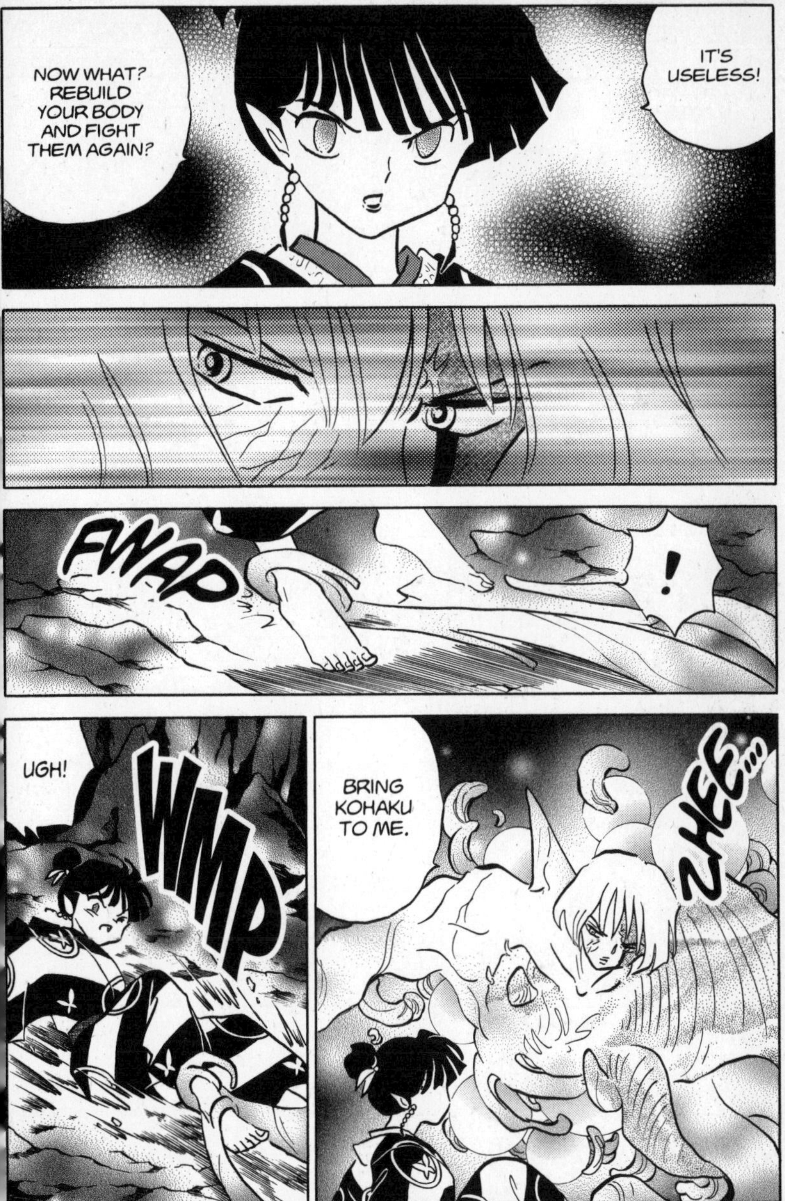
NOW WHAT? REBUILD YOUR BODY AND FIGHT THEM AGAIN?
IT'S USELESS!
FWAP
!
UGH!
WMP
BRING KOHAKU TO ME.
ZHEE...

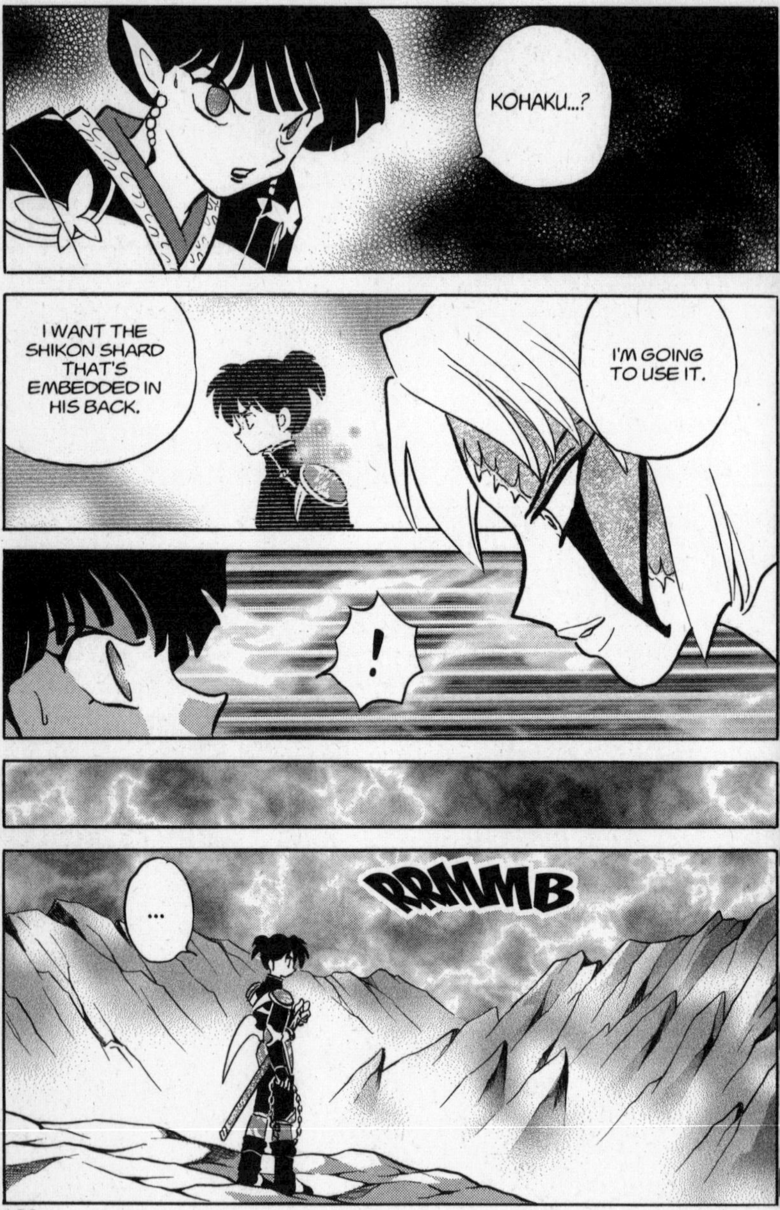
KOHAKU...?
I WANT THE SHIKON SHARD THAT'S EMBEDDED IN HIS BACK.
I'M GOING TO USE IT.
!
...
RRMMMB

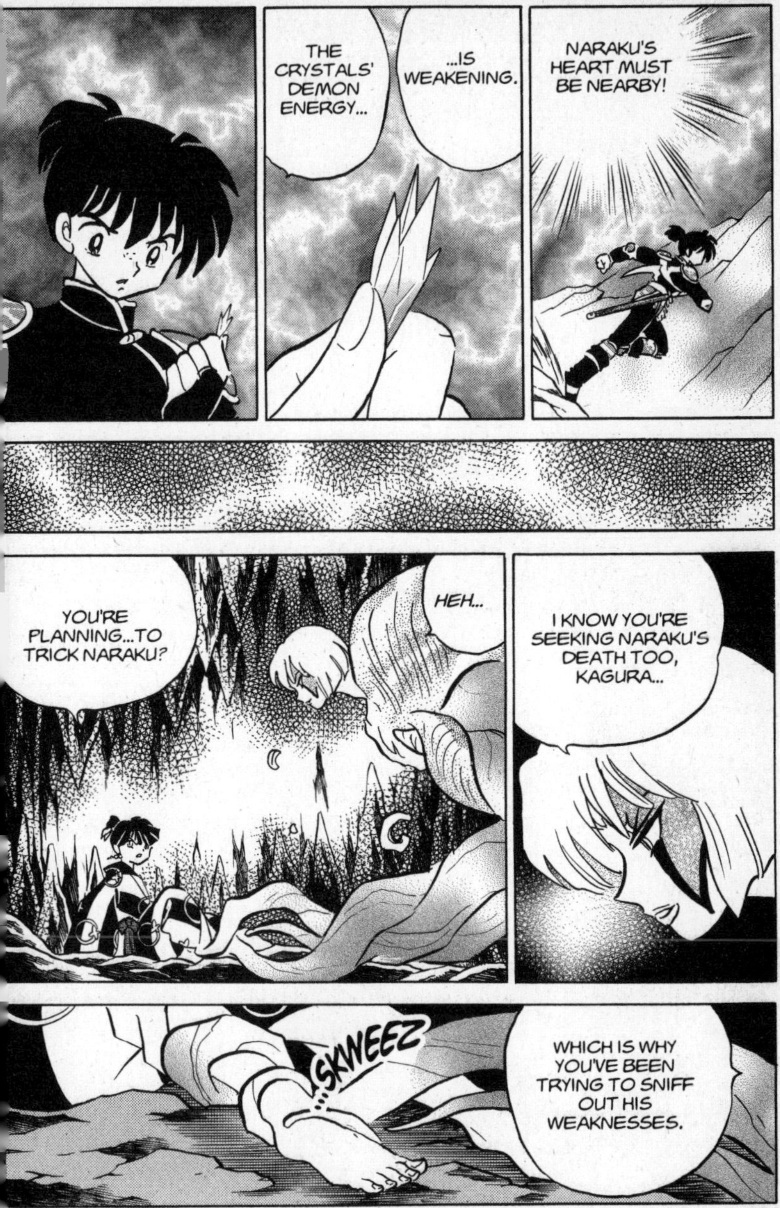
THE CRYSTALS' DEMON ENERGY...
...IS WEAKENING.
NARAKU'S HEART MUST BE NEARBY!
YOU'RE PLANNING...TO TRICK NARAKU?
HEH...
I KNOW YOU'RE SEEKING NARAKU'S DEATH TOO, KAGURA...
SKWEEZ
WHICH IS WHY YOU'VE BEEN TRYING TO SNIFF OUT HIS WEAKNESSES.

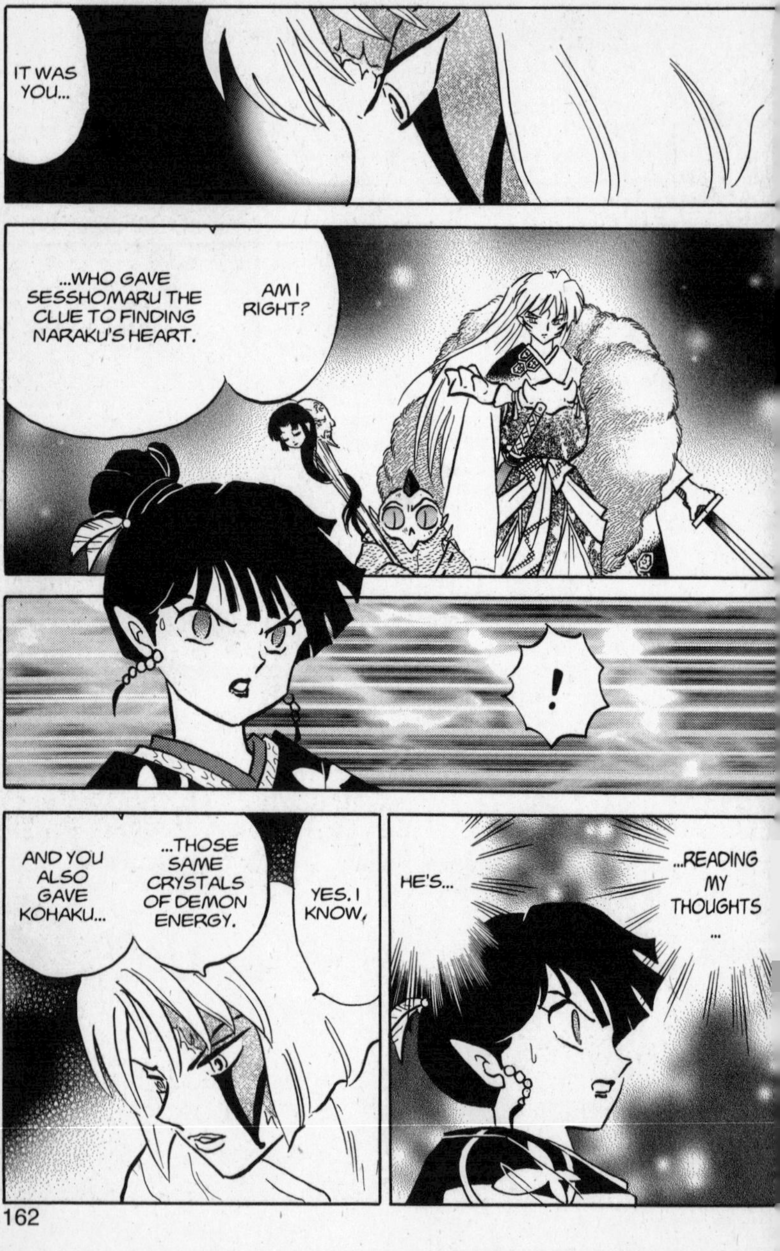
IT WAS YOU...
...WHO GAVE SESSHOMARU THE CLUE TO FINDING NARAKU'S HEART.
AM I RIGHT?
!
AND YOU ALSO GAVE KOHAKU...
...THOSE SAME CRYSTALS OF DEMON ENERGY.
YES. I KNOW,
HE'S...
...READING MY THOUGHTS
...

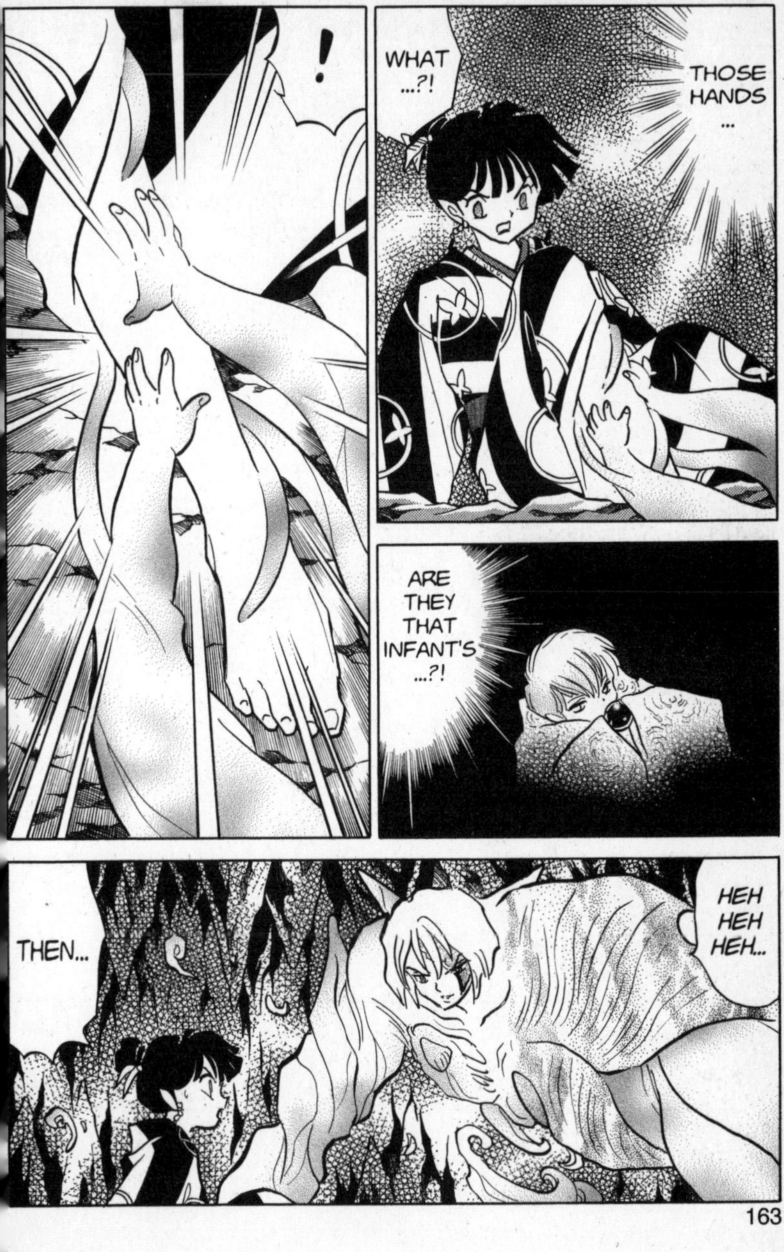
!
WHAT ...?!
THOSE HANDS ...
ARE THEY THAT INFANT'S ...?!
THEN...
HEH HEH HEH...

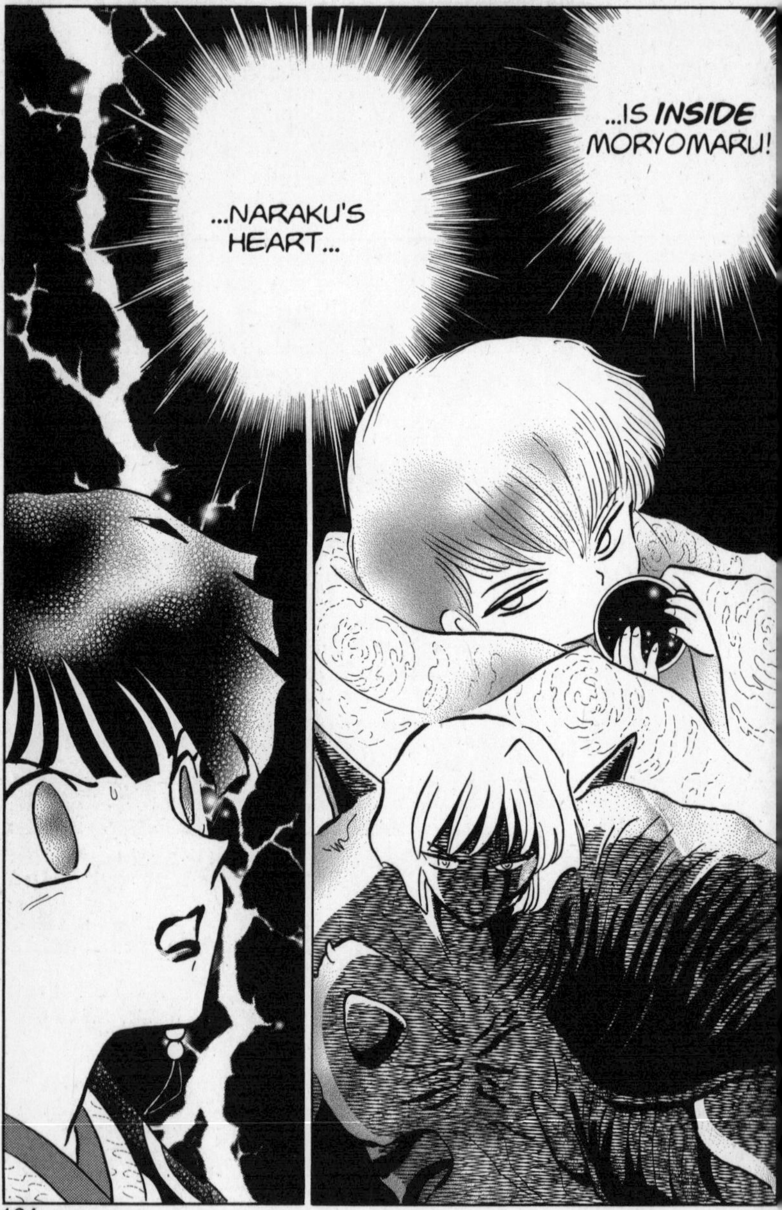
...NARAKU'S HEART...
...IS INSIDE MORYOMARU!

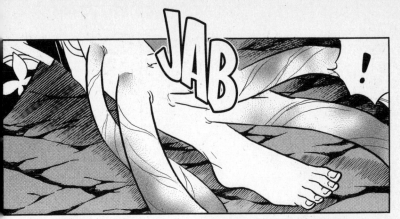

JAB

!

I COULD JUST ABSORB YOU RIGHT *HERE.*

SO WHAT?

S...

...STOP IT!

I'LL DO... WHATEVER YOU WANT...

HEH HEH HEH... THAT'S A GOOD GIRL.

FROM THE MOMENT YOU DEFIED NARAKU'S ORDERS AND RELEASED ME FROM HIS PRISON...

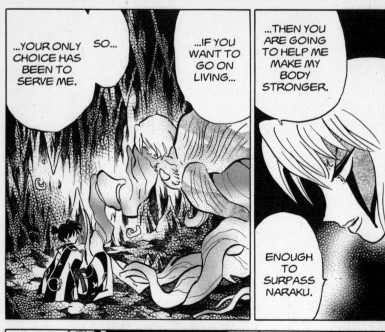

...YOUR ONLY CHOICE HAS BEEN TO SERVE ME.

SO...

...IF YOU WANT TO GO ON LIVING...

...THEN YOU ARE GOING TO HELP ME MAKE MY BODY STRONGER.

ENOUGH TO SURPASS NARAKU.

SURPASS NARAKU...?

YOU MEAN... WITH THE SHIKON SHARD...?

THE SHARD IS SUSTAINING KOHAKU'S LIFE.

IF IT'S REMOVED... HE'LL DIE.

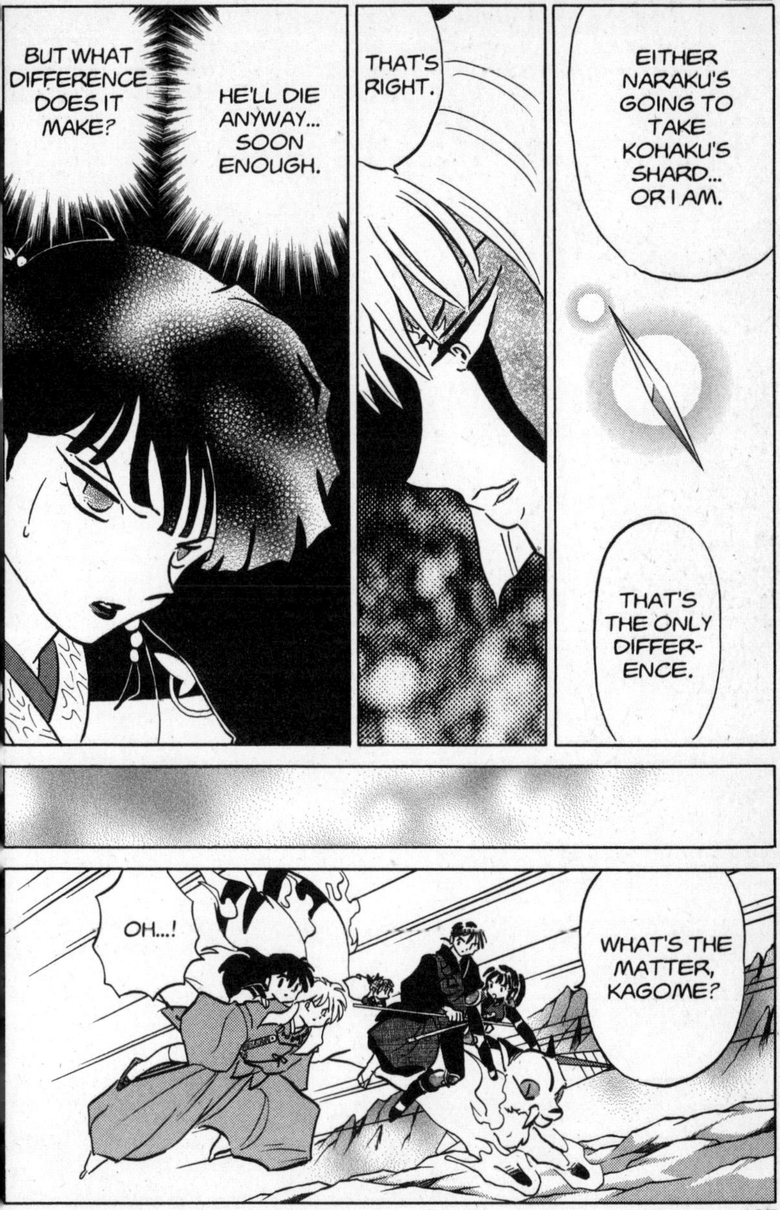
BUT WHAT DIFFERENCE DOES IT MAKE?
HE'LL DIE ANYWAY... SOON ENOUGH.
THAT'S RIGHT.
EITHER NARAKU'S GOING TO TAKE KOHAKU'S SHARD... OR I AM.
THAT'S THE ONLY DIFFER- ENCE.
OH...!
WHAT'S THE MATTER, KAGOME?

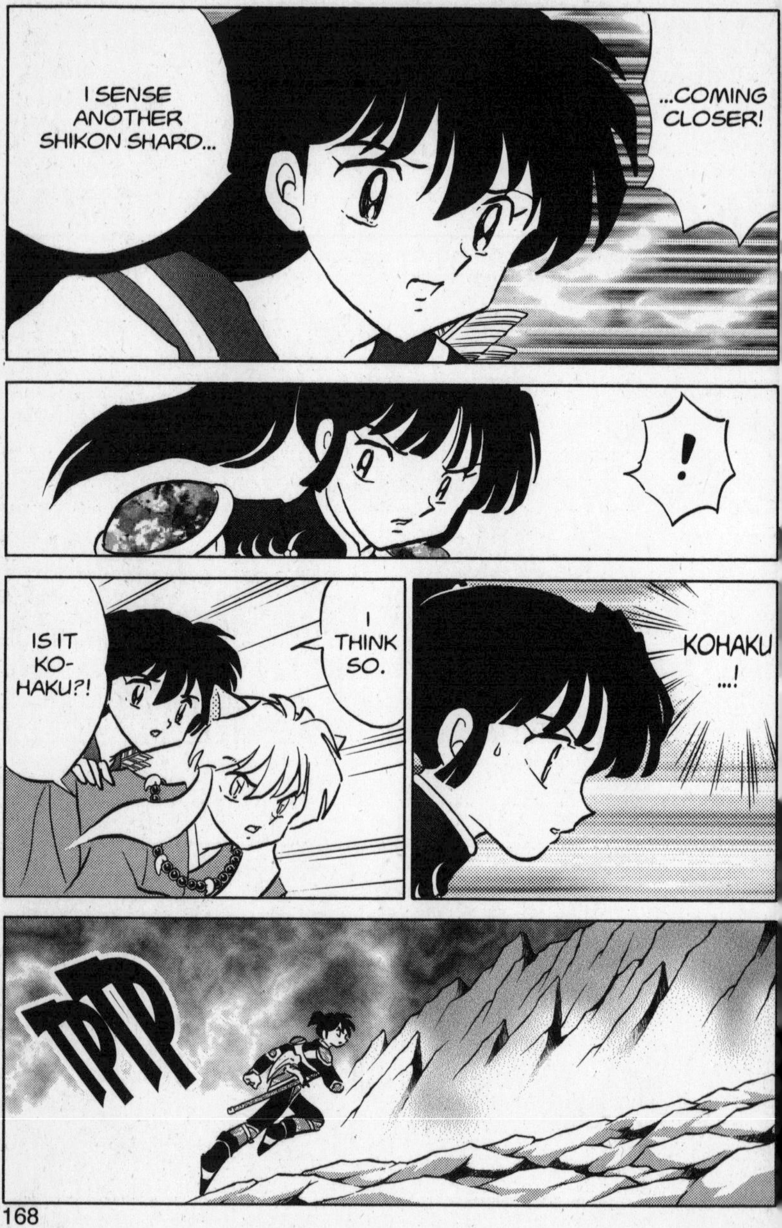
I SENSE ANOTHER SHIKON SHARD...
...COMING CLOSER!
!
IS IT KO-HAKU?!
I THINK SO.
KOHAKU ...!
TPTP

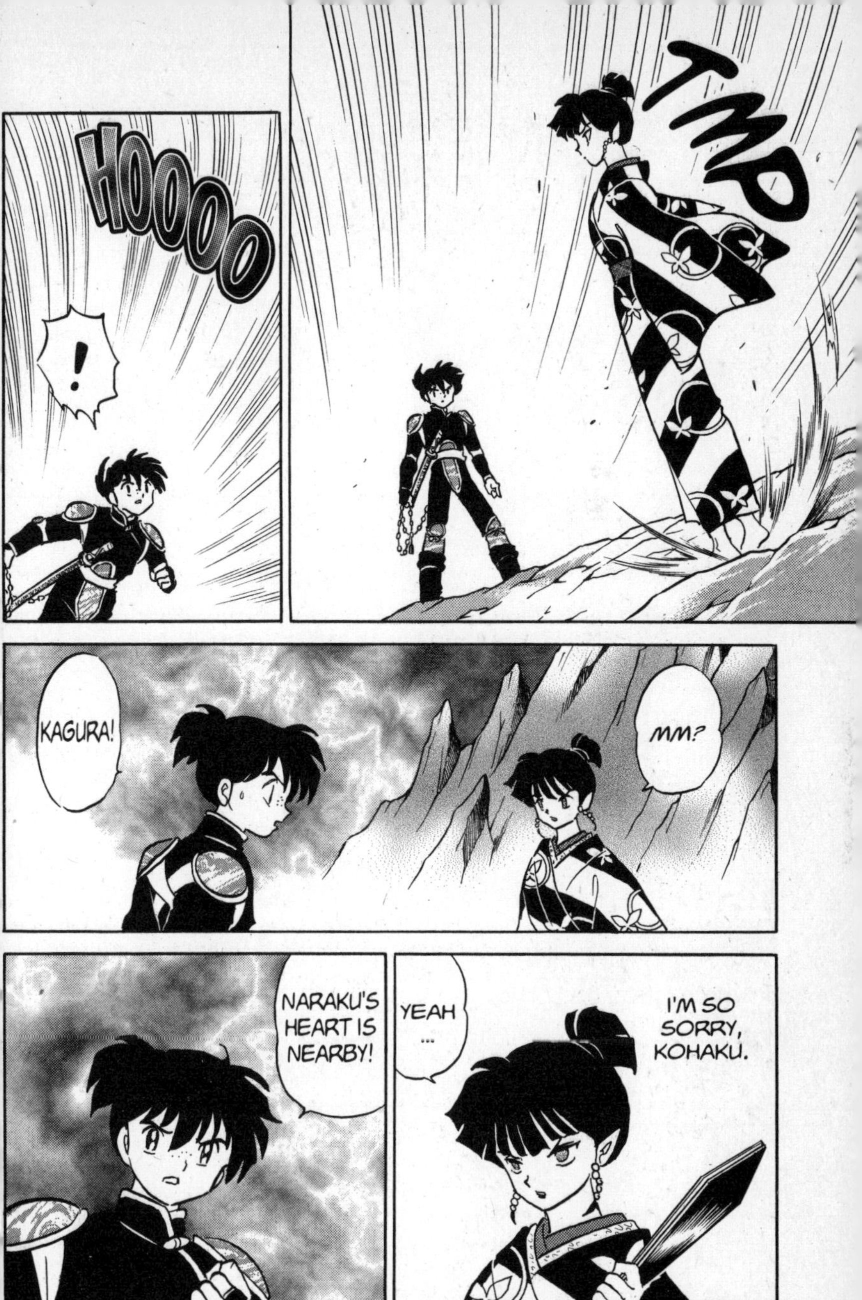
HOOOO
!
TMP
KAGURA!
MM?
NARAKU'S HEART IS NEARBY!
YEAH ...
I'M SO SORRY, KOHAKU.

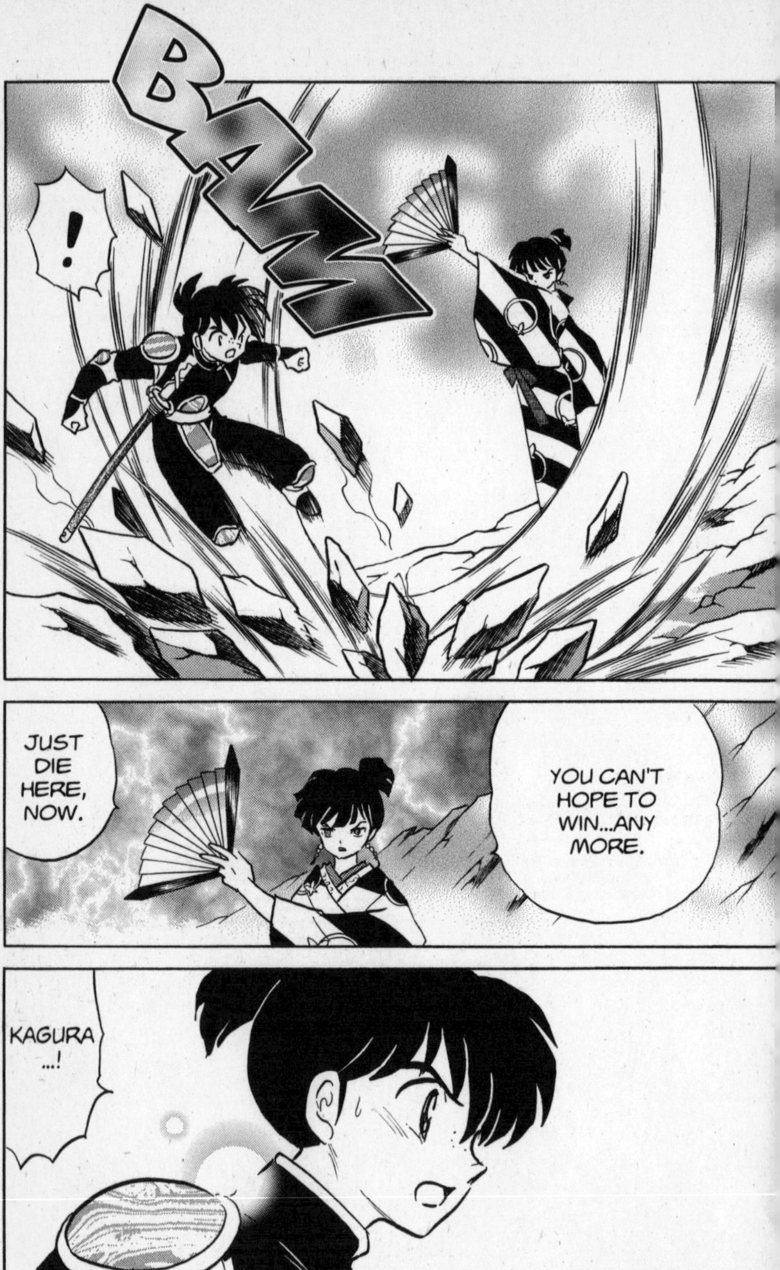
BAM
!
JUST DIE HERE, NOW.
YOU CAN'T HOPE TO WIN...ANY MORE.
KAGURA ...!

SCROLL 10

KAGURA'S DECISION

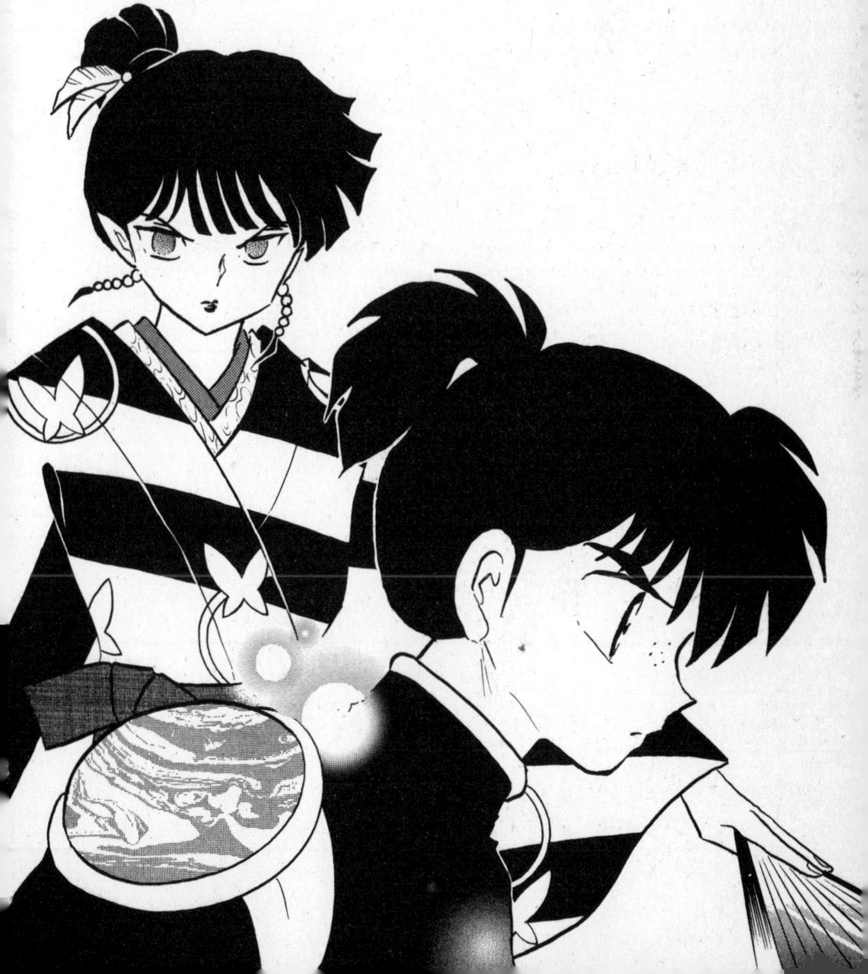

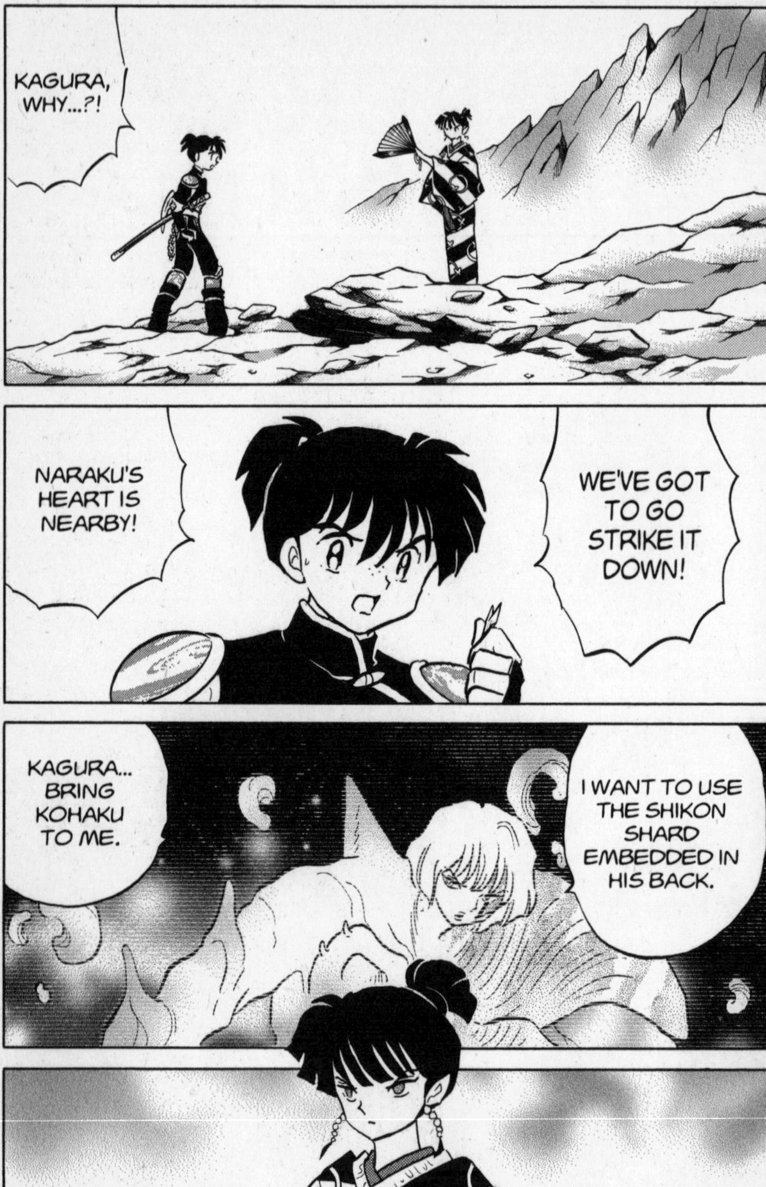
KAGURA, WHY...?!
NARAKU'S HEART IS NEARBY!
WE'VE GOT TO GO STRIKE IT DOWN!
KAGURA... BRING KOHAKU TO ME.
I WANT TO USE THE SHIKON SHARD EMBEDDED IN HIS BACK.

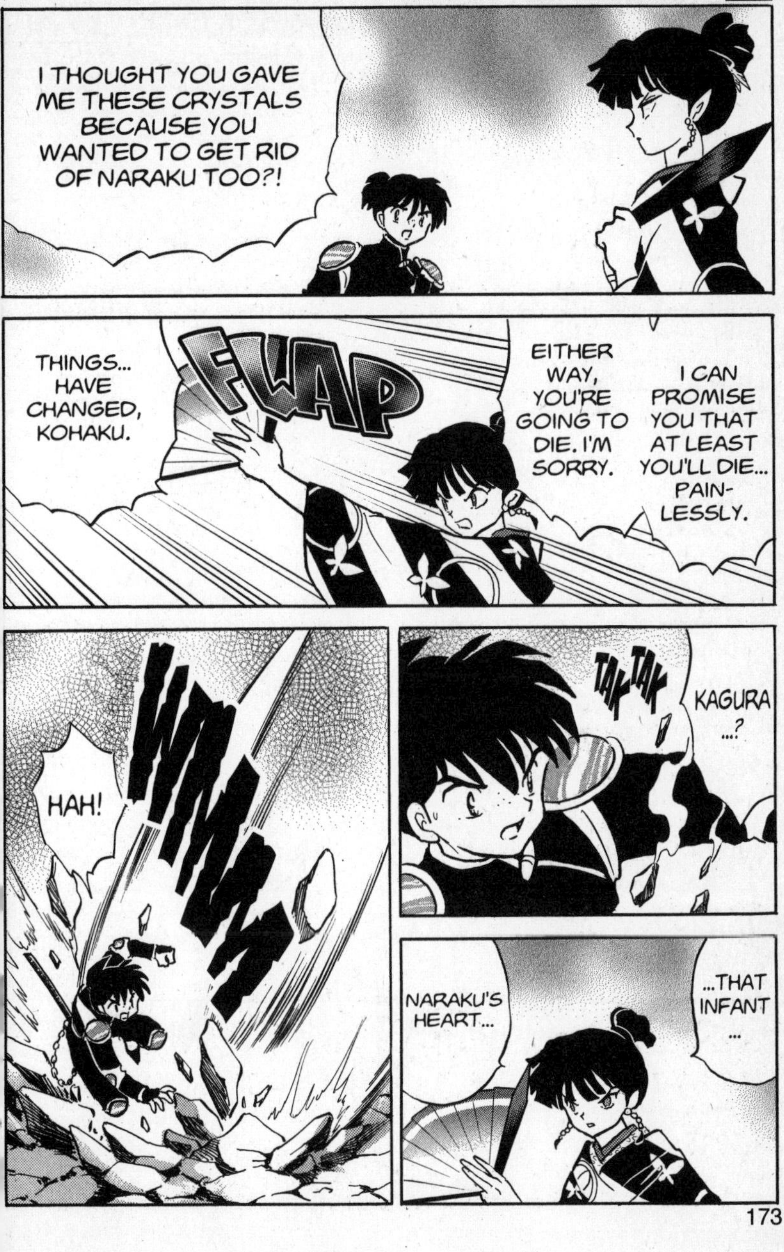
I THOUGHT YOU GAVE ME THESE CRYSTALS BECAUSE YOU WANTED TO GET RID OF NARAKU TOO?!
THINGS... HAVE CHANGED, KOHAKU.
FLAP
EITHER WAY, YOU'RE GOING TO DIE. I'M SORRY.
I CAN PROMISE YOU THAT AT LEAST YOU'LL DIE... PAIN-LESSLY.
HAH!
WHM
TAK TAK
KAGURA ...?
NARAKU'S HEART...
...THAT INFANT ...

...IS NOW INSIDE A DEMON NAMED MORYO-MARU.

HE WANTS TO USE THE SHIKON SHARD INSIDE YOU...

...TO BECOME STRONGER.

SO YOU'RE HERE...

...TO TAKE THE SHARD AND LET ME DIE?

IF I DON'T... I'LL DIE.

THEN... THERE'S NO REASON FOR US TO FIGHT.

I'LL GO WILLINGLY. TAKE ME TO HIM...

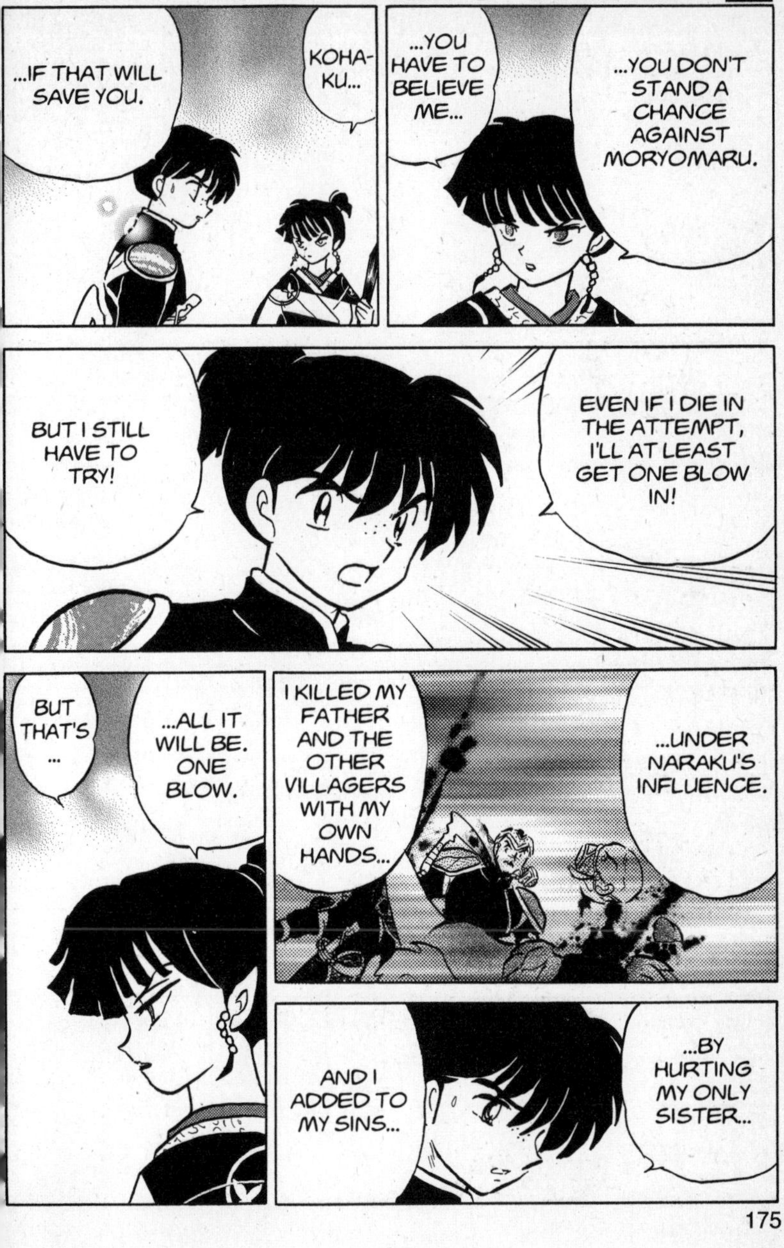
...IF THAT WILL SAVE YOU.
KOHA-KU...
...YOU HAVE TO BELIEVE ME...
...YOU DON'T STAND A CHANCE AGAINST MORYOMARU.
BUT I STILL HAVE TO TRY!
EVEN IF I DIE IN THE ATTEMPT, I'LL AT LEAST GET ONE BLOW IN!
BUT THAT'S ...
...ALL IT WILL BE. ONE BLOW.
I KILLED MY FATHER AND THE OTHER VILLAGERS WITH MY OWN HANDS...
...UNDER NARAKU'S INFLUENCE.
AND I ADDED TO MY SINS...
...BY HURTING MY ONLY SISTER...

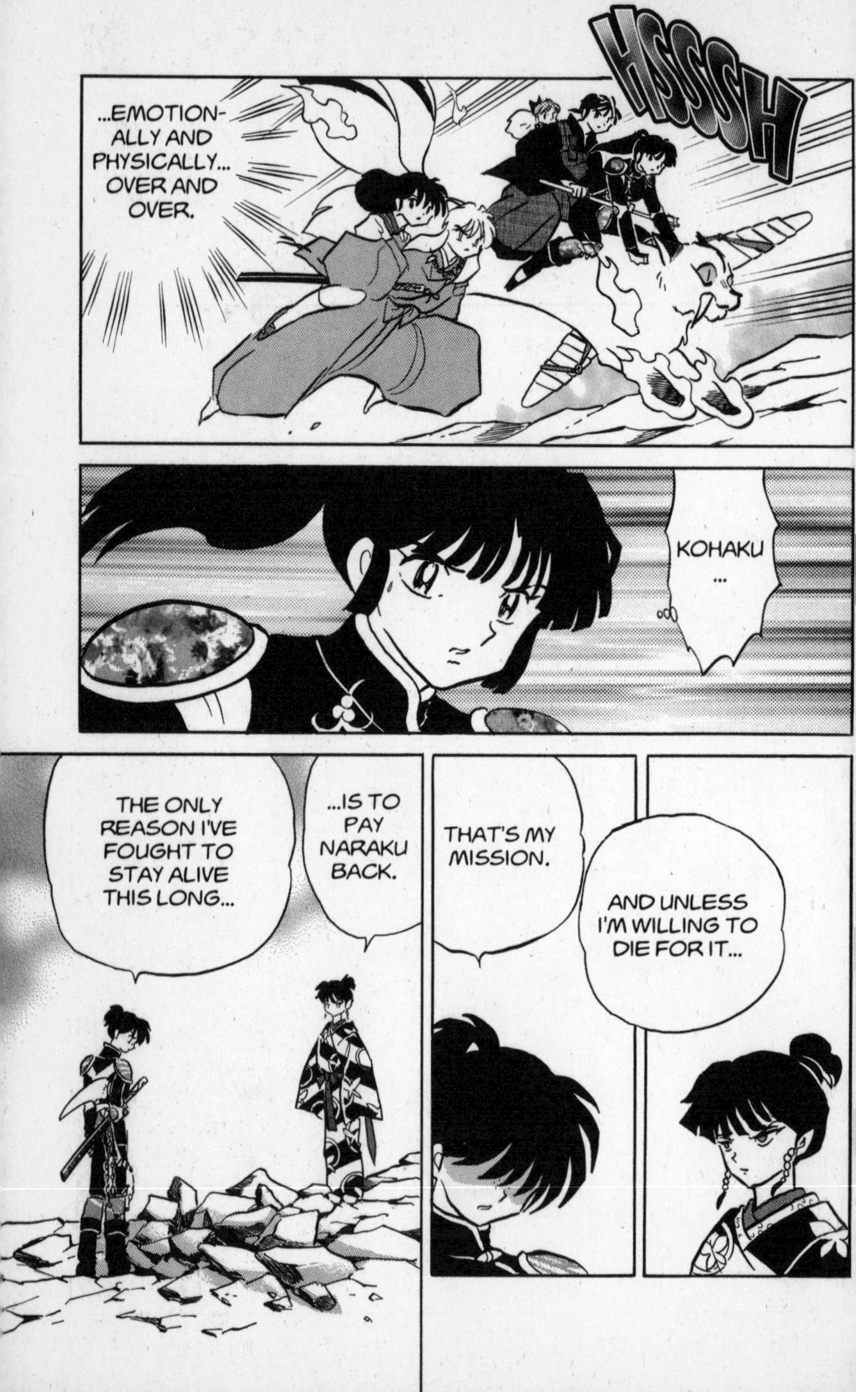

HSSSSH
...EMOTION-ALLY AND PHYSICALLY... OVER AND OVER.
KOHAKU ...
THE ONLY REASON I'VE FOUGHT TO STAY ALIVE THIS LONG...
...IS TO PAY NARAKU BACK.
THAT'S MY MISSION.
AND UNLESS I'M WILLING TO DIE FOR IT...

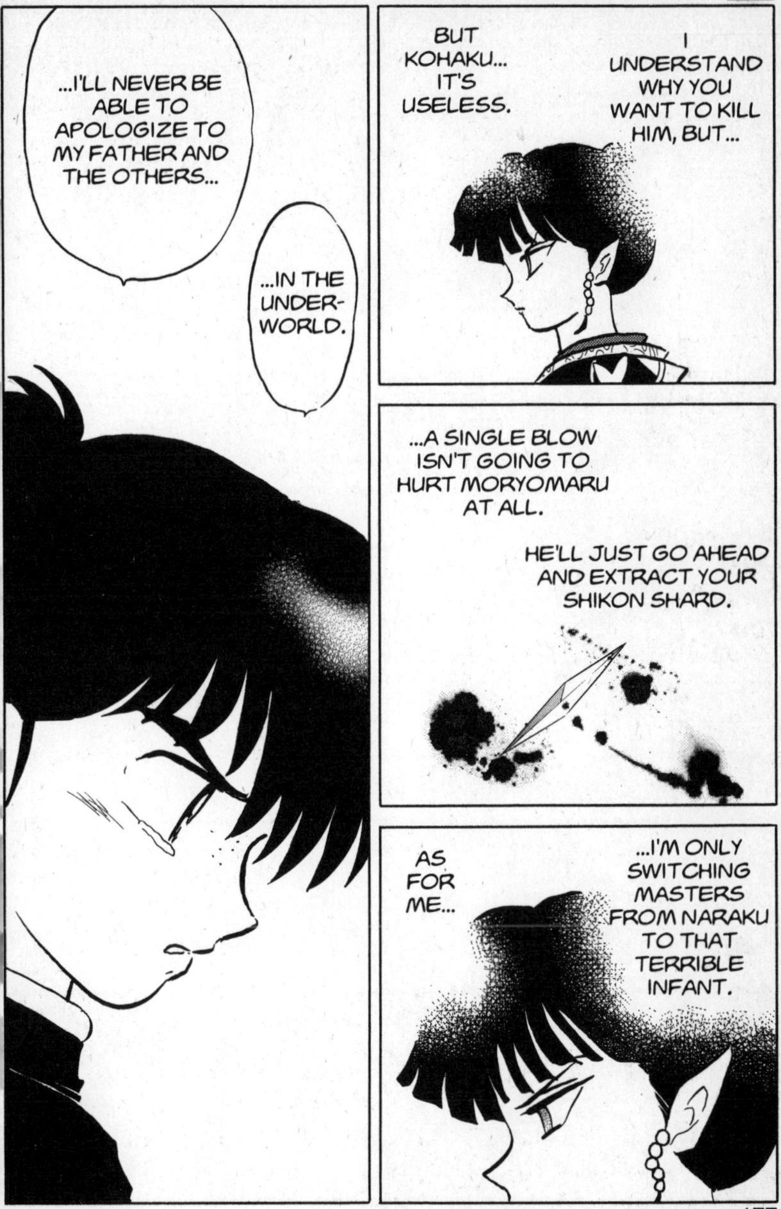
...I'LL NEVER BE ABLE TO APOLOGIZE TO MY FATHER AND THE OTHERS...
...IN THE UNDER-WORLD.
BUT KOHAKU... IT'S USELESS.
I UNDERSTAND WHY YOU WANT TO KILL HIM, BUT...
...A SINGLE BLOW ISN'T GOING TO HURT MORYOMARU AT ALL.
HE'LL JUST GO AHEAD AND EXTRACT YOUR SHIKON SHARD.
AS FOR ME...
...I'M ONLY SWITCHING MASTERS FROM NARAKU TO THAT TERRIBLE INFANT.

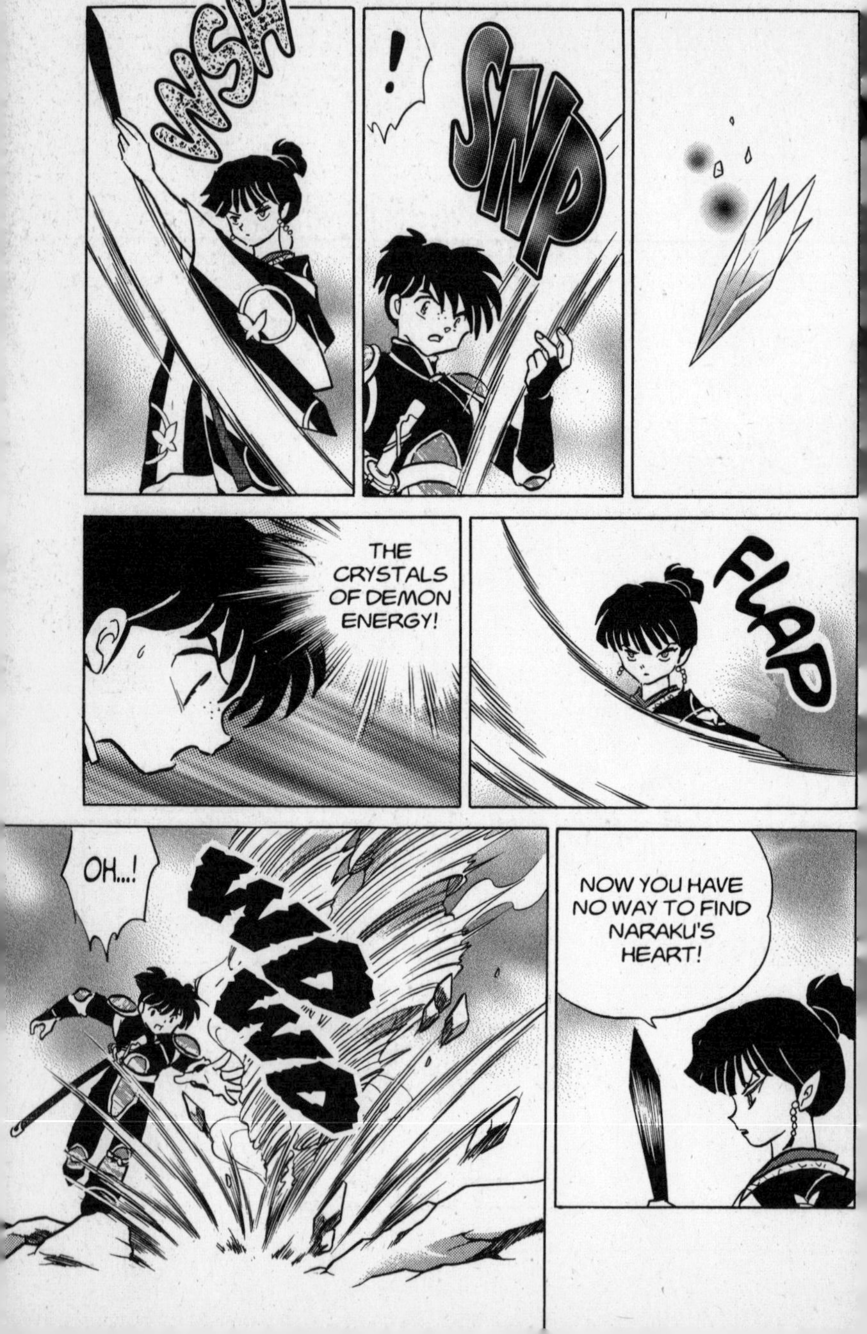
WSH
!
SNP
THE CRYSTALS OF DEMON ENERGY!
FLAP
OH...!
NOW YOU HAVE NO WAY TO FIND NARAKU'S HEART!

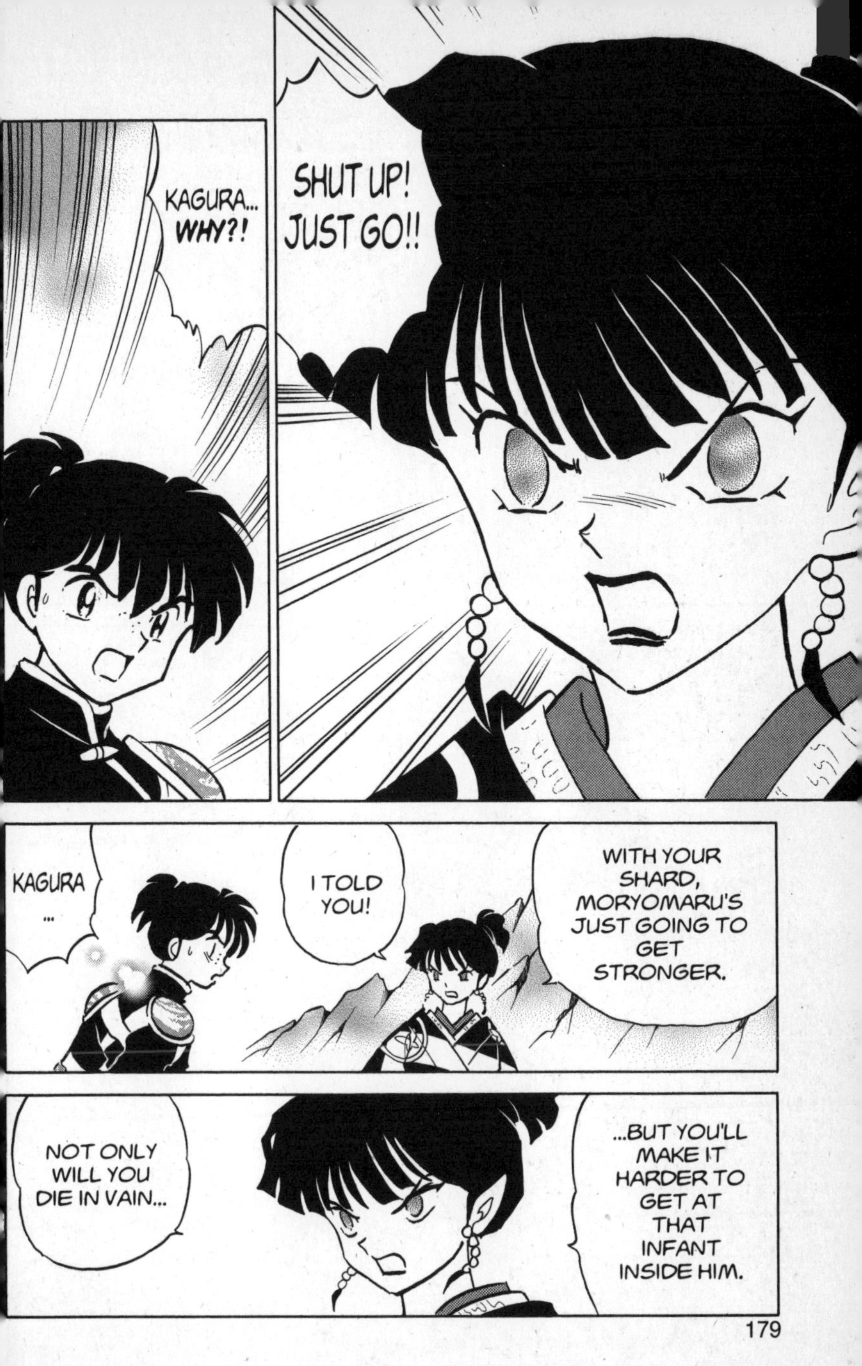
KAGURA... WHY?!
SHUT UP! JUST GO!!
KAGURA ...
I TOLD YOU!
WITH YOUR SHARD, MORYOMARU'S JUST GOING TO GET STRONGER.
NOT ONLY WILL YOU DIE IN VAIN...
...BUT YOU'LL MAKE IT HARDER TO GET AT THAT INFANT INSIDE HIM.

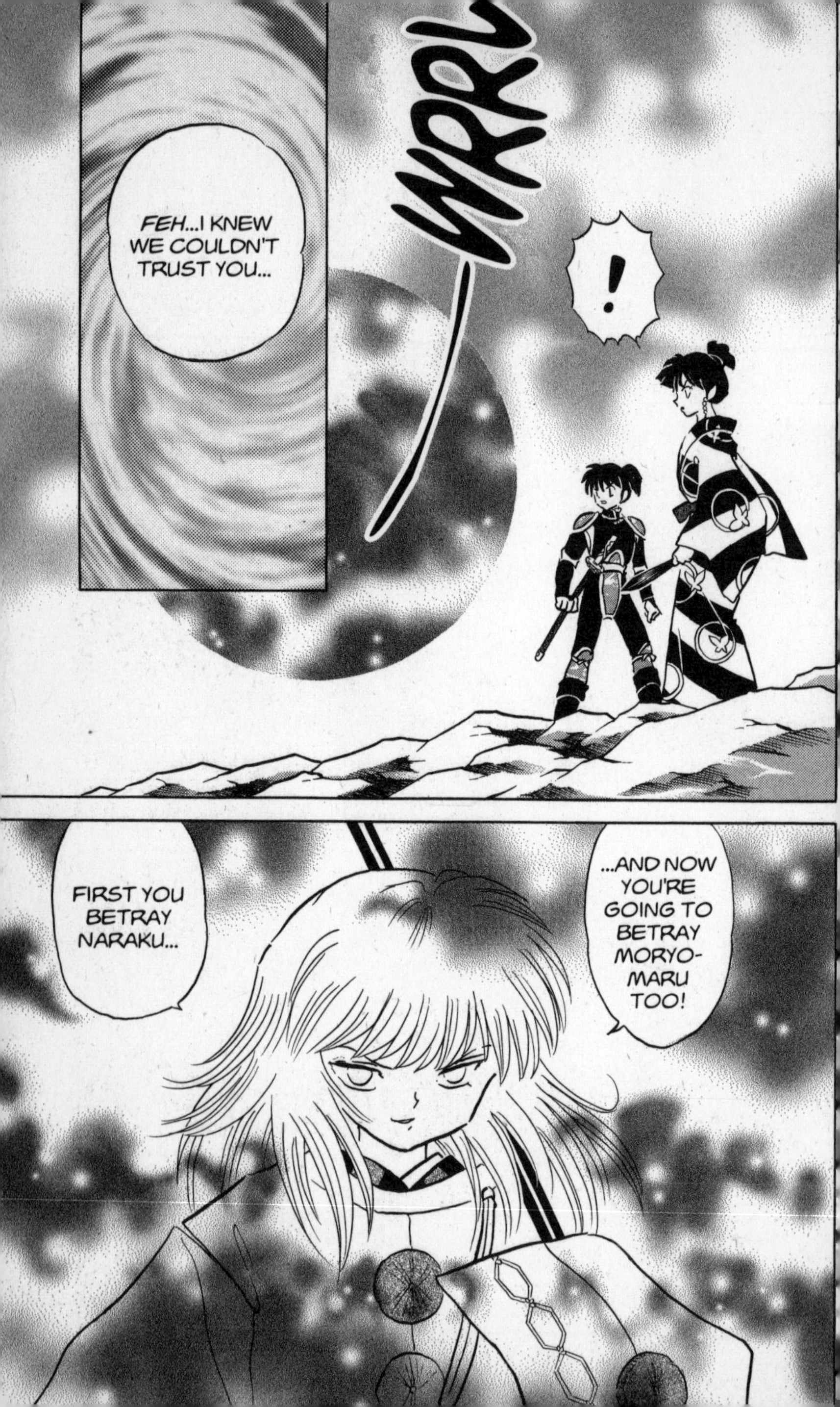
FEH...I KNEW WE COULDN'T TRUST YOU...
WRRR
!
FIRST YOU BETRAY NARAKU...
...AND NOW YOU'RE GOING TO BETRAY MORYO-MARU TOO!

HAKU-DOSHI...!

HEH. YOU'RE ONE TO TALK...

...SINCE YOU'RE TRYING TO BETRAY NARAKU TOO!

?!

I'M FINALLY STARTING TO UNDER-STAND.

YOU AND THAT INFANT WERE ORIGINALLY ONE BEING...

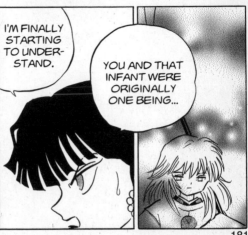

AND MORYOMARU IS A DEMON THAT THE TWO OF YOU CREATED.

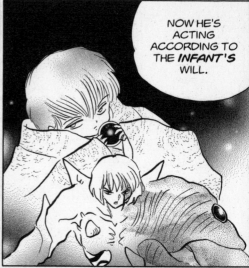

NOW HE'S ACTING ACCORDING TO THE *INFANT'S* WILL.

AND YOU'RE SCHEMING TO SUPPLANT NARAKU!

WELL, KAGURA...

...YOU'RE SMARTER THAN I THOUGHT.

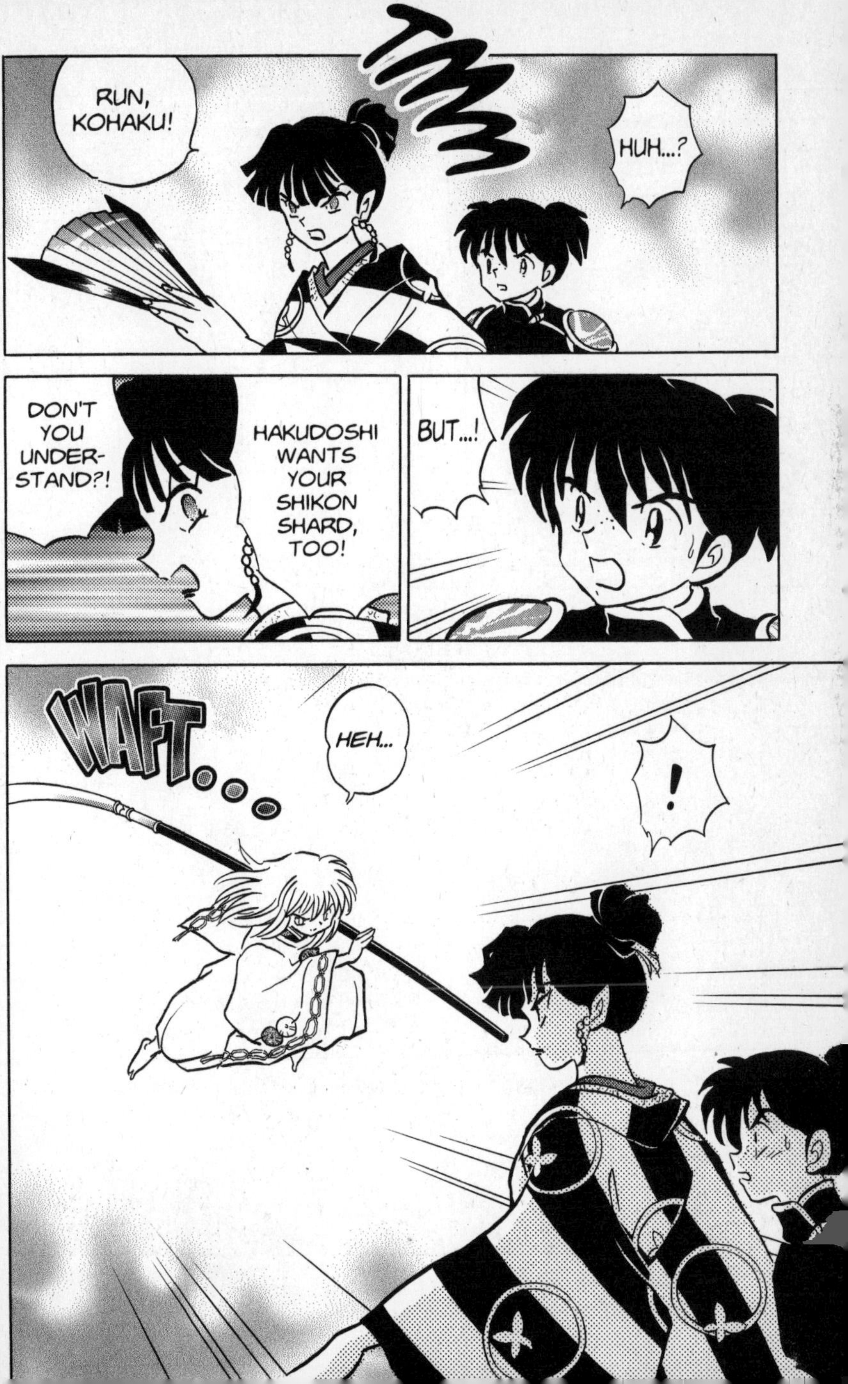
RUN, KOHAKU!
TMM
HUH...?
DON'T YOU UNDER-STAND?!
HAKUDOSHI WANTS YOUR SHIKON SHARD, TOO!
BUT...!
WAFT...
HEH...
!

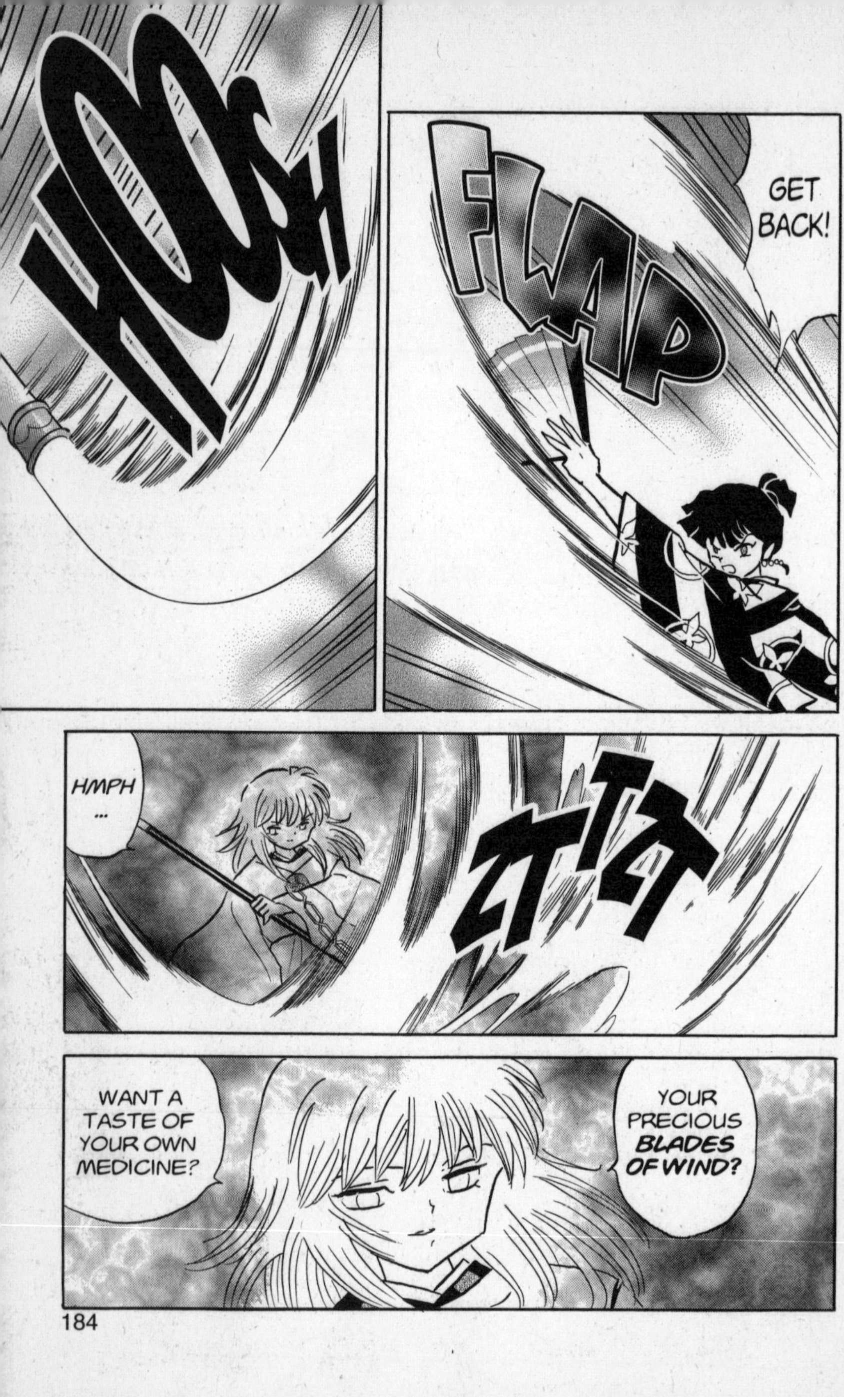
WOOSH!
FLAP
GET BACK!
HMPH ...
WANT A TASTE OF YOUR OWN MEDICINE?
YOUR PRECIOUS *BLADES OF WIND?*

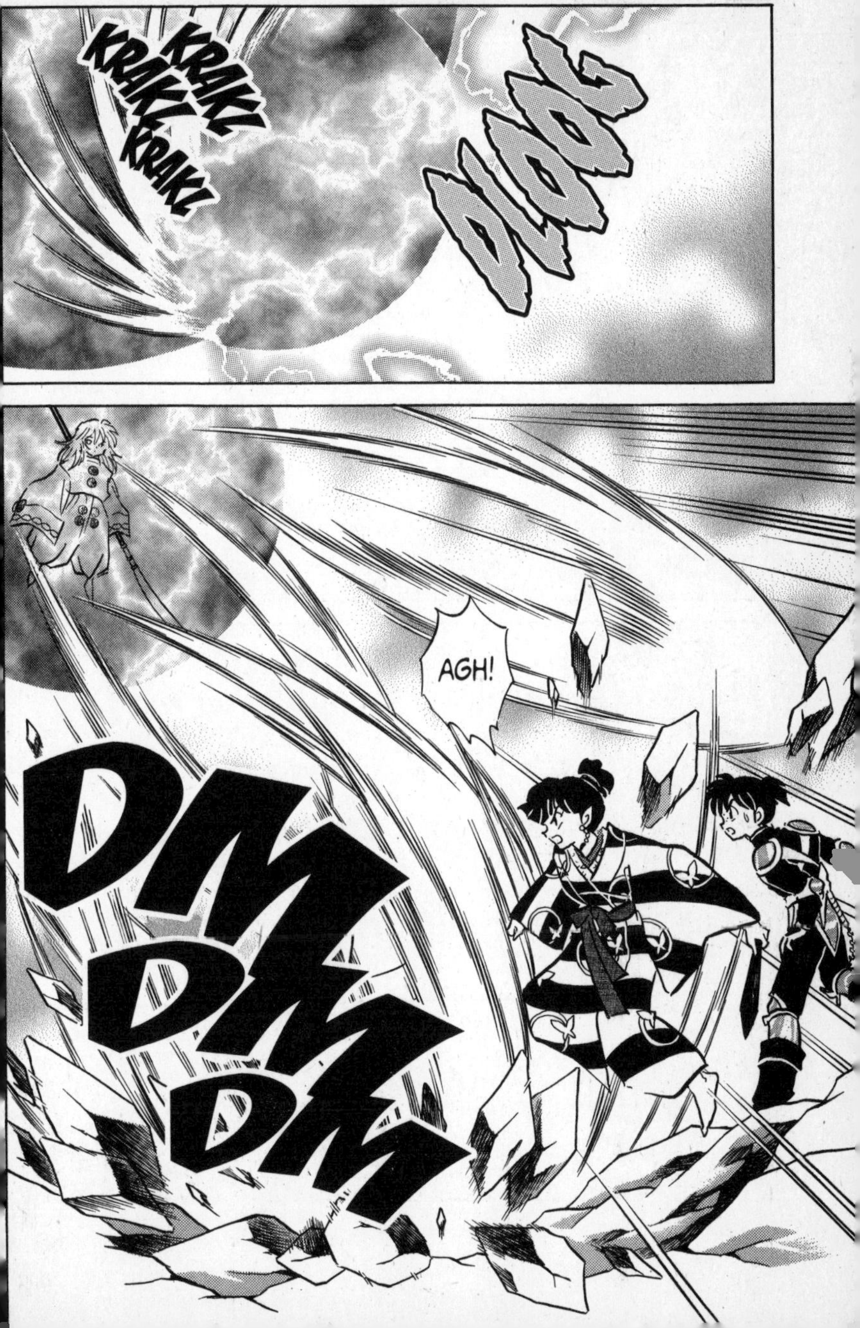
KRAKL KRAKL KRAKL
DJOOG
AGH!
DM DM DM

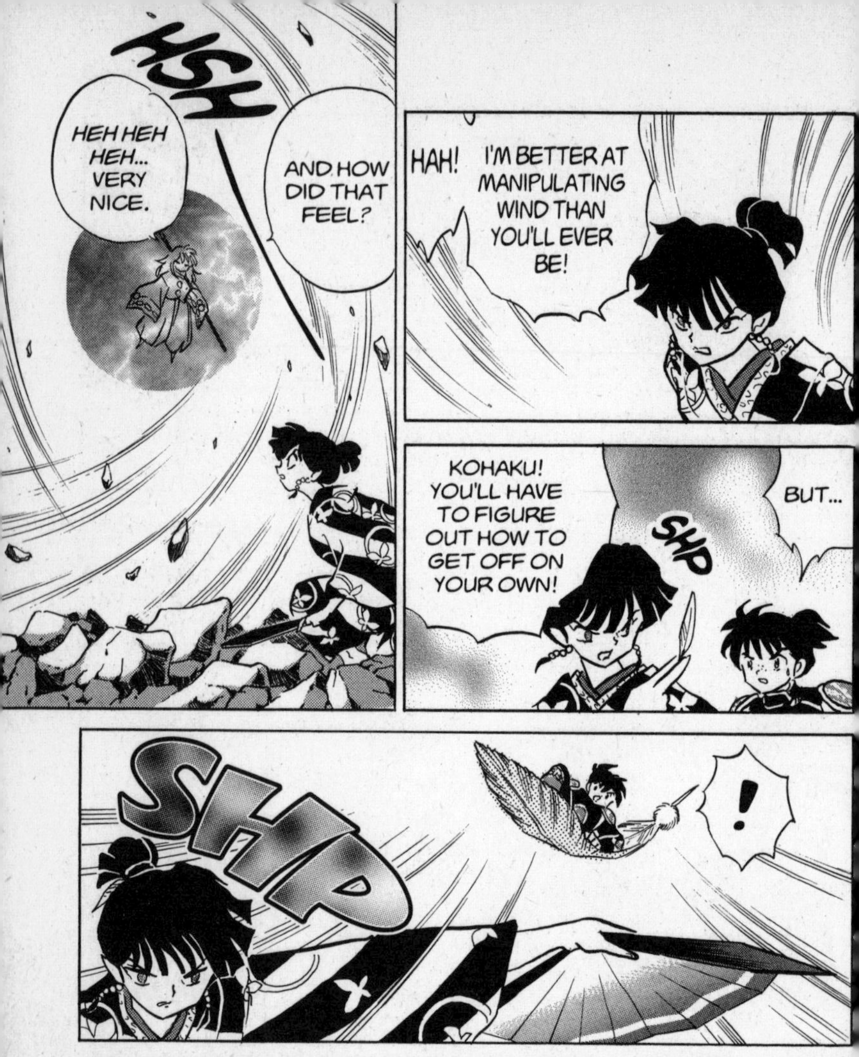
HSH
HEH HEH HEH... VERY NICE.
AND HOW DID THAT FEEL?
HAH!
I'M BETTER AT MANIPULATING WIND THAN YOU'LL EVER BE!
KOHAKU! YOU'LL HAVE TO FIGURE OUT HOW TO GET OFF ON YOUR OWN!
SHP
BUT...
SHP
!
KAGURA!

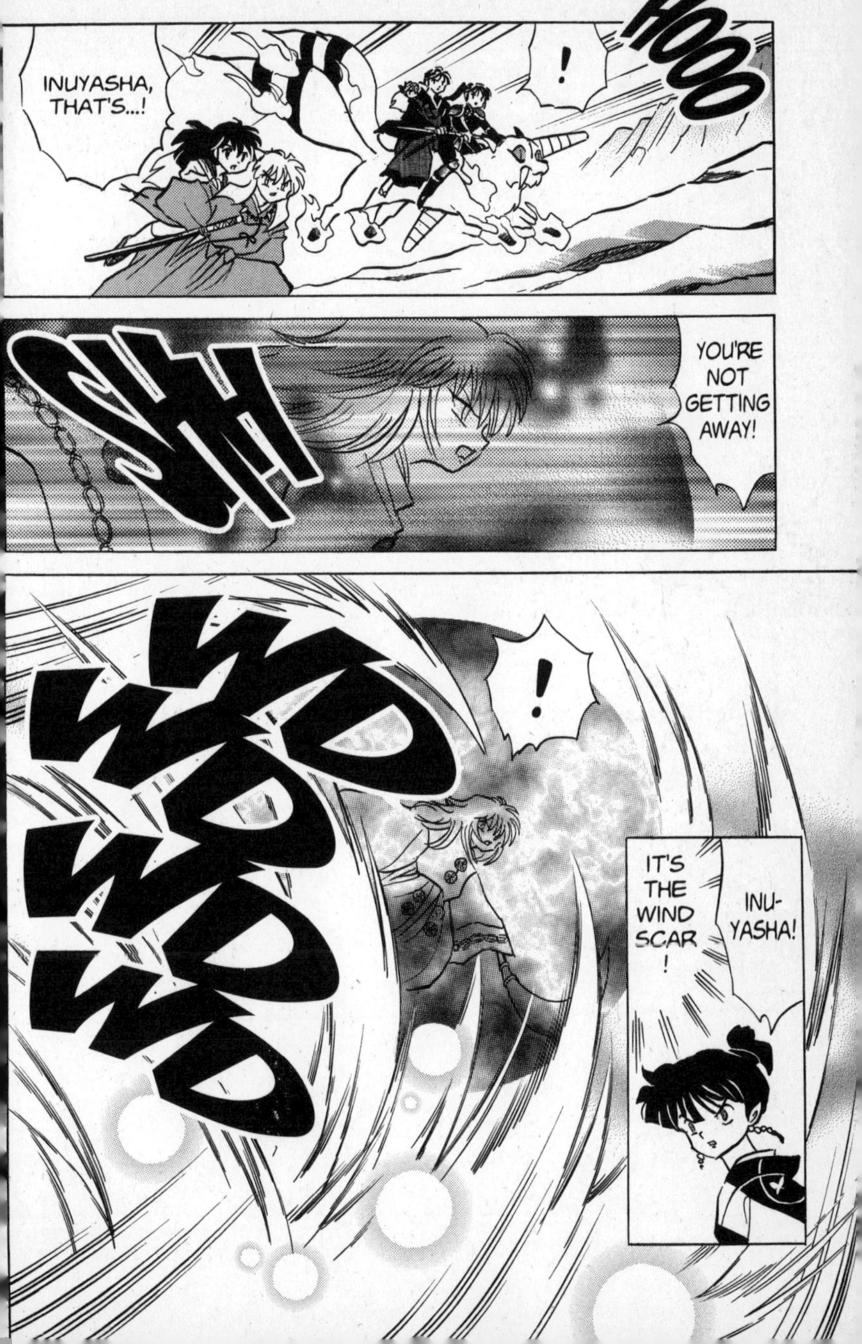
INUYASHA, THAT'S...!
!
HOOO
YOU'RE NOT GETTING AWAY!
!
IT'S THE WIND SCAR!
INU-YASHA!

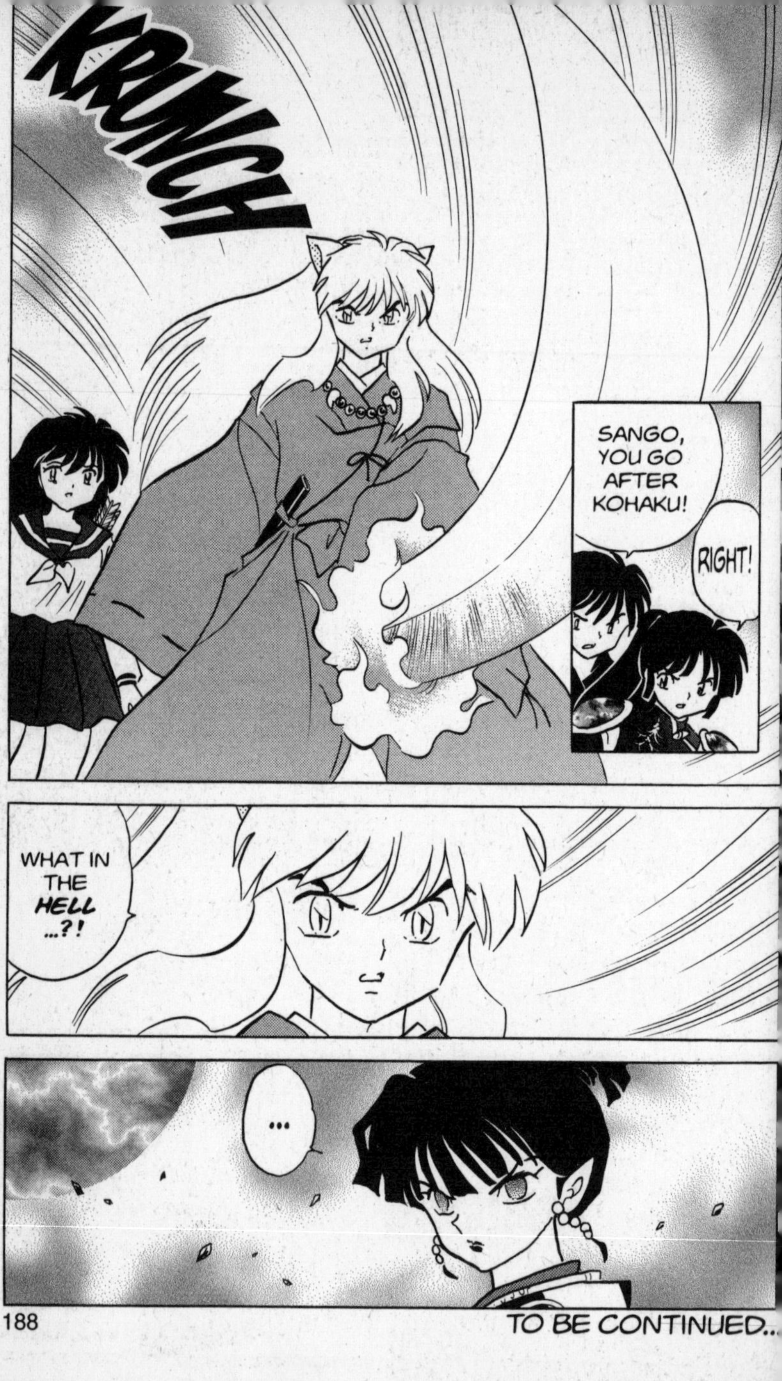
KRUNCH
SANGO, YOU GO AFTER KOHAKU!
RIGHT!
WHAT IN THE HELL ...?!
...

TO BE CONTINUED...

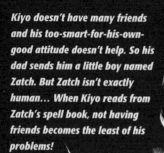